Richard Wright's Travel Writings

Richard Wright in Ghana (1953)

Richard Wright's Travel Writings

New Reflections

Edited by Virginia Whatley Smith

University Press of Mississippi
Jackson

Margaret Walker Alexander Series in
African American Studies

Photographs, courtesy of the Yale Collection of
American Literature, Beinecke Rare Book and
Manuscript Library, Yale University, New Haven, CT
06520. All rights reserved. Permission to quote from
Wright's materials granted by Mrs. Ellen Wright.
All rights reserved.

www. upress.state.ms.us

Library of Congress Cataloging-in-Publication Data

Richard Wright's travel writings : new reflections /
edited by Virginia Whatley Smith.
p. cm.
Includes bibliographical references and index.
ISBN I-57806-347-7 (cloth : alk. paper)
I. Wright, Richard 1908–1960—Knowledge—
Foreign countries.   2. Afro-Americans—Travel—
Foreign countries—History.   3. Travelers' writings,
American—History and criticism.   4. Wright,
Richard, 1908–1960—Journeys.
I. Smith, Virginia Whatley.
PS3545.R815 Z825 2001
813'.52—dc2I
00-047727

British Library Cataloging-in-Publication Data available

Today, as the tide of white domination of the land mass of Asia and Africa recedes, there lies exposed to view a procession of shattered cultures, disintegrated societies, and a writhing sweep of more aggressive, irrational religion than the world has known for centuries. And, as scientific research, partially freed from the blight of colonial control, advances, we are witnessing the rise of a new genre of academic literature dealing with colonial and post-colonial facts from a wider angle of vision than ever possible before. The personality distortions of hundreds of millions of black, brown, and yellow people that are being revealed by this literature are confounding and will necessitate drastic alteration of our past evaluations of colonial rule.

—Richard Wright, *White Man, Listen!*

Contents

Richard Wright Publicizing White Man, Listen! *(1957)*

Introduction

Once author Richard Wright fled the United States in 1946 to live as an expatriate in Paris, France, he entered an arena of intellectual thought and humanistic challenges that transcended the narrow limits of his former American home. As a result of this intercontinental shift, the writer's global experiences to come would lead, by the time of his death in 1960, to his adopting the title of "Twentieth Century Western Man of Color" to complement his self-appointed role of spokesperson for oppressed people worldwide. Not only did exposure to French existentialist philosophy affect Wright's reappraisal of his American identity, but also, by 1957, two world events accounted for his self-definition in *White Man, Listen!* as a "rootless" man of the world. One factor was the recently inaugurated Pan-Africanist movement arising from the Manchester (England) Congress in 1945 to decolonize Africa; a second was Indonesia's lead role, within hours after the end of World War II, in announcing its independence from colonial rule. Attracted by these anti-colonial struggles for human rights, which Wright equated to his ongoing war to achieve equal opportunity for African Americans, he extended his concerns to a global stage involving Afro-Asian and European countries. The result of his multiple travels during the decade of the 1950s was a series of nonfictional productions now categorized by genre as travel literature.

These travel books include *Black Power: A Record of Reactions in a Land of Pathos* (1953); *The Color Curtain: A Report of the Bandung Conference* (1956); *Pagan Spain* (1957); and *White Man, Listen!* (1957)—a collection of essays containing supplementary remarks and speeches made by the author at lectures in Europe about his Afro-Asian travels. Grouped in this body of long accounts are Wright's aborted plans for a fourth travel book on "French West Africa" (c. 1959), which exists in notes, outlines, and a draft.

Contrary to the traditional European and American exploration, colonial, or eighteenth-century travel book, Wright's representation of the master's narrative has taken another shape. Traditional Anglo travel accounts take on such recognizable descriptions as exploration, exile, captivity, and/or excursion literature and have been authored by explorers, scientists, missionaries, and, most frequently, tourists. Since Wright's texts, decidedly non-illustrated in their American productions, were sociologically discursive and politically candid, his publishers, agents, and critics in the 1950s and through the 1980s did not consider them travel books. Yet Wright, an innovator of style who had called for a "Blueprint for Negro Writing" in 1937, not only adopted the genre and its forms but also adapted it into an expression of African American travel writing.

Richard Wright's travel books of the 1950s recapitulate a body of concerns about emancipation from oppressive colonial rule and freedom of religious or gender expression resonating similar cries for human rights by African/African American slaves through their own genre, the slave narrative. Its classic model is that of Frederick Douglass's 1845 *Narrative*. African Americans have also seen the advantage of how this cultural genre with its socio-political message of freedom from enslavement adapts to travel writing. Its earliest expression was inaugurated by William Wells Brown, a slave narrativist, who, in 1852, published *Three Years in Europe, or Places I Have Seen and People I Have Met*.

Wright was familiar with Douglass's slave narrative; however, it is uncertain whether he read Brown's travel book. What is for sure is that Wright magnified, modified, and personalized a nascent and dormant, African American genre by anchoring the motif of travel to a foreign culture as the core of these nonfictions, and presented his readers with his "reactions" first hand. He takes his readers along with him onto the international stage of history to hear the hues and cries of the formerly or presently oppressed people as he witnesses and records in *Black Power* Kwame Nkrumah's anti-colonial initiatives for gaining the Gold Coast's (Ghana's) independence in 1953. In *The Color Curtain*, the author records the surreal convergence of world leaders from twenty-nine black, brown, and yellow formerly or newly-decolonized nations at Bandung, Indonesia, in 1955. He details their efforts to draft strategies to offset maneuvers by the West for neo-colonialist control while, at the same time, protecting their needs for the technological advancements offered by their nemeses of America or Russia. Different in landscape but similar in focus, *Pagan Spain* takes on Franco's Fascist rulership and the way that institutions enforcing the country's Catholic religion constrain women and constrict non-Catholics (Jews and Protestants). *White Man, Listen!* continues Wright's critiques of the East and West in terms of master-slave interdependences but, more importantly, includes his theory of the "frog perspective" defining dominant/subordinate relations between the colonizer and colonized. And "French West Africa," although never reaching fruition, gauges how Wright had again begun to entrench himself in African affairs but this time focusing solely on the French-speaking countries of West, Central, and East Africa.

The essayists in this collection thus respond to Wright's representation of African American travel writing, and how he confirms, resists, adapts, or modifies contours of the familiar Anglo narrative or draws from influences of the African American slave/travel narrative or other domestic or world literatures. They critique his presentation and representation of customs and people, and use a body of interpretive modes from formalist to textual to postmodern to postcolonial theories. Their viewpoints conflict as well as harmonize during their determinations of what is right, what is wrong, what is acceptable, and what is normative about Wright's brand of travel writing. In an essay on *Black Power* (1954), S. Shankar explores how Wright's text not only reproduces Europe and the Otherness of the African, but also its revolutionary, counterdiscourse of the anticolonial narrative emitting from Ghana. Ngwarsungu Chiwengo, on the other hand, says that *Black Power* is about "home" and that Wright's status is that of a homeless, hybrid subject writing into being a hybrid *oikos* (home) in the space between his Western and non-Western identities. And Jack Moore, following the author's footsteps, reevaluates Wright's reactions to the cityscapes of Accra and Kumasi to gauge the accuracy of Wright's "reactions" of feeling displaced in a world of disorder absent of modern amenities.

In the section on *The Color Curtain* (1956), Yoshinobu Hakutani correlates the travelogues and diaries of a seventeenth-century Asian, wandering bard with Wright's humanistic thinking and self-portraiture as a wander-traveler during the 1950s. Virginia Whatley Smith illustrates how Wright's perceived journalistic account is, rather, an eclectic travel book designed for the purpose of warning the West about the East's anti-colonial imperative of resistance.

In remarks on *Pagan Spain* (1957), John Lowe defines Wright as an ethnographer gathering data, and asserts that the form and content of the travel book about his fieldwork experiences in Spain echo both colonial and postcolonial theories of ethnography prominent in anthropology, sociology, psychology, and literature. Keneth Kinnamon, on the other hand, focuses on a section of the travel book to demonstrate how Wright revoices Hemingway's account of Spanish bullfighting in *Death in the Afternoon*. And Dennis Evans, portraying Wright as a "foreigner" in a strange land, paints the author as a humanist figure sympathetic to Spain's marginalized and/or enslaved women, thereby countering Wright's image as a misogynist.

Finally, Virginia Whatley Smith recovers a little-known, unpublished text in draft form pertaining to Wright's plans for a fourth travelogue on "French West Africa," and restages Wright's typical, behind-the-scene activities that ultimately account for the author's self-representation as a self-absorbed existentialist character detached from the subjects of his narratives. Together, these essayists on Wright's four travel books redefine our perceptions of Richard Wright's individual nonfictions of the 1950s as a collective body of travel books as well as inaugurate a lengthy study of a largely-ignored cultural genre known as African American travel writing that, itself, is contemporaneous with postcolonial studies.

After all, it was Richard Wright the foreign traveler who had the prescience of vision as a global humanist and eyewitness to history to pioneer postcolonial studies, and to forecast in *The Color Curtain* (1956) its preeminence in the academy today owing to the post-World War II backlash to colonial rule by black, brown, and yellow peoples. The body of resistance literature and transcultural theoretical studies promoted by such esteemed critics as Edward Said and Mary Louise Pratt, one element being travel writing, fulfills the author's prophecy. This collection of essays not only functions as a seminal study of Richard Wright's travel books, but it also inserts the discourse of African American travel writing into the American canon to receive its due attention as one of the multiple genres of expression used by African American culture.

Many people have lent their financial, scholastic, and/or moral supports that have enabled this project to be realized. At my institution of the University of Alabama at Birmingham, I especially thank Dr. Louis Dale, Associate Vice Provost for Minority and Faculty Affairs, and the committee members of the Comprehensive Minority Faculty Development Fund for sponsoring my quarter-term release from teaching and also for subsidizing my research trips to Natchez, Mississippi; Chicago, Illinois; Paris, France; and New Haven, Connecticut, where Richard Wright lived and/or where his papers are housed. Special thanks also to administrative officials at the University of Alabama at Birmingham and the Department of English for granting sabbatical leave to me for this research effort. Words of appreciation additionally go to Juanita Sizemore, Administrative Associate, Department of English, and T. D. Todd, computer technology expert for the School of Arts and Humanities.

The staff at the Beinecke Rare Book and Manuscript Library, Yale University, deserve accolades for their professionalism and rapid response in locating Wright's manuscript materials and photographs during my in-person visits to the Beinecke Library, or by correspondence of e-mail or telephone. Ms. Ellen Cordes and Mr. Alfred Mueller of the Public Services Branch played distinctive roles in this matter.

Over the years, my professional colleagues and friends have supported this endeavor. To Jerry Ward, Dolan Hubbard, James E. Miller, Mary Kemp Davis, and J. Lee Greene, I thank you for your professional advisements and friendships that kept me moving towards completion of this collection. My good friend Dalia Davis Griggs has been a consistent voice of encouragement as well.

The Wright family members also have been magnificent in granting me access to Wright's personal papers as well as lending their personal time to share knowledge about Wright's life. I express gratitude to Ellen Wright for granting me permission to use Wright's papers at the Beinecke Library as well as for taking me on a personal walking tour of Wright's favorite restaurants and bookstores in Paris. Julia Wright also has been especially helpful during these research endeavors. The Mississippi family members of Wright, too, deserve special recognition for being so hospitable during my visit to Natchez, Mississippi, in August 1999 which enabled me to understand Wright's Deep South roots. To Charles E. Wright, his wife Cora and daughter Cynthia, and to his mother Mrs. Evelyn Wright Davis, I thank all of you for the personal tours! Michel Fabre, of course, holds a distinctive place in Wright scholarship and deserves recognition for directing me to special research locations in Paris as well as for sharing his expert knowledge about Wright with me over many years.

Finally, I thank my family and children for their support of my endeavors over the years, this being only one of several book projects. My support network includes my mother, Mrs. Willie Mae Whatley; my sister, Audrey J. Reid; my nephew, Dennis Reid, and my three children, Khadijyah Ali, Alexis Smith Balkum, and Elworth E. Smith, III.

Richard Wright in Crowd, Ghana (1953)

Essays on *Black Power* (1954)

Richard Wright's *Black Power*

Colonial Politics and the Travel Narrative[1]

S. Shankar

In *Black Power: A Record of Reactions in a Land of Pathos* (1954), Richard Wright turns his attention to a dimension of the diasporic black experience that he had not previously explored in any great detail. What, *Black Power* asks, sometimes explicitly and always implicitly, is the relationship of Richard Wright, this black man of the diaspora, to Africa? *Black Power* is an account of Wright's journey to the Gold Coast during the summer of 1953, four years before the achievement of independence by that country.[2] During his stay in the Gold Coast, Wright not only witnesses first hand the activities of Kwame Nkrumah's Convention People's Party as it campaigns for the achievement of full independence, but also explores (as the subtitle to the book suggests) his "reactions" to Africa.[3]

Wright's title to his book acquires a special resonance for readers who come to the travel narrative after the Sixties when the Black Power movement of which Kwame Touré was a part gave the term popular currency. I have found no evidence linking Wright's use of the term directly with that of the movement of the Sixties. Wright's text, of course, predates the Black Power movement by more than a decade.

It is interesting to note the nationalist overtones of the Black Power movement of the Sixties in this context and to remark that, perhaps independently, the same phrase is applied to the nationalist aspirations of two different black populations. What this correspondence suggests is the continuity of language and historical vision in the African-American political tradition. Indeed, as C. L. R. James asserted in his essay on Kwame Touré entitled "Black Power": "Stokely [Kwame Touré] and the advocates of Black Power stand on the shoulders of all that has gone before.... [T]oo many people see Black Power and its advocates as some sort of portent, a sudden apparition.... It is nothing of the kind. It represents the high peak of thought on the Negro question which has been going on for over half a century" (367). What links together the two uses of the same phrase, then, is the complex political ferment in the black world from Marcus Garvey to Nelson Mandela. Recognizing the resonances of the phrase "Black Power" in this fashion allows us to place Wright's travelogue within the context of this political tradition.

Black Power is a travel narrative and it is with reference to this generic identity of the text, too, that I want to carry out my explorations of *Black Power* in this essay. In discussing the text here, I am interested in posing certain questions regarding the discursive *economy* of Wright's text as a travel narrative written in the colonial context. Elsewhere, I explore in some detail the implications of the term "economy" as it is applicable to texts, but it may be useful to make some schematic points here about the term.[4] What is an economy? As I use the term here, it refers to a *systemic* operation through which *value* is produced and distributed between the different elements that go to make up the system. The term "value" is of central importance to an understanding of "economy." "Value" and "economy" go together as terms. If we were to use a spatial metaphor, and it is only a metaphor, we might call an "economy" a hierarchical structure which is also a machine for producing and concentrating value at specific sites.

I believe the term "economy" can be usefully applied to a text (such as a written narrative) so as to illuminate the functioning of the text in new ways. I make this assertion to foreground the ways in which a text operates as a mechanism for the production and distribution of a certain kind of "value." If we learn to regard the text as an economy, we are able to discern the materialist ways in which the text assigns value selectively, that is, to note how the value-codings of the text have their origins outside the text. This argument cannot be further explored here. Suffice it to note that value signifies plenitude or fullness. With reference to narratives of travel written in the colonial context, I have found the word "economy" especially useful in thematizing certain aspects of both the colonial travel narrative (that is, narratives of travel to colonized countries written by travelers from colonizing countries) and narratives that are deployed counter to it. Applying the term "economy" in this context reveals both the ways in which the colonial travel narrative places different elements in relationship with each other in such a fashion as to produce Europe or the metropolis as a site of concentrated "value," the site of a moral and historical fullness, and the ways in which such a production and distribution of value is contested in counter deployments.

In reading Wright's *Black Power* as a textual economy that is also a travel narrative, then, some of the questions that I propose to ask in this essay are: In what ways does the specific economy of *Black Power* respond to the generic economy—economy of the genre—of the "colonial travel narrative"? That is, how does *Black Power* articulate and rearticulate the value-codings of the *typical* colonial travel narrative? How does the travel narrative become a vehicle for Wright's own "reactions" to Africa? What are the implications of Wright's identification of himself as an African-American traveler to Africa? How does the examination of the economy of *Black Power* help us to re-evaluate the critical responses to the text? There is much to be said about *Black Power* and the notion of a textual economy in this context. I have to restrict my self to only some aspects of this discussion here. In what follows, I foreground certain questions about the specific value-codings of colonial discourse in the relatively uncommon case of a black American's travels in Africa. In the process, we learn something about both Wright's *Black Power* and the functionings of colonial discourse.

I. Outsiders in History

Richard Wright's *The Outsider* (1953) is the story of Cross Damon, a disillusioned black man in Chicago, who takes the opportunity of a train crash that he is involved in to change his identity and disappear in the attempt to remake his life. In New York, under an assumed identity, he joins up with some Communists and finds himself in the midst of a cynical contest for power between Communists and a segregationist. Watching the world with the new freedom that the veil of his assumed identity gives him, Damon comes to a number of realizations regarding the human condition and the exercise of power in such a condition.

Both the Communists and the segregationists, Damon realizes, have understood the meaninglessness of life. Their exercise of power is an attempt to fill the void of human existence. This insight into the meaninglessness of life, Damon concludes, is what permits the monstrously efficient exercise of power on the part of

Communists and segregationists. In his anger at such cynicism, Damon kills both Herndon, the southern racist, and Blount, the Communist. As these murders lead him on to other murders, Damon, ironically, begins to confront his own arbitrary and cynical exercise of power.

The Outsider, even echoing Camus's L'Etranger in its title, can be read as an existentialist novel. Published during Wright's exile in Paris, external evidence strongly invites such a reading. I am more interested, however, in other dimensions of the concept of "the outsider" as it is set forth by Wright. "The outsider" is posited by Wright in the novel as a historical category. Outsiders in the novel are people who have understood the meaninglessness of life and are, therefore, able to detach themselves from the systemic functioning of power and view it from the "outside." Such outsiders may themselves engage in the cynical exercise of power, as do the Communists, or may struggle with the very cynicism of such power, as do Damon and Ely Houston, the hunchbacked white district attorney who befriends Damon and then hunts him down.

In a long declamation towards the end of the novel about totalitarian systems and their origins in an attempt to militate against and invalidate the meaninglessness of life, Damon observes that "As long as this works, it's wonderful. The only real enemies of this system are not the rats [who are controlled] themselves, but those outsiders who are conscious of what is happening and who seek to change the consciousness of the rats who are being controlled" (Outsider 362–3). The outsider, in Wright's novel, is the privileged possessor of an uncommon knowledge regarding power and society, as well as the agent capable of acting upon this knowledge. In Wright's consciously abstract and metaphysical argument in the novel, the outsiders are agents of change, though not always for the better.

In "Richard Wright and the Art of Non-Fiction," John M. Reilly suggests that The Outsider is the expression of Wright's disillusionment with politics. Reilly argues that, in the non-fictional texts relating to the "Third World" that succeed The Outsider (Black Power, 1954, The Color Curtain, 1956, and White Man, Listen!, 1957), the completely individualistic philosophy that Wright tested in the character of Cross Damon of The Outsider during the time of his "crisis" is superseded by his discovery of the "entry into conscious history" of the "Third World" (519).

Reilly's argument regarding an evolution in Wright's thought beyond the individualism of The Outsider to a renewed commitment to politics is certainly plausible. The enthusiasm with which Wright explores the politics of decolonization in the three non-fictional texts of travel is evidence for Reilly's assessment. However, there is also a continuity between the metaphysical meditation of The Outsider and the interpretation of history in the later non-fictional works. This point can be best made by turning to Wright's dedication to *White Man, Listen!* The book is dedicated to Eric Williams, West Indian statesman and author of the book *Capitalism and Slavery*, and to "the Westernized and tragic elite of Asia, Africa, and the West Indies—the lonely outsiders who exist precariously on the clifflike margins of many cultures—men who are distrusted, misunderstood, maligned, criticized by left and right, Christian and pagan—men who carry on their frail but indefatigable shoulders the best of two worlds...." (7).

Like the outsiders of the novel, "the Westernized and tragic elite" of the "Third World" on whom Wright depends for leadership during the process of decolonization, possess privileged access to knowledge. This knowledge is a direct consequence of the elite's existence outside of social structures "on the margins of many cultures." Invoking the metaphor of home at this point, the dedication goes on to describe the elite as "men" who "seek desperately for a home for their hearts: a home which, if found, could be a home for the hearts of all men" (7). Alienation becomes the source not only of knowledge but also of political action of profound historical consequence.[5]

Wright's "tragic elite," we can now see, are ideological exiles. In this they mirror Wright's conception of himself. "I'm a rootless man," Wright tells his reader in the introduction to *White Man, Listen!*, "...I declare unabashedly that I like and even cherish the state of abandonment, of aloneness...it seems to me the natural, inevitable condition of man, and I welcome it. I can make myself at home almost anywhere on this earth..." (17). Living as an expatriate in Paris and exploring the politics of decolonization, Wright discovers in the metaphors of home and exile a semantic field through which to articulate the politics of decolonization. In his own physical and mental condition he finds a connection to the ideological condition of the "tragic elite" of the "Third World." This connection between himself and the "tragic elite" is rendered more meaningful because as a black man Wright, too, exists, in some important respects, outside the ambit of Western culture. Ely Houston, the district attorney, expresses this idea to Cross Damon in *The Outsider* when he suggests that "Negroes as they enter our [American] culture...are going to be both *inside* and *outside* of our culture at the same time" (129, emphasis in text). Discussing the importance of "the outsider" in Wright's later work, Wright's biographer Constance Webb notes, "For many years the theme of the outsider was one of Richard's favorites.... These [the outsiders] were the men dangerous to the status quo, for the outsider was one who no longer responded to the values of the system in which he lived" (313).

"Outsider," "home," "exile"—these are some of the key terms that make up the conceptual baggage that Wright takes to the Gold Coast with him in 1953. Explicit evidence of this baggage is found in two earlier titles that Wright suggested for the text that was finally published as *Black Power*. One of the titles was "Stranger in Africa"; the other was "Ancestral Home" (Fabre, *UQ* 401; 404). The two previous titles identify two important dimensions of *Black Power*. Through the discursive economy of the travel narrative, Wright's text brings the "stranger" to his "ancestral home" and suggests a resolution to his experiences there. The shape of this resolution and the details of the economy that produces it are what I propose to examine now.

2. The Stranger in His Ancestral Home

Soon after his arrival in the Gold Coast, Wright drives into James Town, the slum section of Accra, with Nkrumah. Here he witnesses from the car some women dancing in a manner that seems strangely familiar to him. "And then I remembered: I'd seen these same snakelike, veering dances before..." Wright tells us. "Where? Oh, God, yes; in America, in storefront churches, in Holy Roller Tabernacles, in God's Temples, in unpainted wooden prayer-meeting houses on the plantations of the Deep South...." Bewildered by this sudden echo from his personal past, Wright is forced to confess, "I'd doubted that I'd be able to walk into the African's cultural house and feel at home and know my way around. Yet what I was now looking at in this powerfully improvised dance of these women, I'd seen before in America" (*BP* 56–57).

Thus, Wright confronts early in *Black Power* the question of the meaning of his African ancestry. The semantics of this ancestry are potent territory for Wright. Thinking about the incident of the dancers the next day, he writes, "That there was some kind of link between the native African and the American Negro was undoubtedly true. But what did it mean?" (66). The issue of a connection between Africa and black America comes up often in *Black Power*. In the bus going from Takoradi to Accra, the landscape with its "rich red" soil and black figures going about their work reminds him of the American South (36). In the Old Slave Market Castle in Christianborg, Wright meets Mr. Hagerson who is the descendant of slaves and finds in Mr. Hagerson's features and bearing the reflection of his grandfather (181).

An interesting comparison may be made here with a book by another African-American writer traveling in Ghana. In Maya Angelou's *All God's Children Need*

Traveling Shoes (1987), too, there is a scene similar to the one in which Wright recognized his grandfather's features in Mr. Hagerson. *All God's Children Need Traveling Shoes* is the account of Maya Angelou's stay in Ghana in the early Sixties, about a decade after Wright's own journey to the country when it was still called the Gold Coast.[6] Towards the end of her long stay in Ghana, Angelou travels to a part of the country that she has not been to before. There, in Eastern Ghana, Angelou undergoes two strange experiences. The scene of surprised recognition similar to Wright's occurs on the narrow stairs leading up to the raised market in the town of Keta (203–5). Climbing up the stairs, Angelou is confronted by a woman who mistakes her for the daughter of a friend. When Angelou does not respond to her repeated queries (in Ewe, which Angelou does not understand), the woman begins to get angry. Mr. Adadevo, one of Angelou's companions, has to intervene at this point and Angelou has to produce her California driver's license as evidence of her identity. The woman, finally convinced by the massive force of the California state authority's interpellation of Angelou as a subject, then takes her to be introduced to her friends as the descendant of lost slaves from that region. As the woman leads her up from the dark stairs into the light above, Angelou is astounded to recognize her grandmother's features in the woman's face. Previous to this experience had been another—Angelou's unaccountable disquiet on approaching Keta bridge. As the car approaches the bridge, Angelou begins to get so uneasy that she finally makes the driver stop the car and then walks across the bridge. Once on the other side, Mr. Adadevo asks her if she has heard of the story of the Keta bridge. When she replies in the negative, Mr. Adadevo tells her that until about a century before the bridges in the region were so badly constructed that people were afraid to cross them in any kind of conveyance. Since it was easier in the event of a mishap to reach the other side if you were on foot, the passengers would commonly dismount from the conveyance and walk across (199–200).

The remarkable similarity between the scenes of recognition recorded by Wright and by Angelou does not, however, reflect or lead to a similar interpretation of the scenes by the two writers. For Angelou, who is a traveler to Ghana after Wright, her two experiences in Eastern Ghana become evidence of a fundamental link between herself and her African past that goes beyond the rationalizing ground of "history." This is the implicit message of the incident at the Keta bridge, especially when Angelou experiences a transhistorical, nonpersonal memory in her disquietude upon approaching the bridge.

Considering Angelou's presentation of her link to Africa serves to illustrate the immense difficulty that Wright had experienced previously when faced by the same issue. The comfort that Angelou finds in the connection is never Wright's. In the conclusion to her book, Angelou writes as she describes her departure from Ghana: "Many years earlier I, or rather someone very like me and certainly related to me, had been taken from Africa by force. This second leave-taking would not be so onerous, for now I knew my people had never completely left Africa" (209). The ground of Angelou's transhistorical link to Africa through "my people" is race and it is precisely race that Wright does not, cannot, have recourse to in his exploration of his link to Africa.

This lack of faith in "race" is explicitly declared by Wright in an exchange that he has with Dr. J. B. Danquah, one of Nkrumah's leading African opponents. When Wright goes to Danquah to set up a time for them to meet, the following exchange takes place, as recorded by Wright:

> "How long have you been in Africa?" he asked me.
> "About two months," I said.
> "Stay longer and you'll *feel* your race," he told me.
> "*What?*"
> "You'll *feel* it," he assured me. "It'll all come *back* to you."
> "What'll come back?"
> "The knowledge of your race." He was explicit.
> I liked the man, but not as a Negro or African; I liked his directness, his willingness to be open. Yet, I knew that I'd never feel an identification with Africans on a "racial" basis. "I doubt that," I said softly. (218–19)

And, indeed, such a feeling of his race—a feeling that Maya Angelou experiences—never does "come back" to Wright in *Black Power.* What does come back is an insight regarding culture. In culture, a ground contained within history, Wright finds the connection between himself as an African-American from Mississippi and the Africans. "The question of how much African culture an African retains when transplanted to a new environment is not a racial, but a cultural problem, cutting across such tricks as measuring of skulls and intelligence tests," Wright notes (266). This is not a surprising resolution of the issue for Wright the rationalist. Wright's Marxist background leads him to look for a historical resolution to the question of the connection between Africa and himself. Successfully countering the seductions of the rhetoric of race, Wright remains a stranger in Africa in a way in which Maya Angelou, who discovers a mystic community through "race," does not.

There are also other, related aspects to Wright's self-identification as a stranger in Africa that we can specify from various comments that he makes in *Black Power.*

Wright the traveler is of the West, as he himself repeatedly insists, and it is his acute consciousness of this aspect of his identity that causes him to adopt the attitude to Africa that he does. Thus in a statement like "Today the ruins of their [the Akan people's] former culture, no matter how cruel and barbarous it may seem to *us*, are reflected in timidity, hesitancy, and bewilderment," we find Wright ranging himself quite explicitly on the side of the West, addressing a like-minded audience which is of the West (153, emphasis added).

Another scene of dancing, also in James Town, serves to bring home to Wright the Westerner this acute sense of his difference from the Africans. Poking about in the alleyways of that slum area of Accra, Wright discovers a compound in which men and women are dancing in the dark to the beat of drums. "What's going on in there?" he asks a young man who is about to enter the compound. When the young man observes, "You're a stranger, aren't you?" Wright's reply is, "Yes; I'm an American." The young man invites Wright into the compound and Wright observes the dancers "moving slowly, undulating their abdomens, their eyes holding a faraway look." Wright wants to know why they are dancing and is told that a girl has just died. Wright cannot understand this explanation. "I still didn't know why they were dancing and I wanted to ask him a third time," he writes. Some time later Wright leaves, his confusion at the funeral dancers with "no sadness or joy in their faces" uncleared. His final comment on this episode is, "I had understood nothing. I was black and they were black, but my blackness did not help me" (125–7).

A great deal is at stake in this representative passage from *Black Power*. To illustrate better what is at issue here for Wright, we may compare it to another famous confession of incomprehension with regard to Africa. In *Heart of Darkness*, Joseph Conrad's narrator Marlow is also confronted by a sense of the incomprehensibility of Africa and Africans. Describing at length the jungles of Africa that faced him as he sailed up the river towards Kurtz, Marlow concludes by telling his audience: "The steamer toiled along slowly on the edge of a black and incomprehensible frenzy. The prehistoric man was cursing us, praying to us, welcoming us— who could tell?" (37). These two sentences are only the most explicit expression of that constitutive difference between himself and the Africans that Marlow discovers at every turn in "the dark continent."

In these two sentences is revealed a well-rehearsed method of managing alterity in colonial discourse. The radical disjuncture of alterity poses an epistemological problem for Marlow; it presents him with an entity apparently completely beyond the appropriative structure of his consciousness. The particular narrative of history that Marlow invokes in the same sentence, however, reassigns that constitutive difference-beyond-comprehension that confronts him to a position outside the margins of history. The African is "prehistoric man." What Marlow is telling us in his description of the African scene before him is that the scene is incomprehensible *because* it is prehistoric. History is the knowable, the recognizable, for Marlow; and therefore, in that Western European linear conception of history that begins to acquire especial currency in the late nineteenth century, Africa, which proves itself unknowable, must be outside of history. Marlow believes that the Africans are unknowable because they are prehistoric; I want to venture, however, that it is because Marlow finds them unknowable that he consigns them to a prehistory. In its narrative, *Heart of Darkness* reproduces that economy of colonial discourse which must place Europe and non-Europe, the West and the Rest, metropolis and periphery, in a relationship that achieves the successful assignation of value (historical/cultural/racial) to the first term over the second. By asserting the chaotic incomprehensibility of Africa, Marlow's narrative exiles Africa beyond the margins of ordered human existence. By simultaneously inserting Africa in a structural relationship with Europe, expressed in a linear conception of history, it sets in motion an economy that transfers value to Europe.

Although *Black Power* taken as a whole works towards a less reductive idea of Africa, we may find traces of a similar discursive economy in Wright the Westerner's comments about Africa. Trying to make sense, like Marlow, of the difference of Africa, Wright suggests a resolution that is similar in some ways and different in others. "The tribal African's culture *is* primally human;" Wright argues in theorizing the relationship of Africans to other peoples, and goes on to add—"that which *all* men once had as their warm, indigenous way of living, is his..." (266). Here, in Wright's idea of the primal or the primitive as some kind of a "common denominator" of humanity, the sense of Marlow's prehistory returns surreptitiously: the African is what all "men" are to some extent. What is left unstated but dangerously implicit is the suggestion that that is all the African is but others, through a process of historical evolution, have become more. This complex rendering of Africa and Africans is Wright's own way of "making sense" of all those incomprehensible details about Africa that confront him again and again. It allows him both to render Africa and Africans as different and to place them in a narrative of world evolution.

Wright's typographical insistence on a community between "*all* men" reveals his consciousness of how slippery indeed this evolutionary slope is. Yet, like many other Western travelers to Africa before him, he, too, has recourse, in however self-reflexive a manner, to a certain Africanist conception of the continent (a conception that corresponds to what Edward Said has described as the Orientalist conception of Asia). "The distance today between tribal man and the West is greater than the distance between God and Western man of the sixteenth century" declares Wright at one point (117).[7] Such a distance is what Wright both feels acutely as a Westerner himself and tries to overcome as a black man writing about other black people. Wright's Marxist background suggests to him the problems in turning to "race" as a category for explaining his own relationship to Africa. But it is this same Marxist background, perhaps, which also reinforces his linear conception of history. It sets in motion a discursive economy similar to that we have noted in *Heart of Darkness.*

A passage that appears towards the end of *The Color Curtain,* Wright's journalistic report on the 1955 Bandung Conference of "Third World" nations, captures well his conception of the historical role of the West with which he aligns himself. He writes: "Is this secular, rational base of thought and feeling in the Western world broad and secure enough to warrant the West's assuming the moral right to interfere *sans* narrow, selfish political motives? My answer is, Yes" (185). Here Wright's confidence in the West as the fount of a valued rationality leads him to an open call for Western intervention in the "Third World." A similar apology for Western intervention in Africa is not, in fact, made in *Black Power,* but the idea of the West as the fount of rational thought is very much a part of Wright's narrative of world history in the earlier book as well. Thus, in *Black Power* Wright is often horrified by the examples of religion and superstition that he finds himself confronted with in the Gold Coast. At one point, he records "the pathetic story" of a worker in a gold mine attempting to steal a bar of gold while reciting a magic formula that he thought had rendered him invisible (312–13).[8] At another point, he describes himself as "com[ing] up for air, to take a deep breath..." after going through J. B. Danquah's book on Akan religion with astonished disbelief (218).[9]

In a brief but important scene in *Black Power,* sexual orientation, too, raises the issue of the difference of the Gold Coast for Wright (108–10). At a dance, Wright sees men dancing together in pairs and comes to the horrified conclusion that they are gay. Signifying homosexual practice as Western (without any explanation why), Wright asks himself, "What was *that?* Had I misjudged the African capacity for the assimilation of Western emotional conditionings?...Had the vices of the English public-school system somehow seeped through here?" (108). His host, however, insists that the men are not gay and that it is common in the Gold Coast for young men to dance with each other in this intimate fashion. The homophobic Wright then comes to the conclusion that "Africa was another world, another sphere of being. . . . I'd have to learn to accept without thought a whole new range of assumptions" (110). Wright's travel narrative is able to "decontaminate" the Gold Coast of the imputation of homosexuality only by resignifying it, in this instance, as ontologically of a primitive status in relation to the West to which he belongs. Even in its "vices," the West is advanced. The young men's behavior, as Wright's host informs him to his relief, is a result of "tribal conditioning" and not the terrible vice of homosexuality found in Western countries (110).

Black Power, then, is the ambivalent travel record of a stranger in his ancestral home. Confronted with the material signifiers of black bodies that visually remind him of his own, Wright struggles with the meaning that his ancestry has for him; and confronted by the "irrationality" of African cultural practice, he has recourse in a complex way to his self-identification as a rational Westerner. In situating himself as both inside and outside both of these collective identities, Wright seems to deconstruct in a superficial reading the essentialisms of both. But this is precisely the point at which a linear conception of history as a movement from irrationalism to rationalism appears in Wright the black Western traveler's discourse to impose a problematic structure upon the relationship between "West" and "Africa." Sometimes, as in the case of the young men whose intimate dancing so disturbs Wright, or in the case of the colonial repression indicted by him, the "advanced" condition of the West is seen as being not necessarily better; but at the same time, the West appears as a rational progression beyond "primitive" superstition and practice. Black Power repeatedly describes the contrast between the West and Africa as the difference between rationality and irrationality, science and religion. Indeed, such a contrast between the West and the rest of the world is one of the persistent themes of Wright's later non-fictional works in general. In The Color Curtain, for example, Wright declares after surveying the behavior of Asian delegates traveling to the Bandung Conference in the same aircraft as his, "It was rapidly dawning on me that if the men of the West were political [i.e. scientific and rational] animals, then the men of the East were religious animals..." (69).

3. Politics in a Land of Pathos

At one point in Black Power, Wright describes addressing some Ghanaians at a political gathering held under the auspices of Nkrumah's Convention People's Party. Amongst the words he speaks to his audience are the following: "I'm one of the lost sons of Africa who has come back to look upon the land of his forefathers. In a superficial sense it may be said that I'm a stranger to most of you, but, in terms of a common heritage of suffering and hunger for freedom, your heart and my heart beat as one" (77). In these words of Wright, we find expressed not only that tension between his identity as a black man and as a Westerner that I have discussed above but also his attempt at a resolution to this tension. There is a hint of the dialectical in the construction of the passage. The first sentence introduces Wright's acknowledgment of a common racial history between himself and his African audience. The beginning of the second sentence, on the other hand, emphasizes the historical gulf between them. Abandoning any attempt to reconcile these two positions or even explain them further, Wright introduces a third position into the discussion. What binds his audience and himself, he says, is "a common heritage of suffering and hunger for freedom." Abandoning both (black) race and (Western) culture, Wright chooses to make his stand on the ground of politics. The passage captures very aptly the trajectory of Wright's argument in *Black Power.* This is the same trajectory that is captured by the history of the title of Wright's text. Discarding such titles as "Stranger in Africa" and "Ancestral Home" (amongst others), Wright finally hits upon "Black Power" as expressing that political sensibility that he so wished to emphasize.

It is possible for us to read *Black Power,* then, as the account of a journey not just into a spatial or cultural but also a political geography. Any travel account involves such a journey, but such a journey into politics is an overtly expressed aspect of *Black Power.* In the opening scene of the text, politics is offered as one of the reasons for journeying to the Gold Coast. It is Dorothy Padmore (wife of West Indian writer and anti-colonialist activist George Padmore) who suggests the Ghana trip to Wright in Paris, after an Easter Sunday luncheon. What immediately occurs to Wright in the four-page long scene that follows is a medley of questions ranging from his African ancestry, to whether Africa was underdeveloped, to curiosity regarding Africa's pagan religion, to the meaning of race. The scene even in its brevity is riven by all those ambivalent tensions which go to make up the text of the book itself and which have led to its contrary assessments. Present in the scene is also the theme of politics, understood as a contest for state power. "Kwame Nkrumah, the Prime Minister, is going to table his motion for self-government in July" is the most important reason that Dorothy Padmore gives Wright for going to Ghana, in attempting to persuade him (9).

At first Wright does not pay much attention to this "political" aspect of a prospective journey to the Gold Coast. "I genuinely wanted to know about the political situation in the Gold Coast," he tells us, "yet another and far more important question was trying to shape itself in me. According to popular notions of 'race,' there ought to be something of me down there in Africa" (10). The scene, however, ends with the political part of the journey foregrounded. Learning from Dorothy Padmore that there are African cabinet ministers in the Gold Coast with significant responsibilities, Wright makes his final decision to go.

When Wright departs for Africa from Europe, he leaves from Liverpool in England, "the city that had been the center and focal point of the slave trade" (*BP* 13). The irony of this departure to Africa from Liverpool by a descendant of slaves follows immediately upon the above scene, which itself amends in important ways the premises of colonial travel narratives. If colonial travelers in their roles as adventurers and ethnographers typically profess to pursue material and cultural treasures in colonial territories, Wright departs professing a quest of political treasure. If the economy of *Heart of Darkness*, pursuing and producing cultural "treasure" through its signification of Africa as radically and abysmally different from Europe, transmits value back towards a valorized culture ("English") and valorized place ("London"), *Black Power* through a transformation of such an economy proceeds to accumulate value around a practice ("politics") rather than around a place or a cultural or national identity. Through this emendation, Wright's text revises the conventional protocols of the colonial travel narrative.

But this reading of *Black Power* is complicated by the simultaneous functioning of yet another economy of representation which continues to privilege the West as the site of rationality and secular values in ways I have noted earlier in the chapter. *Black Power* is also a text in which Wright as a Westerner travels from the West to Africa and back. In the functioning of *this* economy the West is the "home" from which Wright sets out on his travel and to which he returns.

Wright's text, then, is a space in which two powerful economies, working in contrary ways, find equal play. The history of the book's title only suggests the economy Wright would like to foreground. The other economy continues to function in the text, and the contrary readings of the book can be attributed to the ambivalent tension within the text because of the simultaneous operations of both economies. In this respect, *Black Power* is both an anti-colonial and a colonial travel narrative.

There are, however, ways in which the operations of the two economies intersect, not to render the ambivalence of the text finally resolved but to hold such ambivalence temporarily in abeyance. The presence of such points of intersection within the text allow it to appear as a coherent, seamless totality to the reader. What is thus brought into being is the semblance of a single meaning. This single meaning, which is put in place by the intersecting economies of the colonial as well as anticolonial travel narratives, bears some detailed examination through attention to the language of the text.

The word "pathos" appears a number of times in Wright's text. The importance of the word is emphasized by the book's subtitle, which is "A Record of

Reactions in a Land of Pathos." Two occurrences of the word illuminate the meaning of the text. One occurrence of the word appears at one of the key moments in the text after Wright, sitting in the galleries, has watched Nkrumah make a speech before the Legislative Assembly "petitioning Her Majesty's Government to enact the necessary legislation for Gold Coast self-government" (169). Witnessing this political act is one of the primary reasons for Wright's journey to the Gold Coast. After the petition, Nkrumah is carried into the celebrating crowd outside. But Wright, watching the scene outside, is apprehensive. He writes: "I could feel the fragility of the African as compared with the might of the British, the naiveté of the African when weighed against the rancid political insight the British possessed, the naked plea of the African when pitted against the anxieties of man holding the secrets of atomic power in their [sic] hands.... And a phrase from Nietzche welled up in me: the pathos of distance...." (170). Pathos, it appears from this passage, signifies what Wright perceives as the vast difference between the British and the Africans, a difference worthy of being expressed in the grand metaphysics of Nietzchean language.

Another striking occurrence of the phrase "pathos of distance" only reinforces this particular meaning. Bibiani is a town centered around a gold mine up on a hill. Walking through the town, the sounds of the machinery of the mine audible even down below where "[i]n the mud huts life was being lived by the imperious rule of instinct," Wright comes across "a tall, naked black boy" defecating on "the porch of his hut." Wright's comment on this scene is: "It was clear the industrial activity upon that hill, owned or operated by no matter what race, could not exist without the curbing and disciplining of instincts, the ordering of emotion, the control of the reflexes of the body. Again I felt the pathos of distance!" (310). The distance, the passage makes clear, is between an instinctual, emotional, reflexive life on the one hand and a rational, industrial life on the other.

What makes the distance between the two "pathetic" is the successful and productive repression of one by the other. Clearly rational life is superior to instinctual life, for it has successfully overcome the other in order to create objects such as mining machinery. I have noted earlier that the epistemological vision of Wright as a traveler involves a linear understanding of history. In this context, rational life appears as a more evolved condition than the life of instinct and Wright's "pathos of distance" is seen to have a historical expression.

The word "pathos" appears in a number of different passages in *Black Power*. In all of its occurrences, the word describes the difference, with an implication of inferiority involved, between Africans, on the one hand, and the British or Westerners, on the other. For Wright, the land of pathos is not only the land of emotions and instincts, but also pathetic in the other, more condescending sense of the term. In *Black Power*, the allusion to "pathos," then, is one more way of constructing "the African" as the Other for the British as well as for Wright himself (in his guise of Westerner). By rendering the Gold Coast "pathetic," Wright assimilates the country and its inhabitants to a powerful Western discourse of alterity.

The history and the politics that are described in *Black Power* may be described as that of a movement from the pre-modern to the modern, from the tribal to the industrial, from the pathetic to the rational. It is in carrying the people of the Gold Coast from the first set of terms to the second that Nkrumah's nationalist revolution, the political phenomenon that Wright has come to bear witness to, is instrumental. The pathos of distance between the two sets of terms is precisely expressed through the rhetoric of distance typically found in the travel narrative. The great geographical distance between Europe and Africa, represented in Wright's narrative of a journey by ship from Liverpool to Takoradi, underwrites the pathetic distance between the two. This distance, it is the business of Nkrumah's revolution to close. It must render the Gold Coast less "pathetic" by focusing authority in the masculine figure of Nkrumah. The nationalist revolution appears then as an overdetermined stage in an evolutionary history.

The single meaning of *Black Power*, brought into being by the play between the twin economies of the colonial and the anti-colonial travel narrative, may now be analyzed in the following manner: the economy of the colonial travel narrative operating through a rhetoric of distance works to produce the Gold Coast as a land of pathos, even as the economy of the anti-colonial travel narrative suggests the Gold Coast may be made to become less pathetic by the politics of revolutionary change. One economy transfers value to the West and the other to the Gold Coast, or at least the politics of the Gold Coast. Through the intersection of these two economies is produced a travel narrative of historical evolution.

4. Conclusion

Kwame Anthony Appiah in "A Long Way from Home: Wright in the Gold Coast" discovers in *Black Power* what he calls a "paranoid hermeneutic" (181). Since Wright discards the comforts of "racial explanation," Appiah argues, he has no reason for being in the Gold Coast and "[b]ecause he has no reason for 'being there,' Wright's reactions seem to oscillate between condescension and paranoia" (180). Appiah finds *Black Power* an ungenerous book in its depiction of the Ghana in which he grew up. Appiah's assessment of *Black Power* is in contradistinction to that of John M. Reilly whom Appiah describes in his essay as "one of the book's more devoted readers" (176). John M. Reilly in "Richard Wright's Discovery of the Third World," as well as in the already-cited "Richard Wright and the Art of Non-Fiction," arrives at a more positive evaluation of *Black Power*. In "Richard Wright's Discovery of the Third World," Reilly acknowledges the bewilderment Wright exhibits when confronted by "African survivals" in African-American culture and his "ambivalence" (Reilly's word) regarding Western rationality (49). Reilly concludes, however, that "with confidence that Africans can *consciously* enter into historical change, Wright concentrates his attention on the liberating consequences of the escape from dependency on ritual and myth. Whatever else he found in Africa pales beside the renewed hope he gained" (51; emphasis in text). What is important to Reilly is that with the publication of *Black Power*, Richard Wright became an exponent of national liberation (52).

Critics, in response to *Black Power*, have assessed the book positively or negatively depending on whether they have focused on Wright's depictions of Africa and Africans (Appiah) or his overt political expressions (Reilly). My own reading of *Black Power* in this essay reveals how Wright's narrative of travel simultaneously assimilates Africa to a colonial discourse of alterity and liberates it from such a discourse by enthusiastically applauding the cause of national liberation. It also reveals how both these aspects are fundamentally related to each other in Wright's narrative. Mary Louise Pratt in reading *Black Power* as a travel narrative suggests that "in *Black Power* Wright directly set himself to work parodying and reworking the inherited tropology [of the colonial travel narrative]" (*Imperial Eyes* 221). The details of this parodying and reworking are what I have examined in this essay. Noting both the successes and failures of Wright's attempt at transforming the economy of the colonial travel narrative offers a way of assessing the full ambivalent complexity of *Black Power*.

Gazing Through the Screen

Richard Wright's Africa

Ngwarsungu Chiwengo

James Campbell states in *Exiled in Paris* that Richard Wright once claimed in his journal that he would write the best book on Africa during his time (185). Wright eventually wrote on Africa, but his travelogue entitled *Black Power* (1954) is one of his most criticized books, especially by Africans who feel betrayed and misrepresented. Concurring, John Gruesser contends in "Afro-American Travel Literature and African Discourse" that the disillusioned and alienated Wright, like William Gardner Smith, Maya Angelou, and Gwendolyn Brooks, fails to represent Africans accurately. Despite his self-declared hybridity, Wright neither identifies nor upholds African tradition, nor does he give Africans a voice or presence in *Black Power*. His only intimate African friend, Peter Abrahams, claims that "Wright wanted to understand the African, but...[he] found the African oblique, a hard-to-know man" ("Blacks" 23). Abrahams describes Wright as a bewildered and disconnected man who did not understand that race does not entail acceptance in tribal Africa. Abrahams claims to love Africa unconditionally. According to him, only outsiders (white people or the Richard Wright types) like or dislike Africa.

Tellingly, Wright declares his admiration for the followers of Marcus Garvey in *Black Boy* (1945), but declines to follow them because of their unrealistic aspirations. Wright contends that he pities them because their dream of returning to Africa could never materialize since "Africa was owned by the imperial powers of

Europe, [that] their lives were alien to the mores of the natives of Africa, [that] they were people of the West and would forever be so until they either merged with the West or perished" (337). While Wright shares the Garveyites' passionate emotions, a result of their exclusion from American life, he accepts his alienation and sees no utopian return to Africa. After all, home is, according to Wright in *White Man, Listen!*, anywhere the mind establishes it. His uprootedness does not distract or perplex him; he welcomes the feeling of aloneness because it is "the natural, inevitable condition of man" (xvii). Although Wright presumes he is a universal man and revels in his deracination, he, nonetheless, claims to be psychologically distant from Western culture as a marginal American hybrid subject who has not been "allowed," as he writes in *White Man, Listen!*, "to blend, in a natural and healthy manner, with the culture and civilization of the West" (47).

Wright's *Black Power* is a travel narrative which, contrary to most accounts economizing on travel, does not have a fixed site of reference, or, as in Georges Van den Abbeele's own words, an *oikos*, a home, "in relation to which wandering can be apprehended" (xviii). Wright, who is both subject and object in his insecure and cold native American *oikos*, has already undergone a journey of dislocation in 1946 when he leaves America for Paris in his search for home. While Wright's British journey in 1953 from Liverpool is the initial point of his departure in *Black Power* and serves theoretically also as the physical point of reference defining and limiting the movement of his travel, Wright lacks an emotional *oikos* since Europe, his exile site of (dis)placement, is a space of both sameness and difference. Wright's home in exile, even as it grants him freedom, preserves his marginality, for, as he writes in the dedication to *White Man, Listen!*, the Westernized and tragic elite of Asia, Africa, and the West Indies are lonely outsiders. As an outsider, Wright seeks "desperately for a home for [his] heart: a home which, if found, could be a home for the hearts of all men" (v). Wright's initial European departure point is, hence, already a problematized space—epistemologically, socially, and historically constructed as the land of exile while Africa is his point of origin. The years spent in Paris separate him from his black constituency and his native home, America, so defined by time. Indeed, Jan Vladislav claims in "Exile, Responsibility, Destiny" that one's history, the history of those who surround one, and language make a place home (15). Yet, Wright's position in America, according to Paul Gilroy, is an uncomfortable one, for he is "inside but not organically of the West" (151). Although Wright considers his European departure site as home, for him, unlike for his fellow Western travelers, the West is the socially-constructed point of destination since it is solely his physical *oikos* and not his racial and initial geographical

one. Wright himself wonders in *Black Power* whether his destination is not the original point from which he is exiled. Though Wright's journey is instigated by a
genuine interest in the political developments in pre-independence Gold Coast, it
is his desire to probe his racial connection to Africa that compels him to journey
to Ghana. In Appendix D of *The World of Richard Wright*, Mrs. Padmore in her "Letter" dated March 13, 1963 writes that Wright went enthusiastically to Africa not
only "to observe the environment and atmosphere at a time of liberatory struggle, but also partly in a mood of curiosity to know and understand the people
from whom his ancestors had sprung" (Fabre 257). According to Padmore, he was
also anxious "to understand why it was that Africans had sold other Africans into
slavery" (258). Wright's voyage is not about discovering the Other in the Ghanaian
"contact zone" or reassessing the self and home; rather, it is about understanding
the moment of severance, searching for the self in one's original historical place
of reference and then reconstructing the self in the mirror of that racial self.

Because the fortuity of birth had made him racially of African descent, Wright,
who disdains racialist theories—although his existence is marked by blackness—
needs to know just "how much of [him] was African" (*BP* 11). Wright's journey
to Africa is, as indicated in the "Apropos Prepossessions" section, a quest and a
probing of the African American border identity through his assessment and comprehension of the African. His voyage is an attempt to confirm the rupture of exile
or the historical connectedness between his present Western experience and his
African past which Wright proclaims in *12 Million Black Voices* (1941) as retracing
the journey of the African American in American society. *Black Power* is not a journalistic travel book that provides information merely on the political situation of
Ghana. Instead it is, as Wright claims, "a first-person, subjective narrative on the
life and conditions of the colony and areas of the Gold Coast" (xiv), a decenter-
ing of the Other and inscribing of the self. Like *12 Million Black Voices*, it is a book
about the African American's odyssey from a metaphorical oral past to literacy
and history. It is a mirror in which America can see herself and remember. It is
only by curing herself of a collective forgetfulness that America can understand
the historical and social ties that unite her inextricably to the African American
becoming. The West's collective forgetfulness, symbolized by the lower class am-
nesic, English woman in *Black Power*, erases the horrible European history of colonial conquest. Despite the dire deeds the West historically committed against humanity, this woman signifying Europe ironically solely recalls of that past the fact
that Europe had lifted the colonies and now has "had enough of carrying them

[blacks] on [its] shoulders" (18). By exposing Western hegemony, debunking the white man's burden fallacy, and projecting the numerous faces and positions of black minorities, Wright foregrounds the restrictive and arbitrary marginal position that the African American occupies within Western society. It is only by looking at the African through the eyes of the African American that America will truly comprehend how African American identity is socially constructed and ultimately intertwined with that of other Americans. Wright tells his white readers in *12 Million Black Voices:* "Look at us and know us, you will know yourselves, for *we* are *you*, looking back at you from the dark mirror of our lives!" (146). As Wright writes himself into being, he displaces the gaze from the African black object to the white subject who becomes the object of the former's gaze. On the other hand, when Wright looks at Africa, his gaze posits Western centrality and power, and the Africans' stares, as he interprets them, define him as a Westerner and as an Other. *Black Power* is, hence, foremost a travelogue of an exile's return voyage "home," an assessment of his insiderness, and a geographical positioning of himself as a becoming-self-within-the-world.

Black Power unfolds with a lengthy digressive account of the historical slave trade triangle, and Wright's reflections on the city recalling the initial journey of (dis)location. His singular journey is juxtaposed to the collective middle Atlantic voyage of former slaves that began the original rupture. Because Liverpool (the location from which Wright sets forth for Africa) was a focal city in the slave trade, his journey is both a moment of questioning the "drab respectability" of the West, of remembering how the African American was considered a commodity, and of reconsidering the distorted ontological nature of the African American. Through the act of writing this travel narrative, his "Reactions in the Land of Pathos" extirpates Wright's identity from both "social and racial heredity" and defines him as an outsider. Indeed, Jack Moore contends in "Black Power Revisited: In Search of Richard Wright" that while Wright captures his emotions, he, nonetheless, reshapes and distorts his perceptions to conform to his role of outsider. Moore invites readers of *Black Power* to read it "as a novel focusing on a character named Richard Wright playing a familiar role, the outsider, the baffled native son foreign to the land of his ancestors' birth" (185). Wright himself, quoted by Michel Fabre in *From Harlem to Paris,* states that to be a free Western subject he could not trust and align himself with Africa on mere trust and blackness since Africa had been a "fifth column, a corps of saboteurs and spies of Europe" (192). Because Africa was a continent from which he needed to be free, Wright questions this continent not at a human level but in relationship to the Western world. By using the mediation of the Other African, Wright, as Michel de Certeau theorizes in *The Writing of History*, inscribes his self within the newly-created African text which configures his relationship with the African Other, the past (212). Africa, therefore for Wright, is merely a background against which African American subjectivity is construed and negotiated through the gazing, reading, and remapping of Africa and the projection of the African American experience into history.

Gazing at Africa is for him the fathoming of the depths of history and the reconstructing of one's memory through a reverse transatlantic journey. When he attempts to bridge the moment of rupture of the exile from his original geographical space and race, his desire is not achievable because his memory cannot operate without Western, Africanist discourse. Yoshinobu Hakutani claims in *Richard Wright and Racial Discourse* that Wright's portrayal of Africa is balanced and one in which he seeks the commonalities of African and Western culture (169). Wright also claims to be free from ideological influences; yet, the site from which he departs determines his very perception of the world bipolarized into nature and culture and self and Other. Van den Abbeele purports that it is the point of initial departure that "acts as a transcendental point of reference that organizes and domesticates a given area by defining all points in relation to itself" (xviii). Because the point of *oikos* is considered the origin and absolute end of this movement, Wright's critique and perception of Africa is rephrased within Western ethnographic categories since the people he foremost desires to see in primitive Africa are the pagans. By gazing at the "primitives," the "pagans," Wright's subjectivity and experience are centered and his color rendered invisible. He becomes, as Pile and Thrift contend in *Mapping the Subject*, "the subject position . . . setting the frame for the meaning of the encounter with the other" (41). As he gazes through the Western screen, Wright's memory resists the creation of a collective black myth because it would validate his sub-citizenry. Collective memory would bind him to immutable blackness and Otherness. Disruption and amnesia can alone affirm his selfhood. Like the colonial master, his Othering of Africa allows him, the Westernized logocentric subject, to demarcate himself from African negativity. Yet, his problematic status in Western society, despite his Westernization, sustains his exilic condition within both African and American societies. Although he gregariously attaches himself to the Western collective consciousness, he remains a border citizen defined by the phenomenological gaze of Westerners and an American through the gaze of the Africans. *Black Power*, delineating the existential angst of an African American's exile, is a travel book in the classical sense (travel by road, ship and car, maps, et cetera); yet, it is foremost an eclectic neoslave travelogue combining characteristics of the travel genre, the literature of exile, and the slave narrative.

From the onset of his journey, Wright is aware of the power of Western ideology to determine the image of Africa; he is aware of the discrepancy between image and representation. Wright's awareness of the alienating nature of Western metaphors and the invented identities of Africanist projects is skillfully illustrated by his poem "Afterword: A Film" and by his use of films in the novel *Native Son* (1940). By associating in *Native Son* intelligence with money and manipulation, and using the African's nudity, barbarity, and proximity to nature as a foil to the Westerner's sophistication, culture, and opulence, the films *(The Gay Woman* and *Trader Horn)* respectively establish a manichean, racial opposition positing white superiority. Bigger Thomas, reminiscing about the movie *The Gay Woman*, marvels how "whites are smart people; they knew how to get hold of money, millions of it. . . . Sure, it was a game, and white people knew how to play it" (36). Bigger's alienation and metaphoric nature is, as Wright claims in both *White Man, Listen!* and *12 Million Black Voices*, a Western invention and social construct. Wright contends that "the name 'Negro'" in America means something not racial or biological, but something that has been purely socially constructed and specific to the United States (*12MBV* 30). Black selfhood, as W. E. B. Du Bois ingeniously explains in *The Souls of Black Folk*, is the creation of another's dream. Inextricably defined by his blackness, the double-conscious African American grasps reality and himself through the thoughts and actions of others. As Wright dramatizes in both "Afterword: A Film" and *Native Son*, the African American is America's metaphor (*WML* 72).

Because Wright believes the African American does not have any cultural or racial affinity with Africans, his attitude towards Africa and Africans in *Black Power* is ambivalent. Wright the Pan-Africanist claims in *White Man, Listen!* that African Americans are Americans and that their history transcends the lives of their grandparents and the immediacy of their own. But the stories by their slave ancestors and freed foreparents recall a time when neither whites nor blacks inhabited the Americas. Despite their oral history, African Americans are still separated from Africa. The African American and the African share a common history of racial oppression, but time has torn them apart. Wright writes in *Black Power* that although the past constitutes the present, he can only engage intellectually, not emotionally, with Africa: ". . . faced with the absolute otherness and inaccessibility of this new world, I was prey to a vague sense of mild panic" (175). Because he cannot establish an emotional connection with the African, and because the ambiance is entirely foreign and unfamiliar, the African is to Wright a symbol of foreign, enigmatic, and absolute Otherness. The only connection between the African American and the African that Wright accepts is the suffering and oppression which both groups have endured.

Wright's ambivalent attitude towards Africa is manifested in his interactions with Africans. Nina Kressner Cobb corroborates in "Richard Wright and the Third World" that Wright's initial attitude toward Africa was a combination of "hostility, sympathy, repugnance, and condescension" (230). In *The World of Richard Wright*, Michel Fabre also claims that "Wright's initial outlook on African culture was that of a "Western-educated, Marxist-oriented agnostic, quite conscious of the differences between Afro-American and African social, political and cultural conditions" (192). He further contends that Wright had read no African writer and was not aware of the existence of the "negritude" movement before his exile. Although he is said to have developed closer contacts with French-speaking Africans in 1947 under Sartre's instigation, he really did not have ongoing personal contacts with either Léopold Senghor or Aimé Césaire. Wright never sought them out because he didn't find "an echo of his own" in the objectives and tenets of negritude (194). Despite his relationships with Alioune Diop, the founder of Présence Africaine, and Senghor, one of the founding fathers of negritude, Wright preferred to rely on secondary sources. His African experience was limited to exchanging views and obtaining information on Africa from the South African Peter Abrahams and the Caribbean George Padmore, who were both exiled and alienated Africans in England. The influence of his friend Padmore further distorted Wright's perception of Africa since the former cautioned him against reading lyrical African literature and/or its tenets of negritude. How then can Wright, aloof and distrustful if not ignorant of Africans and African culture, give Africa a voice and excavate the African past entrapped within the veil?

Black Power's introductory epigraphic paratexts also betray Wright's ambivalent attitude towards Africa. Although he and Kwame Nkrumah both certify that he is an honest, serious, and responsible writer free of Communist influences and fit to mold the material from which the destiny of blacks will be shaped, he betrays his political and ideological stances prior to inscribing his self. Wright's gesture of declaring his theoretical postulates, motives, and assumptions is but a means to manipulate the reader into believing that he has no other motives to repress in the text. While he contends to utilize a Marxist approach on purely scientific grounds and does not explicitly advocate the Western commercial expansionism of early travel writings, he, nonetheless, presents the West as the apex of civilization, enlightenment, and progress. Wright's disenchantment with both Communism and capitalism stems from the reluctance of both systems to acknowledge his subjectivity and his right to freedom. He writes that fortuity of birth "had cast [him] in the role of being of African descent" (11), and that he was, thus, accounted as being of African, that is of Negro descent. The words "fortuity," "role," and "accounted as" connote the accidentalness and arbitrariness of his blackness as defined by the West. Western man, according to him, needs to cast suspicion upon the very sense of "justice and freedom which he himself helped to instill in men" if he desires to maintain world control (xii). His assertion that Communist power is the direct result of Western racism and abandonment of its democratic ideals (called by Communists "Capitalistic contradictions") illustrates, once again, his sympathy, appreciation, and embracement of Western principles. Since the aim of the book is primarily a reexamination of "a slice of African Life" and Western racial attitudes, Wright's voyage to Africa is solely a pretext to explore the essence of the African American and his role within Western schemes of development. What Wright historicizes in *Black Power* is not his encounter with Africans but the development and rise to manhood of the African American.

Wright's account of Africa in *Black Power* fails to efface the West as the speaking subject. Instead of showing the West its "hard and inhuman face" as mirrored in the consciousness of those "who live outside its confines" (2), the voices within the narrative present the West as the alluring paradigm of humanness. The African voice never emerges from the text. Instead, the African American voice, situated between the first and the third worlds, struggles to define its place in the world. It emerges, determines, and controls the narrative. Although *Black Power* as a travelogue provides descriptive sequences of sites, it is subverted from the very beginning. It is, above all, an immersion and ascent narrative modeled on slave narratives. *Black Power* does not focus on the mythical African "Other" and the space to be appropriated or put to good use. On the contrary, it delineates a circular journey (immersion) of a hybrid black "self" split in twain and similar yet different. The outbound journey to the Gold Coast is not an encounter with the self, but a probing into the racial self to determine the similarity or difference between the authentic African and the African American. This sub-text, increasingly important as Wright fashions his self, is foregrounded in the fictionalized narrative at the introductory pages. When Dorothy Padmore suggests to Wright that he visit Africa, his mind, he writes, becomes suddenly overwhelmed with questions about Africa: "Africa! I repeated the word to myself, then paused as something strange and disturbing stirred slowly in the depths of me. I am African! I'm of African descent.... Yet I'd never seen Africa; I'd never really known any Africans; I'd hardly ever thought of Africa" (9).

He also questions whether his being of African descent would enable him to "feel and know something about Africa on the basis of a common 'racial' heritage. Africa was a vast continent full of 'my people.'... Or had three hundred years imposed a psychological distance between me and the 'racial stock' from which I had sprung?" During this consciousness struggle over heritage, Wright also realizes that: "My emotions seemed to be touching a dark and dank wall.... *But, am I African?* Had some of my ancestors sold their relatives to white men?" Wright wonders how much of this African presence was in his blood. Did the one-sixteenth, one-eighth, one-fourth, or one-half drop of Negro blood determine his identity? And if so, how much of him was African? Finally, he weighs and questions the West's construct of Africa as the Other: "Was Africa 'primitive'? What did being 'primitive' mean?" (9–10). One of the most provoking questions he struggles with is "Would the Africans regard me as a lost brother who had returned?" Unfortunately, *Black Power* fails to capture the African consciousness through Wright's gaze in order to project the West's inhumanity. But this is a sign of the condition of Wright's humanity, individualism, and freedom. After all, it is literacy and his participation in conscious history that allow him subjectivity.

Wright's immersion and ascent narrative unfolds on the theme of travel with a letter of invitation from Kwame Nkrumah, a prologue entitled "Appropos Prepossession," maps of North Western Africa and the Gold Coast, and epigraphs by Countee Cullen, Walt Whitman, and Robert Briffault. These documents voice both the authenticating matter of slave narratives as already noted by Kwame Appiah in "A Long Way from Home: Wright in the Gold Coast" as well as the form's mutable kinship to travel literature. While authenticating documents generally validate the existence and intellectual capacities of the author delineated in the "tale," *Black Power's* authenticating matter, and especially Kwame Nkrumah's letter, certify that Wright is "a fit and proper person to conduct research on the social and historical aspects" of Ghana. "Through a splendid inversion of the strategy of authentication," Wright, claims Appiah, "seeks legitimation from a black man" (189). Wright seeks recognition from a black man because *Black Power* posits the blackness Wright and Nkrumah share as well as their different historical courses. Although both the African American and the African are defined by each one's blackness, Wright's dedication "To the Unknown African," alluding to the "irreducibly human," "simple and terrifying vision" of the African, invokes the African's absence of humanity. The juxtaposition of the idealized portrayal of Africa and the speaker's distant position to the continent in Countee Cullen's poem "What is Africa to Me?" also foregrounds the African American and the African's sameness and difference. Similarly, the juxtaposition of Walt Whitman's concept of brotherhood and Robert Briffault's theory of cultural determination positions the narrator as "One three centuries removed/From the scenes his father loved." The "Apropos Prepossessions" (meaning "pertinent biases, supposedly to impress us favorably in advance"), also posits Wright as subject, and announces his subjectivity. It is the subject's emotions, experiences, and historical space that transcend the immediate concerns. Wright asserts his control over the material when he writes, "The interpretation of facts, their coloring and presentation are my own, and, for whatever it is worth, I take full responsibility for them" (*BP* ix-x; 4).

Wright frequently refers to his minority status and his deprivation of freedom by means of America's authenticating strategies. Yet, the African American's assumed sophistication creates tension between the African and the African American in this very same authenticating matter and throughout *Black Power.* The Africans are lack (bereft of subjectivity) while Wright, as Frederick Jameson in *The Prison House of Language* claims of Frederick Douglass's narrative, is presence. Like Douglass, Wright is one of the two terms opposed in the text which "is apprehended as positively having a certain feature"—culture, consciousness and presence (qtd in Gates 222). This childish African, consequently, needs the assistance of the West. The latter has the alternative of helping Africa "nobly" or losing it (condemning it therefore to absence). The first-person narrator who distances himself from the Africans through the use of the deictics "the Africans" further reinforces the divide between the African American and the African. Having inscribed his self in writing, Wright asserts his subjectivity and presence while confirming the Otherness of the African and his lack. The author, hence, writes "the conclusions arrived at in these pages might well startle or dismay those who dote on 'primitive' people" (*BP* 8), a non-cultured people whom he bounds and maps in an immutable space. The authenticating documents of *Black Power* validate the author and the authenticity of his narrative. They also displace the subject of inquiry by marginalizing the African.

Africa remains a blank space for Richard Wright. To Marlow in Joseph Conrad's *Heart of Darkness* (1902), it seems to have changed when he remarks that Africa is no longer "a blank space. It had got filled up since [his] boyhood with rivers and lakes and names. It had ceased to be a blank space of delightful mystery—a white patch for a boy to dream gloriously over" (5). Despite his desire to understand Africa and the nature of his blackness, Wright's Africa is a doubly-removed and distorted metaphor because he never gazes at nature but sees through the dreams of others. He refuses, he writes, to idealize the African past by espousing the counter-racist precepts of negritude and Egyptology; yet, his thoughts are covertly governed by Western racialist postulates. Wright claims that he politely listened and "mulled" over the sentences of those who spoke of racial essentialism, but he invariably reverts to his universalistic mode of thinking by preempting race. Disillusioning himself that his ideological stance is raceless, this "double-conscious brother" believes (as he claims) in the absolute objectivity of his narrative whereas his perception of self and Africa is predetermined by Western Africanist discourse. His vision is marred, for it is filtered through his readings—judiciously chosen among the more objective "historical facts presented by the British themselves" (*BP* 13). Cognizant of the Eurocentric nature of his readings, Wright acknowledges in his travelogue that "so unimportant were Africa's millions deemed that no real account of that long campaign was ever fully or properly recorded" (14). In addition, a true account could never exist in an ahistorical country where, according to him, "whatever history was buried in this hot and wet earth must have long decayed, melted back into the red and ravenous clay" (123). Albeit the *Encyclopaedia Britannica* he consults stresses the fauna, gold, and diamonds and only describes the people as of the "Negro race"; Wright never rectifies the history of blacks because his Africa has already been fabricated by popular Western literature. He expresses the desire to see "this Africa that was . . . conjuring up in [his] mind notions of the fabulous and remote: heat, jungle, rain, strange place names like Cape Coast, Elmina, Accra, Kumasi" (2). His perception—informed by the Africanist metaphors drawn by the Western writers Conrad, Gide, Freud, Gobineau, et cetera—precludes an African presence and posits the latter as a negative from whom he needs to distance himself through Cartesian discourse. His failure to demystify and alter Western discourse, or at least to subvert it, stems from his inability to create his subjectivity except by foregrounding his Otherness. After all, the manichean binarism within which he is enmeshed forecloses the possibility of subjectivity without these oppositional spaces.

As Wright travels to Africa and the Gold Coast, Africans are never actually present to corroborate (or contradict) the literary, philosophical, and anthropological works he has read. The texts supplant his actual experience, and therefore limit and confirm his construction of the African according to the images of Western discourse. As Elizabeth Mudimbe-Boyi writes of Bernard Dadié's travelogue of *An African in Paris*, Wright's perspective, likewise, objectifies Africa and monopolizes the word which fosters "the emergence of an encratic language—the language of a hegemonic culture that establishes and determines a hierarchical set of relationships between Self and Other" (31). His Africa is thus apprehended by Western metaphors of bestiality, ignorance, simplicity and "primitiveness." His very landscape, unlike the visual descriptions of John Barrows identified by Mary Louise Pratt, is not inviting (*Imperial* 63). Rather it is repelling and impenetrable because it refuses to open up to him. It "reaches smack to the top of a tall mountain." The air is "wet, sticky, yeasty," and the clouds are "sagging" (*BP* 261). Wright's perception of the world is not formed by his subjective experience. Entrapped by the very rhetorical and ideological structure he seeks to undermine, he is incapable of constructing a self distinct from Western technology, individualism, democracy, literacy, and humanity. His inability to trace a black subjectivity without Western paradigms is foreshadowed by Justice Thomas of the Nigerian Supreme Court. The "evolué" Justice Thomas, civilized and Westernized, ensures that his lengthy connection with Europe is recognized, and that he is differentiated from "[t]hose cannibal natives running naked in the bush" (21). Wright despises him and diagnoses Thomas as suffering from "Frantz Fanonian alienation (dis)ease" because of Thomas's desire to emulate and measure his achievements by British demeanor and intellectualism. Wright rejects any identification with Thomas, his Westernized alter ego. His own sexual disinterest is superior to Thomas's uncontrolled sexuality.

Primordial and colonial Africa are also of no interest to Wright in *Black Power.* The ramifications of the slave trade structure the narrative. As the ship sails forth, Wright compares his journey to that of former slaves; only this time, there are, "no handcuffs, chains, fetters, whips" (19). Echoing Sartre's *Black Orpheus,* Wright wants to reveal the African's vision of the West to the world. One can but wonder through whose eyes? His travel discourse on the African continent is not naive, innocent, or subjective. On the contrary, it is informed by literature. When he takes the train to Liverpool and looks out to the British landscape, he assesses it through the literature of D. H. Lawrence, Arnold Bennett, or George Moore. Similarly, the African landscape is constructed through his reading of Conrad. Like the primordial world of *Heart of Darkness,* Wright's description of the African sunset is described as a "majestic display of color that possessed an unearthly and imperious nobility" (*BP* 26). The ship *per se* is said to slice "its way through a sea...that stretched limitless...toward the murky horizon" (27). Like Conrad's river which is silent, heavy, and "seems to beacon...before the sunlit face of the land a treacherous appeal to the lurking death,...to the profound darkness of his heart" (*Heart* 33), Wright's ocean also possesses "a quiet but persistent threat of terror lurking just beneath the surface," so he would "not have been surprised if a vast tidal wave had thrust the ship skyward in a sudden titanic upheaval of destruction" (*BP* 26). Wright even compares the hotel where he later stays to a hotel in a Conrad book. Because Wright ignores the laws regulating the African world and is incapable of deciphering African faces, which are riddles to him, he alleviates his anxiety by foisting both African and Western landscapes into literary constructs to endow them with meaning.

Wright fails to investigate the laws of African society; rather, as he gazes at the mirror, the African faces and huts mirror his being. He reads in this mirror how he himself is judged. The African body confirms his difference. This moment of disclosure imparts his shared objectification with the African—the Western world, superimposed on the African, is the measurement of the culture he beholds. Though Wright is aware that the metaphor of Africa is simply a projection of Western desires, he readily confines Africa within Western discourse because his Western gaze places Africa and Europe within a nature-versus-culture dichotomy. The African's close relationship with nature and lack of sophistication is constantly emphasized. When Wright strays off the main roads, he perceives, "black human beings who had so completely merged with the dirt that one could scarcely tell where humanity ended and the earth began; they lived in and out of the dirt, the flesh of bodies seeming to fuse insensibly with the soil" (*BP* 67). Having the impression that the Africans were the oldest people on earth, Wright feels a sense of sadness at knowing that the culture of these people "so organically dependent upon the soil and climate of West Africa, so purely woven out of the impulses of naked men, could never be reconstructed." The Africans themselves are not tangible beings. On the contrary, when he sees them, he writes that they "appeared unsubstantial like figments of a dream that would vanish upon close inspection" (75).

The African's very body, a paradigm of the primordial man, is diseased and abnormal. Where Conrad sees legs, arms, "black shapes," "black shadows," "bundles of acute angles" and strings of "dusty niggers" (*Heart* 14), Wright sees "tube-like teats," mutilations, and hideous bodies (*BP* 14). Describing women's breasts, Wright reports that some "have such long ones" that they "simply toss it over the shoulder to the child on their back" (48). When breasts cease to draw his attention, he is attracted to tribal marks. The very body of the African is repulsive and inhuman as evinced in Wright's description of beggars. Some are so deformed that it is painful for Wright to look at them. Several, he states, had "Monstrously swollen legs, running sores" and broken limbs. The "empty-sockets" of blind men "yawned wetly" in the hot sun (51). Uncivilized in manner, these men and women, too, would defecate and urinate like animals in public. The African, as he contends when discoursing on the beggars, "had surely overdone" his deformation "in terms of Western sensibilities." Wright is moved not to compassion, but to revulsion (51). This bestial and barbaric representation of the African, paradoxically, is not reflected in Wright's pictures in the 1956 Dennis Dobson edition of *Black Power.* Most of the Africans are dressed and beautiful (I dare say), and even seem to be civilized. Wright contradicts himself and betrays his own indoctrination when he writes that, to his relief, most Africans, except for a few, did not "deliberately disfigure or deform their bodies" through scarification and that circumcision was taboo (70).

Animal-like, these Africans are incapable of romantic love as Thomas Jefferson notes in *Notes on the State of Virginia.* For a man who had only lived with the Ghanaians for a few months and had neither experienced a sexual encounter nor had the time to observe African couples, Wright confirms Appiah's charge in his misreading of African sexual practices. Amazingly, Wright asserts that, among Africans, "there is no sighing, no longing, or other romantic notions in a young man seeking a wife; kissing is not a part of courtship, and is unknown except among chaste Christians" (116). The author associates "sighing and longing" with chastity and Christianity, and sexuality with paganism. These Africans, responding to needs that Wright cannot fathom, choose, moreover, not to concentrate their passions on sex. Failing to manifest their affection in the usual Western manner, they become, in Wright's opinion, asexual despite their "uninhibited instincts" and the numerous children which they propagate.

The African's "uninhibited instincts" are merely a reflection of his puerility. Although Wright is offended by the colonialists' racist jokes about the African's simplistic intellect, he himself considers them "jungle children" (261). He refers to the African on several occasions as a child living in fear. Lacking intellect, this childish African is incapable of transcending the mood of his environment. Because he dwells in the past, his mind is static and is, hence, incapable of apprehending concepts. He, therefore, loves images, movement, dreams, and personalities, but cannot understand realities, forms, or abstractions. When he attempts to conceptualize within the limits of tribal life, he works with fetishistic material. The Convention People's Party female militants, illiterate and myth-minded, rightfully pledge their allegiance to Nkrumah, but to Wright, seemingly are incapable of understanding the binding nature of "an abstract oath taken to a flag or a constitution." The women can only grasp a human symbol that they can "see, hear, speak to, [or] check upon his actions" (61). Wright's skepticism about the intelligence of potentially-educated Africans is also evident when he cautions his Western readers that educated Africans (if intelligent and capable of reflection) would eventually be angered by the nature of their Christian education. According to him, the African is, on the contrary, all "emotions and instincts because he believes straight forwardly" (299). Child-like, the African lives in an unconscious state and is not aware of dreaming. His bounteous environment encourages him to center on his emotions and thus, paradoxically, hinders his development. He lives, says Wright, "in a waking dream" (159). A dreamer, he fabricates fictions that, according to Ken Frieden, signify everything and nothing. Since the African's reality is but a dream, he lives without the confines of logic, never discovering but inventing meaning. Incapable of distinguishing fantasy from reality, he never supersedes the infantile stage.

Furthermore, the African who situates himself within a different temporal space, according to Wright, has a different sense of time than the Westerner. The latter defines time in terms of past, present, and future; the former is constantly seeking meaning in the past. The Africans, according to Wright, "are static; they move and have their being, but it's the kind that bends back upon itself" (264). Wright discovers the African's cultural difference and obsession with the past when he ventures into a theater to observe how Africans are influenced by artificial Hollywood dreams. While educated Africans pretend to display their understanding of Western values in the Legislative Assembly, they make no pretenses in the obscurity of the theater when they mock the Western world and interpret it at will. They are disinterested in the morality and the plot of movies; instead, they relish the elements of surprise, the improbable, and the action. Unlike Westerners who pursue new frontiers and unceasingly look to the future, Africans are forever realizing their lives in mythical, original moments and always seeking past fulfillment. Africans are not moving towards a teleological destiny but persistently seeking the original moment. Wright asserts that Africans—even Western-educated ones who have written works he acknowledges to have not read—are incapable of producing literary works because their circular concept of time forecloses any possibility of Africa having a literature, albeit oral. The Africans' need to repeat the original act curbs their development and stifles their desire and need for technological advancements. With a mythic time that constantly returns to the past for justification, authenticity and truth, no true progress is possible because the African's eyes are riveted on the *zaamani,* the past. As John Mbiti claims, his future and progress are auctioned.

Although the title of the travelogue *Black Power* denotes the empowerment of blacks, Wright's Africans lack the power to capture their being through words. Because they lack intellect and are child-like, they are portrayed in *Black Power* as speechless. Their utterances are insignificant and dismissible even though Wright purports to understand them. Wright, after all, declares that "the African was about the only man really believing in his [vision]" (132). Wright is, therefore, not interested in African voices but in static pictures that lend themselves to a multiplicity of interpretations. He frequently takes pictures but rarely listens to those voices he came to register. He laments that Ghanaians are reluctant to explain themselves or talk about their customs. However, when he is given the opportunity to ask questions, he retreats to his books, having failed to understand his interlocutors. For example, when an educated African inquires whether Wright has understood his explanations of funeral rites, the latter never replies. Rather than rely on his own observations or the interpretations of his informants, he turns, instead, to Western anthropological literature to substantiate and clarify what he has directly experienced. When he seeks to understand African psychology ("debilitating," according to his earlier assertions), he solicits the assistance of a missionary—the very imperial agent he castigates in *Black Power.* After briefly interviewing a servant, Wright presumes that he has penetrated the African mind, paradoxically achieved through the translation (with all the difficulties implied) of the missionary Lyod.

Wright does interview several Africans but never allows them to be projected into history. He never fully expounds upon Nkrumah's political speeches. On the other hand, he extensively records his own Convention People's Party speech that centers on slavery, his American identity, and his group's keen awareness of human suffering. What emerges from Wright's attendance of political rallies is not a better understanding of the Ghanaian vision of freedom, but his own interpretation of their intentions and the workings of Ghanaian politics which, according to him, "smacked of the dreamlike, of the stuff which art and myths are made" (82). He silences the leaders of political parties in his interviews because he emphasizes mostly his own introspections and interpretations. Wright's immediate concern is not the African's interpretation of societal structures and values. Mr. Baako's and Mrs. Cudjoe's interviews are the only African accounts that enlighten the reader about the Convention People's Party. Even then, Mrs. Cudjoe is dismissed because she is supposedly "simple, direct, and factual." Incapable of grasping "abstract ideas, she could not give [Wright] broad, coherent descriptions" (102). Wright merely summarizes Nkrumah's most important speech (petitioning for self-government) but accentuates his own appropriation and interpretation of the speech. According to him, it is "calm, competent, and calculated" to please and reassure the British. He judges the speech of Dr. Danquah, the opposition leader, as superficial because it merely pecks "away at Nkrumah's motion without ever getting beneath the surface of the situation." Wright dissects and analyzes it to conclude, "England had laid her hand upon [Danquah's] spirit," but Danquah lacks both the intellect and the discourse to convey the experience (172). When the educated African finally does speak to Wright, he is accused of cupidity. During a conversation with Mr. Hagerson, Wright wonders why the latter is eager to talk. "Most Africans," he muses, are not "communicative unless it's for material reasons" (181).

Meanwhile, the uneducated African pidgin speaker is incomprehensible because of his limited vocabulary. Although Wright suspects that Pidgin English most probably stems from the African's adaptation of English to the tonal Twi language, he resents it. He vows to never speak it, most probably, because its limited vocabulary betrays the limited intellectual capacities and abstract concepts of Africans (for example, the word "pass" is used to convey material and psychological comparatives as well as the impertinence of a young man). According to Wright, the corporeality of the African and his lack of voice are rooted in his very religious beliefs because he interacts with the invisible world and seems addicted to "a form of physical lyricism." He is prone to speak with a physical movement such as "[protesting] with a stiffening of his neck" or "arguing with his legs" (110–111).

The African's non-verbal medium of expression perhaps explains why Wright had limited contacts with traditional Africans, and also his reluctance to let them speak for themselves. Even when he has the opportunity to hear them, he fails to do so. Wright asks a boy whether his grandfather remembers a lot of history. When the old man starts to tell him, Wright abruptly ends the conversation by thanking the boy for his kindness. On the other hand, Wright patiently listens to fabulous tales such as the foolish and blatant lies by an African royal informant about the king's stool. Also, an anecdote by an African king about his army of ants seems to be a fairy tale to Wright. Tellingly, Wright never listens to the traditional Africans because their words do not signify meaning. How could they? The tribal mind, he writes, is "sensuous: loving images, not concepts; personalities, not abstractions; movement, not form; dreams, not reality" (264).

He only mulls over other people's comments, and quickly reverts to his habit of raceless thinking. Moreover, it is clear in *Black Power* that Wright also distances himself racially from the African. According to him, his very blackness signifies his alienation from the continent and his very body stands for foreignness in the eyes of the natives. Wright's travel to Africa is not a pilgrimage of identity, but an odyssey to confirm the African American's racial and cultural difference.

Wright posits himself several times as an American—and thus human—through documentation which he incorporates in his travel book. This documentation also functions like the authenticating matter associated with slave narratives identified by Robert Stepto in *From Behind the Veil*. Wright's speech to the Convention People's Party is replete with distancing deictics such as "your country," "your great and respected Prime Minister," while he foregrounds himself as one of "the lost sons of Africa." He is a stranger who uniquely shares with the Africans a heritage of suffering and desire for freedom. The crux of his speech is, therefore, not about the African experience, but the African American experience of slavery. Five paragraphs out of eight are devoted to the African American experience. The distance between the two nationalities is further reflected in the excerpt from *The African Morning Post* bearing a headline reading "Odikor's Death Being Investigated." The missing letters, the presentation of facts, and the format of the article display both the unprofessional and superficial journalistic reporting hindering even the best of the Ghanaian newspapers. This lack of professionalism widens the intellectual breach between the African and the African American. Wright comments that "the Gold Coast press differs sharply from the press of the African American Negro. If one ignored the names [of African American newspapers], one would never know that the press was giving news of black people" (*BP* 187–188). This remark surely suggests the likeness of African American presses to white presses, and therefore, their superiority in journalistic reporting and sameness in terms of quality. The limited influence of Africa on the African American is certainly conveyed in Wright's observation that both the African newspaper and the African are locally specific and that "African ideas and culture do not fare well on alien soil, and the African has no hankering for foreign parts" (188). The United Missionary Alliance letter requesting a territory in Ghana for missionary work equally stresses the African American's degree of enlightenment, for they, too, are returning to Africa to civilize and bring religion to the Africans. Wright deplores their interference; yet, he underscores the remoteness of America from the colonies and the African experience. These internal documents extend the postulate advanced within the authenticating matter appended to the travel account, and also establish a general context of power for both as well as a particular self/Other relationship.

While the Africans, the unindividuated puppets animated by ancestors, fail to write and produce literature because of their lack of aspirations for future accomplishments, the African American, according to Wright, transcribes his future and desires in writing, thereby creating his subjectivity. Although African American identity is preserved by the oral tradition, humanity is defined solely in terms of Western logocentricity. Thus, *Black Power,* like ethnographical writings, produces "a kind of authority that is anchored to a large extent in subjective, sensuous experience" because the ethnologist "experiences the indigenous environment and lifeways for [him]self, sees with [his] own eyes, even plays some roles, albeit contrived ones, in the daily life of the community" (Pratt, "Fieldwork" 32). *Black Power* has a similar authority because it is Wright who sees and hears. However, instead of conveying his impressions in a scientific discourse which, according to Pratt, effaces "the speaking and experiencing subject" who "look[s] into and/or down upon what is other" (32), Wright appropriates the ethnological text and posits it as the result of his personal objective scientific investigation. His utterances are consequently never genuine because they only perpetuate, in their intertextuality, an *a priori* ethnocentric perspective. Although his observations shift from narrative to factual generalizations as in some travel writings, his generalizations are far from being personal generalized empirical descriptions; they are paraphrasings of his scientific ethnographical research. When Wright explicates the significance of some funeral rituals after conversing with an educated African youth, his assertions seem to derive from that conversation. But the reader is soon disillusioned when Wright stops on his way home at a bookstore to purchase some literature on the subject. What better way to spend one's afternoon in Africa, he affirms, "than in reading what they say about their 'dead'" (213). Wright's knowledge of the African concept of death is not derived from his experience, but mediated through his readings; it is a knowledge that comes from "thumbing through old pages" (213). Before he summarizes Dr. Danquah's book, Wright points out the culture's temporal concept and pattern of thought that differentiates him from the Africans. After establishing that he (contrary to the African) expresses himself directly, he summarizes Dr. Danquah's book in formal academic style, replete with quotations, paraphrases, and sources. Through the essay, Wright distinctly inscribes his intellectual Cartesian self which distances him from the mythically-minded African. Even though he resorts to an African literary voice, he belittles this "muddy metaphysics" of African riddles (215). When he does meet Dr. Danquah, a self-declared Christian and ancestor worshipper, he concludes that the latter's comprehension of reality is "too profoundly different" about religions. Moreover, his grasp of life is "essentially poetic; it was close to that which our fantasies and daydreams would have reality be" (222).

Wright continually juxtaposes his Cartesian discourse to the African's mythic discursive practices. His text prefigures African culture as object and situates the analysis. His voice prevails throughout the text; yet, it never subsumes the voices of the various historical and ethnographical texts interspersed throughout the narrative. Through this discursive practice Wright becomes the objective intellectual guided by Cartesian logic. It is thus that he posits his Western intellectuality. After all, does he not write, "Men create the world in which they live by the methods they use to interpret it" (118).

Black Power does not allow African voices to emerge, participate in, or dominate this interplay of voices. When they are heard, it is merely as raw data—recorded and interpreted. Wright's own speech is controlled and distant, distinct from the emotions of the Africans. It is the voice of logic and not one of dreams. Generally when the African voice is heard, it is that of the educated hybrid African, the slave and mulatto families disputing at the Christianborg slave market, or the traditional servant, politician, and/or the king. These African voices do not shed light on their own existence, but instead, on the nature of slavery and the African American's struggle. Thus, the servant's discussion on death evolves into the discussion of slavery and its *raison d'être.* Slavery, according to the servant, is punishment, for the ancestors have abandoned the enslaved. Had he been innocent and good, they would have assisted him. Slavery, to this man, is exile—or death since the servant is severed from his clan. While the textual African voices betray their alienation and confusion about Christianity and the West, they primarily mirror African American essence and the African's relationship to the West. Although the gist of Wright's dialogic text relegates the African voices to the margins, Wright's dominant voice expresses much compassion and sympathy for those Africans who see him through their gaze as Other American.

Wright insightfully analyzes the psychological impact of colonialism on the African psyche, hegemony under colonialism and its exploitative nature, and the conflicting nature of Christianity within this imperialistic system. But these analyses are comprehended only through Western power and its institutions which are able to inflict sufferance upon the African American's condition. Because Wright positions himself between the two binary poles of whiteness and blackness, he distances himself from both the African and the Westerner. He widens the gap when he confronts the African's emotions, lack of physical control, and instincts that must be suppressed in order for industrialism to emerge. Yet he empathizes with the African because of the suffering the two both share. He may criticize the Africans' huge gaudy umbrellas, their thirst for blood and women, their waste of property, their barbaric justice and never-ending retinue of slaves, "yet, withal," he concedes that "they are a human lot, intensely human" (307). Conversely, he acknowledges that the African American has retained some of the African's basic and primal attitudes towards life—human, and not racially induced—only because he has been excluded from the Western system. He further sympathizes with the Africans when he sees them carrying heavy loads on their heads as they unload a European ship. He visualizes the enactment of slave labor, only this time with no whips or guns. Because exploitation of the African reflects that of the African American slave, their similar experiences of oppression allow Wright to visualize and theorize the American condition. Again when he attends a Wesleyan Methodist Church, he contrasts the women's earrings with paganism and questions the genuineness of Western religion. The African's religious gyrations and celebrations of death are, according to Wright, more authentic than the money grabbing Western religion which he reflects is paradoxically connoted in the name of Christianborg castle. An atheist, Wright claims that he prefers the singing of Paul Laurence Dunbar's secular song "When Malindy Sings" to the Gold Coast hymn which only elicited a cough of embarrassment from him. Because Christianity has stinted the pagan's sense of pride, Wright claims that his idea of a Christian "was the poor pagan who lived the terror of life" because he "had no Christ to die for [him]," and thus "had to sweat and suffer it all" (134).

Wright's neocolonialist discourse is also more dictated by his Western experience rather than being based upon the African's. His political recommendations to Nkrumah are thus flawed because they are not totally the result of his observations during his travel, but the outcome of his experience of living in the United States. Westerners, as he clearly states in *White Man, Listen!*, must address their racial issues at home prior to attending to the African world where only "psychologically crippled" and "white misfit" Americans venture. Wright thus refuses to recommend Western doctrines to Nkrumah as a solution to Africa's woes. Until Westerners have set their own houses in order with their restless populations, until they have "resolved their racial and economic problems, they can never—no matter what they may say to you at any given moment!—deal honestly with you" (*BP* 345). The houses the West needs to put in order are its racial relations with the African American. The West should not be trusted. Foreign money, especially, should not be accepted because it would tie Africa to Western control and ideas. At all costs Africa must, according to Wright, "be chary of other slaveries no matter in what guise they present themselves" (350). Wright's desire to free Africa stems foremost from his desire to erase the theme attached to blackness by freeing her from her traditional past.

Wright's will to distance himself from Africans and his condemnation of the West are all signs of his desire for freedom. Like Frederick Douglass, Wright ascends towards freedom—both economic and human. Although condescending, Wright's travel response letter to Nkrumah—which ironically legitimizes the latter and his actions—should be read as Wright's manifesto of freedom. The letter attests to both his freedom and his body of knowledge and, therefore, his intellect. Indeed, despite the racial segregation to which the African American is subjected, Wright emerges from this letter, and the book, more human and more sophisticated than the African because of his literacy and intellect. By legitimating Nkrumah's political action and advising him, he, like Frederick Douglass, reverses Nkrumah's legitimation in the authenticating documents. Through this act Wright not only controls his history but also affirms his subjectivity and his vision. The letter, thus, attests to both his freedom and his body of knowledge. Unlike the emotional and sensuous African, Wright rationalizes his condition and that of the African. He assumes the voice of the abolitionist in exhorting his people to freedom and in the process proclaims their humanity. Through his distanced, intellectual travel account of his encounter with the African, Wright establishes his emotional and intellectual kinship with the West, albeit his skin color. This kinship is frequently accentuated in his references to his American identity. His freedom, in addition, is ritualistically enacted in his return voyage. Unlike the slave woman who sheds a pearl tear in bondage, Wright returns to the West a free man—both literally and figuratively, now that he has discovered that Africans enslaved other Africans because "Life is all that life has in Africa" (159). To Africans, the African American's ordeal was justified because people had value only in that they were a kind of currency. He, thus, fittingly ends the book underscoring the difference between the African and the African American when he declares, "Your fight has been fought before. I am an American and my country too was a colony of England. . . . It was old Walt Whitman who felt what you and your brother fighters are now feeling" (351). By referring affectionately to Walt Whitman with the epithet "old," Wright underscores his familiarity with and bondage to the poet because of their collective American history. The African's struggle to integrate "human civilization" and to seek freedom by becoming a member of a universal culture is not an original endeavor but one already accomplished by others. Walt Whitman's poem, "A Boston Ballad," depicts America's liberation and, hence, projects and encompasses Wright within Western history by collapsing the divide existing between the African American and his white American counterpart. Like his predecessors who wrote slave narratives, Wright reclaims his humanity as a black man who has adopted Western civilization and has moved from the African sensuous, fictional system to a scientific Cartesian one.

Despite Wright's distorted vision filtered through Western screens, he struggles to create a new language of hybridity between the interstitial space of colonialist discourse as "an uneasy member" of the Western world. However, he fails, although he raises questions and makes condemning assertions about Western discourse in order to mint a language that can determine black humanity without Western discourse. Though he occupies the space of the subaltern within and without the manichean binarism as a dominant/resistant subject, his gaze is entrapped within the gaze of the colonialist. His voice continues to be marginalized and "caught by time, culture within [the West's] wide sway of power" (2).

As Wright denounces Western ethnocentric discursive practices, egoism, and thirst for power, he decenters the Western self. Through his perceptive analysis of the alienating relationship of the dominant culture and the colonized, his voice of resistance frays a new path towards breaking the illusory manichean binarism. As Wright gazes at Africans, he rewrites Western presence like the colonialists who, according to Simon Gikandi, shape their identities by inventing and excluding the colonial subject whom they consider a figure of alterity. While he posits himself as a Westerner he, nonetheless, concedes that African beliefs cannot explain the disdain and discrimination of the West. As he tells Africa, he diffuses Western knowledge. According to Wright, as fantastic as some African beliefs may be, they remain bodies of knowledge to be respected. Later in his letter to Nkrumah, he questions Western philanthropic designs and exposes their drive to dominate and exploit the African continent.

Through Wright's travel narrative the West is submitted to the subaltern's gaze, and the black man also comes face to face with his own past, future, and Other selves. Caught within Africanist discourse, Africa is the Other, the mirror that reflects the horrifying image of the West and destiny of Africans. Wright discovers that he felt "an odd kind of at-homeness, a solidarity that stemmed not from ties of blood or race, or from [his] being of African descent, but from the quality of deep hope and suffering embedded in the lives of [Nkrumah's] people, from the hard facts of oppression that cut across time, space, and culture" (342). During this circular journey or immersion narrative of his return to Europe, Wright discovers an emotional *oikos* through his shared experience of oppression with Africans. Yet, "home" remains an abstraction because Wright's real home is in the West. This home, to be regained by his return, remains enigmatic for his travel affirms that the West is the initial point of reference, the original home, but yet is an *oikos* where the African American lives a marginalized experience. If both the African and the African American are to be selves freed from stereotypes and oppression, they must of necessity walk into the twentieth century. This march, according to Wright, can materialize only by placing African personality at the center and reorganizing that personality. While African American identity is the overriding theme of his travel book, Wright, the socially-defined man of color, perceptively understands that his own image and that of the African are co-dependent. *Black Power*, like most travelogues, is, hence, rightly a neoslave narrative about African American identity and, by extension, the projection of African identity. Like the missionary about whom Wright writes who yearns to "'save,' that is, to remake *his* own image," Wright also attempts in *Black Power* to save, foremost, himself from his sense of not belonging to the world in which he was born (158). *Black Power* is, hence, a travel narrative about "home" and Wright's endless homelessness as a hybrid subject writing into being a hybrid *oikos* within the interstices.

"No Street Numbers in Accra"

Richard Wright's African Cities

Jack B. Moore

Reprinted from *The City in African American Literature*. Eds. Yoshinobu Hakutani and Robert Butler. Madison: Associated U P, 1995. 64–79. Permission by Associated University Presses.

Two strong images of African life are projected in Richard Wright's *Black Power*[1] before he begins explaining why he wanted to travel to his ancestors' homeland, and both refer to an older, non-urban Africa. He dedicates his book "TO THE UNKNOWN AFRICAN... who, alone in the forests of West Africa, created a vision of life so simple as to be terrifying, yet a vision that was irreducibly human." The anthropological validity of Wright's thinking that earlier African vision to be "simple" is questionable, but his picture of the "primal" African existing far outside the city is clear.

Next, he quotes an excerpt from Countee Cullen's famous poem "Heritage," in which the black American search for identity transports "One three centuries removed / From the scenes his fathers loved" back to a land remembered as jungle, a terrain of mind that possessed a "Jungle star" and "jungle track" when it was a kind of paradise where "birds of Eden sang." The place seems like a version of the pastoral replete with a "Spicy grove" and "cinnamon tree": Africa before the white man, before colonial empires, before the age of technology. Though Africa

45

contained vast and great cities before whites seized political control of the continent, Wright does not mention these yet. The Africa that captivates his dreams is
peopled with "Strong bronzed men, or regal black / Women" who are jungle people, free people. His own progress to manhood, humanity, and artistry directed
him away from small towns and agricultural regions to big cities like Chicago,
New York, and Paris. Trying to find out "am I African?" (10) he would soon voyage
to Accra, the Gold Coast's (Ghana's) biggest city, no forest or jungle of Edenic
flocks and sweet redolence. And that posed problems for Richard Wright.

At the start of *Black Power,* Wright describes himself sitting at lunch in the city
of his choice, Paris, on a quiet, pleasant day. He is sipping coffee and staring "at
the gray walls of the University of Paris that loomed beyond" his window when
Dorothy Padmore asks him why doesn't he go to Africa? His answer, *"Africa?"* is
italicized indicating his shock. "But that's four thousand miles away!" he protests.
He describes himself feeling "on the defensive, feeling poised on the verge of the
unknown." The intensity of his response is caused partly by the disparity between
the city where he is placed—Paris, here presented as a city of calm and beauty,
Paris in the spring (it is Easter Sunday and "footfalls from the tranquil Paris street
below echoed upward")—and the terra incognita that frightens him even as it
lures him to it "as something strange and disturbing stirred slowly in the depths
of me" (9). Africa is the land of mystery, "fabulous and remote: heat, jungle, rain"
(10). Paris is one of the most culturally distinguished cities of Western civilization,
a symbol of great art, traditionally a city treasured as a center of learning (suggested by the great and ancient school whose walls Wright says "loomed" near).
Great distance separates this Paris in Wright's mind from the cities of the Gold
Coast: "Cape Coast, Elmina, Accra, Kumasi" which are for him not even cities
but only "strange place names" he thinks of after "conjuring up" the jungle (12).
Yet the story he will tell in *Black Power* is a travel narrative of a journey to the city,
the African city.

First Wright had to travel through two English cities which, like Paris, represent something of the Western world that had been his home. London and Liverpool illustrate the unpleasantness, the cruelty, and exploitiveness that hopefully
he would not find duplicated in the Gold Coast. London is cold so that in his
boat-train, Wright "huddled in his macintosh" and longed for the heavy coat he
had packed in his trunk. His discomfort in London partly results from the cold,
partly from viewing the depressing landscape outside his train window which he
says "was as bleak as any described by D. H. Lawrence or Arnold Bennett or
George Moore" (13). London is a counterimage to his imagined picture of the

warm Gold Coast which, according to the *Encyclopaedia Britannica* he consulted, "was vivid, replete with dangerous reptiles, gold, and diamonds...and teemed with mineral and agricultural wealth" (12), another image of African land outside the cities.

Liverpool "was the city that had been the center and focal point of the slave trade; it was here that most of the slavers had been organized, fitted out, financed and dispatched with high hopes on their infamous but lucrative voyages" (13). Liverpool had sent ships to Africa and then across the Atlantic between 1783 and 1793, carrying over 300,000 slaves "whose sterling value has been estimated as being over fifteen million pounds" (17). Though the city looked "calm" and "innocent" now, Wright knew its "foundations...were built of human flesh and blood." Though skies were sunny on the June day Wright went through immigration and customs in Liverpool, Wright was cold as he had been in London. English cities offered "massive and solidly built buildings" (18), visible signs of a technologically advanced civilization, but they still chilled Wright who knew the slave trade had helped build them and that "Until 1783 the whole of English society, the monarchy, church, state, and press backed and defended this trade in slaves." Even after the trade was legally abolished (if not completely stopped) the cities were maintained by the imposition of colonial rule throughout West Africa, creating "a vast geographical prison whose inmates were presumably sentenced for all time to suffer the exploitation of their human, agricultural, and mineral resources" (17). And now that prison was being destroyed. No wonder Wright was excited, and apprehensive.

It is hard to know what Wright really expected to find in the Gold Coast once he actually arrived there, since what he imagines about it depicts a pastoral Africa long past, if it ever existed, that had been replaced by an abolitionist's nightmare. The colonial West African prison he describes resembles the notorious image Stanley Elkins put forth in *Slavery: A Problem in American Institutional and Intellectual Life* that compared slavery to something like a concentration camp, many of whose inmates learned to shuffle and grin like Sambos in order to survive, a depressingly deterministic concept. Just before he disembarks from his ship he tells a West African judge "I don't expect to find anything there that's completely new" but that seems more bravado than prediction. He had by this time already seen plenty that was new in his first Gold Coast city that under its "blanket of blue mist... seethed with activity" even early in the morning. The "forest of derricks, cranes, sheds, machines" (*BP* 33) he observes seem to mirror Wordsworth's description of London in the morning in his sonnet "Composed Upon Westminster Bridge," with its "Ships, towers, domes, theatres, and temples" open to the sky. But all industrial devices Wright saw in Takoradi were operated by black men. The vision appears to corroborate a hope he had stated earlier when he conjectured what would be the consequences of colonialism's death since "machines had a nigger-loving way of letting even black hands operate them." Perhaps free Africans could benefit from the industrialization that for so long had fueled the growth of the West. "Africans were talking boldly of hydroelectric plants and the making of aluminum" (19).

Wright's pleasure at seeing the activity of so many black workers, at being guided by Mr. Ansah who owned a lumber business employing two hundred (black) men who cut, dressed, drew, and shipped timber "to all parts of the world," at not being in the minority for once, is short lived. He is embarrassed in a modern store staffed by Africans when he is asked what part of Africa he came from and he answers he does not know, because "you fellows who sold us and the white men who bought us didn't keep any records" (35). Here Wright is wounded by something in his past and Africa's, and now the city suddenly does not excite him nearly so much, nor give him cause for pleased wonder. He is glad to return to the docks for the city's heat and humidity make him feel as though his "flesh was melting from [his] bones." He boards a government bus and rides at first "slowly through streets clogged with black life" (36). The word "clogged" suggests his feelings of gummy torpor. He could have selected many other far more positive terms—described streets "vibrant" or "rich" with black life. Even the more neutral word "crowded" would have been less despairing than "clogged," but would not have so accurately depicted the city's impact on him.

Then within a few minutes Wright leaves and learns that "African cities are small and one is in the 'bush'—the jungle—before one knows it." This is not for him a source of delight. There is in *Black Power* no expressed reverence for village life although individual villagers please him. The "mud huts...[n]aked black children....Black women, naked to the waist," and finally the "rich red" soil "like that of Georgia or Mississippi" momentarily delude him "into thinking I was back in the American South." Wright seems overwhelmed but definitely not dazzled by the "kaleidoscope of sea, jungle, nudity, mud huts, and crowded market places" that cause a deep conflict within him, a "protest... against the... strangeness of a completely different order of life" (36). At this early moment of emotional crisis (and Wright will experience many others as he seeks black power) he has "the foolish feeling that I had but to turn my head and I'd see the ordered, clothed streets of Paris" (37). The nudity Wright objects to here seems not simply a comment on African sexuality (though he does not appear in *Black Power* to have greatly understood that) but on African lack of civilization—in the Western sense founded upon successful and power-laden use of advanced technology. The order he apparently yearns for is the proper and potent arrangement of that technology, embodied in the high civilization of Paris. When Wright left Takoradi he discovered himself soon in the bush, but what he does not acknowledge (and this will cause him greater confusion throughout his stay in the Gold Coast) is that the African city as he experiences it contains within its confines elements of the traditional life he associates with his concept of the bush or village. He observes this but he does not comprehend it.

Wright's life in the chief city of the Gold Coast, Accra, provides a greater source of disappointment than Takoradi. He recognizes little of this African city's colorful vitality but instead slogs through it daily in increasing despair. His life in Accra makes even bolder an act of will the hope he projects sporadically throughout his sojourn in the country, and almost heroic his hortatory letter to Nkrumah at his trip's end calling for a democratic revolution independent of the West (including Russia) but fought for by "The People" (351).

Accra was the Gold Coast's capital city when Wright arrived there, sprawling flatly out from the ocean without a good port, containing about 350,000 inhabitants most of whom were relatively poor by Western standards and packed into what were originally three smaller towns once known as British, Dutch, and Danish Accra: essentially the Jamestown, Usshertown [sic] and Christianborg sections of the more modern city. Physically, like many of the chief West African cities during the time of Wright's visit (1953) Accra differed from many European cities (and the American cities Wright knew best such as New York, Chicago, perhaps Memphis) in lacking tall buildings, large enclosed spaces (like big theatres or sports arenas) and probably most importantly, extensive, mechanized industrial sectors and middle-class suburban areas. The city's sprawl was low and flat, comprised of few-storied offices and stores downtown, acres and acres of small, shed-like houses and small, rather basically constructed apartment buildings, a large low-lying open market area and several smaller markets, and on the outskirts of a city, small pockets of wider, fine homes neatly landscaped, often owned or lived in by expatriates. Wright's travel text of *Black Power* underscores the confusion he incessantly felt in Accra and the Gold Coast by not containing some coherent, broad, familiarizing vista of the city. Wright never draws back and studies its greater topographic details; he never orients the reader or himself to its generalized contours. Thus he is never led to consider or discuss some of the African city's imminent problems, such as underemployment in an area of concentrated, accelerating population with a minuscule industrial base. I do not point this out to suggest his lack of astuteness. He was perceptive about some of Ghana's future political issues: how would a democracy evolve in a land where the will of the people had been rigidly suppressed for generations; how could that deterministic pressure be removed? How could tribal ways fit into a participatory democracy? I wish merely to describe his skill in creating (or reporting on) a personage in his text who is honestly confused by what he sees in the city but who strives to surmount his confusion to establish some link to a land he wishes to admire but is ill-prepared to understand in its complexity.

Physically, Accra devastates Wright, thus diminishing the original, excited resolve he felt contemplating his trip back, and increasing his anxiety. Accra fortifies his doubts about Africa's chances in the new world he thought it was entering. His first morning in the city after a night's sleep in a "beautiful bungalow...built expressly by the British authorities for the creature comforts of the new African ministers" (47) located in pastoral hills outside the metropolitan area, he takes a taxi and plunges directly into Accra. "There were no sidewalks; one walked at the edge of a drainage ditch made of concrete in which urine ran. A stench pervaded the sunlit air" (48). He describes the market (ordinarily one of the African city's most fascinating attractions) selling bits of products, with "carts piled with cheap mirrors...and cheaply framed photos of Hollywood movie stars" and concludes "Was it a lack of capital that made the Africans sell like this on the streets?" (49).

On this first day and frequently throughout his time in Accra "The sun was killing" (49). Periodically he will make remarks such as "It was hot. I felt exhausted" (64). His hopes for some communion with Kwame Nkrumah start caving in while the city's heat makes him feel more strongly his discomfort in the city. In the text immediately following his claim that "The Africans had been so trained to a cryptic servility that they make you act a role that you loathed, live a part that sickened you," he notes depressingly that "At midday when the tropic sun weighs upon your head, making you feel giddy, you discover that there are no parks in Accra, no water fountains, no shade trees, no public benches upon which one can rest from a weary walk. There are no public cafes or restaurants in which one can buy a cup of tea or coffee" (178). He does not add, nor does he have to, "...as there are in Paris." He finds an absence of structure in the city which at times resembles an expressionistic landscape contorted to erase direction and order. "There are no mail deliveries. You went to the post office each morning for your letters" (111). Worse, "Houses have no street numbers in Accra" (176).

He observes two funerals in Accra but no baptisms or marriages. At one funeral he observes men and women dancing and keeps asking "Why?" (125–126) and at the other he watches a parade of city people with a boy carried on a palanquin and "men in red firing muskets"; as they pass, he stands "feeling foolish and help-less in the hot sun," concluding that "I had understood nothing, nothing" (130). Always the artist, Wright turns Accra into the embodiment of his futility. Like a man with a mouth filled with bad teeth who probes his tongue at his most ex-posed nerve, he moves from his cool bungalow into one of the worst sections of Accra surrounding the decrepit "Seaview" (actually "Sea View") hotel where he will reside waiting for a call from Nkrumah. Though the hotel is adjacent to the ocean, "No breezes blew here to freshen the air. My skin was always oily and wet and tiny mosquitoes bit deeply into my arms and ankles." The toilets howl when flushed, the air is constantly humid, "there were flies, greasy food, splattered walls." He grows accustomed, he says, to "the early morning stench of home-made soap . . . the vapors of excrement drifting into the hotel from the open drainage ditches outside."

From his balcony he can look down and see "Africa in all its squalor, vitality and fantastic disorder." Though he seems to enjoy watching the fishermen at work nearby, squalor and disorder seem more apparent than vitality in the streets around the Sea View where he finds "but a few trees," no grass, and "no flowers" (80–82) in the "maze" of the surrounding region. Even the city's wealthy black bourgeoisie who lived at the city's fringes on paved streets in large, fine houses "enclosed by high concrete walls the tops of which held barbed wire and jagged shards of glass to keep out intruders" had no flowers or landscaping around their homes, accord-ing to Wright. Their houses were widely separated and their yards "usually over-grown with weeds or . . . bare or littered with rubbish" (179). Predictably, his depres-sion increases. At one point he complains, "My money is melting under this tropic sun faster than I am soaking up the reality about me," but his narrative demon-strates that the city is draining him also of the ability to understand what the Africans "are thinking and feeling" (136–7). And what surrounds him is not nec-essarily reality.

Because *Black Power* is ostensibly non-fiction, it is easy to consider its descrip-tions of physical facts and conditions as mere reporting, descriptions of a sort pre-sumably any informed observer might make. Elsewhere I have dealt with the ben-efits proceeding from examining the book as a novel with a central character, an outsider who explores territory strange to him and is disconcerted by it. Even journalistic reporting, however, contains themes and motifs that need analysis to see what patterns they fit into. Anyone writing about West Africa might mention the heat, though it is interesting how many of the best novels of traditional African life outside the cities do not describe it as an overpowering force. Certainly the "Africa my Africa" of so many nostalgic African poems is not a stupifyingly hot land. But heat pervades Wright's memory of Accra, along with decay to an extent suggesting that he is not simply delivering a weather report, but using it as a novelist would present these conditions symbolically to describe the climate for progress in the city that is about to become the capital of a new land of the free—if its citizens can free themselves of the various kinds of torpor that colonialism and tribalism have imposed upon them. Wright seems to turn the heat into an unnatural force, though of course it is quite natural to the region, a power mortifying (in the sense of bringing to decay) the land, perverting natural life cycles: "I was told that vegetables grew so swiftly in this hot and red earth that they were not really nourishing! Lettuce refused" (as though it had a life and will of its own) "to form a head here...Other vegetables turned into soft, pulpy masses" (206–207). It is almost as though Wright were describing that foul heat that carried with it evil, turning love into lust, that the Elizabethan playwrights and poets wrote about. Only in the Gold Coast it operates upon other animals in the kingdom. "The heat makes insect life breed prolifically: mosquitoes, ants, lizards, and myriads of other creatures swarm in the air and underfoot. A lump of sugar left in a saucer will draw ants in an hour even to the second floor of a stone building" (207). The heat acts like bad magic.

Queerly, as the heat drives life forward too fast or engenders a prolixity among bugs that is treated as malfunctional to man, together with the dampness, it tears down man's paraphernalia of civilized existence. One morning like many others in Accra, Wright awakens more tired than "When I had gone to sleep. I was gripped by an enervation that seemed to clog the pores of my skin. I was about to pull on my shoes when I discovered, to my horror, that my clothes were getting mildewed, that my shoes were beginning to turn a yellowish green color. I scraped at it; it was mold" (160). As Wright declines, he finds the city world around him rotting. In his hotel room he picks up his nail file and is shocked that it is red. Like objects in a horror film, everything in his toilet kit is "a deep, dark red. I rubbed my fingers across the metal and a soft mound of wet rust rolled up...What could last here?" He wonders what would happen if the "Gold Coast" were isolated from the West "for ten years?" (123). True, the Old Slave Market in Christianborg is crumbling, its walls rotting and columns broken into rubble (180), but that is made to seem not a symbol of the old life's death, but of the constant decay of matter in the city where Ghana's new life will soon be constructed and centered.

Wright also visited the Gold Coast's second largest city, Kumasi, less than half as populous as Accra at the time of his trip there. Though fewer than 200 road miles inland northwest from the seacoast city, Kumasi seems to belong to a different world. "A brooding African city... You get the feeling that the white man is far away... This is the heart of historic Negrodom" (272). The terrain leading from Accra to Kumasi prepared Wright for a different city. The route departing from Accra after a short time spirals up a palisade from which it is possible to look down almost level with rain clouds at the flat lands leading back to the capital. The road then seems to ride the crest of this high plateau winding through some small villages before slowly curving down and then heading directly to Kumasi. Wright's taxi tunneled through heavily wooded forests dense with great, tall cotton trees whose thick, grey trunks looked hard as iron. These trees seem driven like dynamo shafts into the ground the sun's rays rarely reach. Their roots drip down from branches big as trees themselves about twenty feet up from the earth. Whole jungles of thick vines and creepers and green ferns festoon down from the lower limbs that are still much too high to scale, hairy tendrils crawling with bugs and animated by flapping insects and butterflies. The sight is striking and it is possible to feel swallowed up by these forests especially if one drives through them in the dusk or dark. The day I drove this route I followed for a long time a wobbling Volkswagen "Bug" whose bowlegged wheels shivered under its tottering and crumpled body. When I could finally pass its arhythmic and unpredictable veering, I noticed a sign on its side saying "Safety First Driving School." About a fourth of the way to Kumasi just beyond Korforidua, I saw a sign with three vultures squatting on it directing visitors to the "President Nixon Business College." I felt Wright would have appreciated these incidents.

Wright is ambivalent towards Kumasi, from which "perhaps millions of slaves were marched down to the coast and sold to white traders" but where centuries later "Negroes stood stalwart against the British in war after war" (272) culminating in the ferocious siege of British troops huddled in the fort at Kumasi after their commander boldly demanded the Ashanti Golden Stool, symbol of Ashanti nationhood. Wright respects the old Ashanti kingdom for defending itself, even though at the time unsuccessfully, from British political domination; yet in the history lesson the city provides him with an opportunity to deliver, deplores also the region's complicity in the slave trade. Thus in local history he finds examples of both the African search for freedom from European outsiders and its accept-

ance of an internal system of oligarchic power he abhors. He even finds a form
of slavery alive in the present Asantehene Queen Mother's court. From his hotel
window he can see below him the streets of Kumasi "alive" but the family he observes seems still to live in the old, traditional (non-twentieth century urban) fashion: their front yard is a "combination of bathroom, kitchen, dining room, and
living room." The mother is "nude to the waist," another woman fans "a charcoal
fire," a "tall, black girl" pounds corn in a wood vat (274).

Suddenly Wright is "enervated from the heat and dampness again." In Kumasi
"There is little or no sun.... Weather broods over the city; always it feels like
rain, looks like rain, smells like rain" but only "a fine drizzle falls" (279). Wright
feels that from the sky the city must be invisible. The people of Kumasi are as
much a puzzle to him as had been the people of Accra. Kumasi is more black
than Accra had been, but no more reassuring to his search for the foundations of
African political freedom. The life of the Asantehene's court makes him suspi-
cious and sometimes angry, and he cannot figure out "why do most of the people
spit all the time?" (283). He tries to spit as he claims the Ashanti do, and only
dribbles saliva down his shirt.

The Ashanti kingdom radiating around Kumasi is rich in black history of defi-
ance which Wright is careful to recount, but now its chiefdom appears superstitious and conniving to him. His description of the city underscores what must
have been his disappointment in finding no sense of brotherhood with the Akan
nation, no communion. Where he early describes the city as "vital" (272), before
long he is complaining that the foul rainy "Weather dominated everything, created
the mood of living... tinted the feelings with somberness, with an unappeasable
melancholy." He looks out his window and claims "there is no sky" (283), and
when it is not raining the sky is simply cloudy and he sees "huge black vultures
wheeling" in it "all day long" (272). The hotel at which he resides is "dank and
musty." It is an "African hotel" which by now connotes that it is inefficient and
unpleasant. Kumasi's wealthy West Africans can live otherwise, he discovers, when
a young local man points out to him a "big white house ... that looked like a hospital surrounded by a high cement wall" (301). He is told the owner of the house
has grown rich from political corruption. Elsewhere he sees a new housing development for more ordinary citizens, "neat, new wooden houses" in a "plot over-
grown with tall weeds." But no one lives in this surrealistically depicted sub-section
of Kumasi because the homes "cost too much. Africans can't buy or rent them."
They stand finely built, "solid," empty (300).

Open markets selling a variety of goods—food and drink, household equip-ment, clothes and textiles, livestock—dot the neighborhoods of most West African cities, and each city contains a central open market. These markets are (or were when Wright visited Kumasi) a focus of African city life. No matter what your station in life, if you were African you gathered at some time in the market. The central market was the Times Square of African city life. What Wright experi-enced when he finally visited Kumasi's central market, in his phrase "decided to descend into the maelstrom" (defined by dictionaries as a dangerous "whirlpool of extraordinary size or violence"), reflects his state of mind much of the time he was in the Gold Coast and his perhaps unconscious but natural tendency to denigrate the African city in comparison to his idealized European city. "It was a vast masterpiece of disorder . . . filled with men and women and children and vul-tures and mud and stagnant water and flies and filth and foul odors." Immediately he thinks Paris's large "*Le Marche aux Puches*" (its famous Flea Market) "and *Les Halles* would be lost here." Paris had been lovely and peaceful, civilized; the mar-ket at Kumasi represents for Wright "that indescribable African confusion" where he hears "a babble of voices" and sees "men and women and children, in all . . . de-grees of nudity" (294) (the streets of Paris had been "ordered, clothed" [37]).

Perhaps since he is writing in effect a travel narrative it is easy to forget how solipsistic Wright's description is here. What he calls a "babble" is actually many people speaking in their own languages that he cannot understand. The "babble" is in his mind, not on their tongues. Much of the disorder and confusion he per-ceives in the market is similarly in his mind. Market life is rather rigidly codified and operates according to rules of customary regulation. When I retraced Wright's steps and traveled to Kumasi, of course, I visited the market. My notes as it hap-pens do not stress disorder or confusion. "The market is like a bowl from half-way up its sides and when I blurred my eyes I could see black masses swirling smoothly, like the flow of protoplasm you see in films of magnified amoebae—black amoe-bae." I mention my notes here definitely not to prove my view of the market su-perior to Wright's—I am not so foolhardy—but simply to indicate the difference in my perception which might have many causes (my own background, the fact that I lived a while in Africa before journeying to Kumasi, the fact that I had pre-viously read Wright's account for example). I did experience temporary disorder in the market when the shoppers and vendors became agitated as a short, naked man whose body was lathered with sweat and speckled with blood that dripped from his torn eye suddenly appeared running and crashed into several stalls trying to escape "the mob" (my notes) pursuing him. I held my two-year-old daughter in my arms and dashed behind a car when he glowered at me. Some people in the crowd laughed and a woman standing next to me holding a bolt of cloth giggled. Then the man dashed at a policeman and the policeman ran from him and the crowd laughed even more loudly. I did not. The very black man still dripping deep red blood like sweat as he ran, disappeared down an alley. The crowd buzzed for a short time, then shopping resumed as usual. The market, it seemed to me then, had assimilated this incident. That was my tinctured perception at the time.

Leaving Kumasi and heading north Wright enters in his rented taxi a "forest jungle . . . not as thick as it had been about Kumasi; the air was less heavy and I felt almost normal for the first time in many days. The heat was there . . . but a horizon opened out to all sides" so that the jungle did not make him feel "hemmed-in" (297). In a small village he attends another funeral and asks the Information Service member who has accompanied him "Just how many" human sacrifices "are needed" now "when a member of the royal family dies?" and he is told "That depends upon who dies" (298). Back in Kumasi, Wright reports that he cannot see the sun but he can feel its heat through a white mist. "Scores of vultures wheel silently over the city" (299). He has seen in it no more cause for hope than in Accra.

Richard Wright was primarily a creative writer and *Black Power* is at least as much a creative as reportorial travel work. It demonstrates how creative a supposedly reportorial work can be. His African cities are as much constructs of his creation, of his mind, as they are real places on real maps, or more to the point, on real territory. His Accra and Kumasi exist in the shadows of his Paris, and probably his New York and Chicago, too—and certainly his London and Liverpool. Accra and Kumasi are symbolic cities prefiguring Ayi Kwei Armah's Accra in his post-Nkrumah novel *The Beautyful Ones Are Not Yet Born* that also focuses on (now) Ghana's political hopes for the near future, and perhaps Africa's as well. Physically and symbolically, Accra is remarkably alike in both narratives though Armah's city desperately awaits rain as Wright's does not. Otherwise, Armah's Accra is even more insistently depressing than Wright's, and possibly filthier, filled with excrement, urine, mucous, rot, rust, spit, foul odors, sweat, grease, and encrusted filth. There cannot be a page of the novel without some ugly description of what makes up the city, of what the book's obsessed protagonist focuses on in the city. In his work office "Sometimes it was possible to taste very clearly the salt that had been eating the walls and the paint on them, if one cared to run one's hand down the dripping surfaces and taste the sticky mess. . . . Everybody seemed to sweat a lot, not from the exertion of their jobs, but from some kind of inner struggle that was always going on" (20). Even the money smells like corruption, "a very old smell, very strong, and so very rotten that the stench itself came with a curious, satisfying pleasure" (3). "Oozing freely," an "oil-like liquid" drips from a sleeping man's mouth and becomes "entangled...in the fingers of the man's left hand" (5). The polish of a much-used banister "was supposed" to "catch the rot. But of course in the end it was the rot which imprisoned everything in its effortless embrace" (12). A once "gleaming white" garbage receptacle now "covered over thickly with the juice of every imaginable kind of waste matter" (7) contains the boldly printed message KEEP YOUR COUNTRY CLEAN BY KEEPING YOUR CITY CLEAN. But Armah's Accra is foul and its inhabitants nearly all as filled with the decay as its streets and buildings. His novel concludes with possibly one man's salvation during "Passion Week," but political hope for Ghana's future seems gleamless, bleak in the presence of such moral and physical disintegration. The sign on a poda-poda bus delivers his psycho-social-political message: "The Beautyful Ones Are Not Yet Born." Still, when Armah's unnamed, detribalized, deracinated protagonist, an exile in his own homeland, decides to return home to an "aching emptiness" that "would be all that the remainder of his own life could offer him" (160), he seems to have performed an act of moral heroism. He has just aided the escape of a corrupt friend during a coup ("for the nation itself there would only be a change of embezzlers and a change of the hunters and hunted" [160]) by disappearing with him down the toilet hole of a latrine, repeating and parodying the legendary hero's journey underground to knowledge. Later, at sea, he jumps from the boat sailing his friend away and swims in an innertube back to the beach where he finally lies cold but vaguely free. Perhaps his brief break from passivity, his determination to follow his will and perform an action instead of passively submitting to the forces of rot that appear to control life in his Accra, will enable him to stand against the history of defeat he has experienced in the city. Even so, no ultimate victory is certain: "He walked slowly, going home" (180).

The Accra Wright constructed or created or saw is not as bleak as Armah's nor is his conclusion to *Black Power* as tentative. Both books are in the naturalistic tradition demonstrating the difficulty or impossibility of overcoming deterministic environmental and social forces that trap individuals and entire societies. In this hostile scheme the city is a power that seems to drag humanity down with it through its own disorder and decay. It is also a symbol of the disintegration and corruption of its inhabitants, of their irrationality and sometimes their craziness even while it is the locus of their dreams.

Wright's art is tricky in *Black Power*, whether he knew it or not. Travel literature traditionally presents a "true" picture of strange sights but has for a long time— maybe from the beginning—blurred the distinction between fact and fiction: re-member John Smith's *A True Relation*, his *General Historie*, or Melville's *Typee*, other travel books about westerners visiting exotic technologically underdeveloped lands. The blur is perhaps more self-consciously achieved in modern travel books such as those by Paul Theroux, V. S. Naipaul and John Krich. In many ways, *Black Power* is part of this tradition thought of as recent and so well represented in Paul Fussell's *The Norton Book of Travel. Black Power* purports to be and is about the Gold Coast on the eve of its independence from Great Britain, but it is also a highly subjective account of an exile's journey to the land of his long gone ancestors, a quest of the self in search of itself. The central landscape of this quest is not the fabled jungles of African and black American legend, but cities of Africa today which are also cities of Wright's imagination: the two may be but are not neces-sarily the same. Neither Accra nor Kumasi is really ready for a successful revolu-tion, and for Wright that is what African independence demands. As cities of the mind, neither is a place Wright can call home. They threaten to envelop him, drain him, drug him, erode his self. As a device to achieve objectivity, which can be seen as another way of asserting the self, he relates chunks of Gold Coast his-tory, but with this he mixes myth and what he considers superstition, which only further erases the distinctions between fact and fiction. The cities which he por-trays as places of disorder and confusion reflect or are projections of the disorder and confusion he experiences in his own quest (an American, and African, descen-dent of Du Bois's doubled Negro, an exile fresh from Paris). He fills his book with dialogue which should lend a travel book or reporter's account verisimilitude, but which here also makes his story seem like fiction. He employs what Mikhail Bakhtin called "polyphony" to communicate his "hidden message,"[2] different voices he, the constant stranger, hears along his way, that orchestrate his ambiguous journey during the Gold Coast's solidly historical event.

At the conclusion of his journey and his book, Wright sets down a letter of advice to Kwame Nkrumah, perhaps because he has lost personal contact with him completely. He concludes, despite all the evidence he has delivered seemingly to the contrary, that he "felt an odd kind of at-homeness, a solidarity" in the Gold Coast that has nothing to do with race. The link he feels is psychological or emotional, forged "from the quality of deep hope and suffering embedded in the lives of your people" (*BP* 342). Wright has suffered, yet he hopes. This letter also reverses the drift of *Black Power* in its hortatory optimism, its strength and confidence of statement, in advising Nkrumah how to achieve the revolution necessary to re-store the Gold Coast (and Africa) to greatness in the modern world. Wright's forceful charge seems doubly ironic. Throughout his text he has questioned the ability of Gold Coast leaders to command this kind of revolution, and the capacity of their constituency to follow their guidance. Furthermore though he concurs with the "*African* path" Nkrumah has so far followed (350), his text consistently questions primary components of that way—tribal structures and African religions for example.

By turns patronizing, naive, and wise, Wright's words to Nkrumah fit best into the scheme of *Black Power* as a revelation of Wright's own human condition. A victim of racial and class oppression, he fought with the hardness and discipline he calls for in the Africans, to escape the deterministic traps of recurrent victimization. He attempted to chart his own path to freedom by not slavishly following the Western or Marxist way. In exhorting Africans to become "MILITARIZED!... NOT FOR DESPOTISM BUT TO FREE MINDS FROM MUMBO-JUMBO" (347), he is confessing what he tried to achieve in his own life as a writer. The "hope and faith!" (354) he terminates his quest with were virtues necessary for him to maintain his struggle to determine his own identity and fate against the controlling forces he knew opposed him or any human. His letter demonstrates he knew Africans shared his needs in their dubious political battle.

In his double quest which becomes a journey beyond reason, Wright achieves self-definition not through the cities he departs from in Europe or discovers in Africa, but by not succumbing to them. Perhaps only fables of his construction, like African riddles, they may illuminate reality when deciphered.

Richard Wright with Mochtar Lubis, Jakarta, Indonesia (1955)

Essays on *The Color Curtain* (1956)

The Color Curtain

Richard Wright's Journey into Asia
Yoshinobu Hakutani

Partly because of America's independence and isolation from the other continents, and perhaps, because of its development and evolution from the older cultures, the mode of writing in America has historically been noted for its time lag. Howellsian realism and the turn-of-the-century naturalism, for example, were in vogue two or three decades later than their counterparts in Europe. Poundian imagism, a modernistic literary movement under the influence of Asian poetics, originated in London in the early 1910s, but its full impact on American poetry came at least a decade later. What we today call postmodernity in American literature is no exception. Understandably, none of Richard Wright's travelogues, which appeared in the mid-twentieth century, was favorably reviewed. What the literary public failed to see in these travel narratives was not only that they represented postmodernity, but also that America after World War II had a hegemonic "superiority complex" over the other cultures.

The uniqueness of *The Color Curtain: A Report on the Bandung Conference* (1956), one of several travelogues which Richard Wright published in the 1950s, can also be gauged in its subject matter. While Wright was primarily concerned with European colonialism in *Black Power: A Record of Reactions in a Land of Pathos* (1954/1956), his account of travel to the Gold Coast/Ghana, he deeply dealt with Eastern and African religions and Catholicism in a later travel book entitled *Pagan Spain* (1957).

The Color Curtain brought together all the issues which Wright had investigated differently in his other two works. By traveling by ship and airplane across the oceans and, more importantly, across the boundaries of race, culture, religion, and philosophy, Wright went to great pains to write an unprecedented postmodern, postcolonial travelogue.

I

On the surface, *The Color Curtain* seems an autonomous, independent travelogue, but its epiphany originates in its predecessor *Black Power.* It was among the Ashanti peoples of West Africa with whom Wright visited that he came upon what he called "[the African's] primal outlook upon life, his basically poetic apprehension of existence," a Zen-like revelation. With this primal outlook on human life, Wright traveled to Asia and specifically Jakarta, Indonesia, in 1954. "What the social scientist should seek for," Wright argues, "are not 'African survivals' at all, but the persistence and vitality of primal attitudes and the social causes thereof. And he would discover that the same primal attitudes exist among other people; after all, what are the basic promptings of artists, poets, and actors but primal attitudes consciously held?" (*BP* 266–67).

After Wright's travel to Asia, his interest in Asian culture and Zen philosophy in particular intensified. In 1959, a young South African who loved haiku described the form to Wright, who, in turn, borrowed from him the four volumes of *Haiku* by R. H. Blyth (Fabre, *UQ* 505), a well-detailed study of the genre and Zen philosophy. Indeed, the primal, poetic vision of human existence in nature Wright seized upon in his African journey was reinforced by his view of Asian culture, religion, and philosophy. As a political discourse, *The Color Curtain* brings home a prophetic argument that Asians and Africans must acquire the basic ideas of democracy and freedom from the West. As an epiphany, it gives the admonition that they must uphold the African and Asian primal philosophy of life and reject its antithesis of Western materialism.

This primacy of the spirit of nature over the materialistic pursuit of Western culture finds its genesis in Wright's earlier essay "Blueprint for Negro Writing." In this postmodern manifesto, one of his theoretical principles calls for an African American writer's exploration of universal humanism, an examination which is common among all cultures. Says Wright,"Every iota of gain in human thought and sensibility should be ready grist for his mill, no matter how far-fetched they may seem in their immediate implications" ("Blueprint" 45). After a journey into

the Ashanti kingdom in 1953 when he was forty-five years old, Wright wrote in
Black Power:

> The truth is that the question of how much of Africa has survived in the New World is
> misnamed when termed "African survivals." The African attitude toward life springs from a
> natural and poetic grasp of existence and all the emotional implications that such an atti-
> tude carries; it is clear, then, that what the anthropologists have been trying to explain are
> not "African survivals" at all—they are but the retention of basic and primal attitudes to-
> ward life. (266)

Wright's encounter with indigenous Ashanti peoples as an outsider and foreigner,
an African American and Westerner, convinced him that the defense of African
culture meant the renewal of Africans' faith in themselves. He realized for the first
time in his life as a Westerner that African culture was buttressed by universal
human values, and he cited instances in *Black Power* of such values as awe of nature,
family kinship and love, faith in religion, and sense of honor that had made the
African survival possible. For the purpose of writing haiku as well, this primal
outlook had a singular influence on his poetic vision.

Before discussing Ashanti culture, he quotes a passage from Edmund Husserl's
Ideas, which suggests that the world of nature is pre-eminent over the scientific vision of that world, the pre-eminence of intuition over knowledge in the search
for truth. This relationship of human beings to their world is somewhat remindful
of Emerson, who emphasizes the pre-eminence of the spiritual and transcendental over the material and empirical. As Emerson urges his readers to realize their
world rather than to attain material things, Wright defines the primal vision in
African culture as the pre-eminence of spirit over matter.

Similarly, Wright's interpretation of the African philosophy recalls a teaching
in Zen Buddhism. Unlike the other sects of Buddhism, Zen teaches that every individual possesses "Buddhahood" and all he or she must do is to realize it. One
must purge one's mind and heart of any materialistic thoughts or feelings, and
appreciate the wonder of the world here and now. Zen is a way of self-discipline
and self-reliance. Its emphasis on self is derived from the prophetic admonishment
Gautama Buddha is said to have given to his disciples: "Seek within, you are the
Buddha." Zen's emphasis on self-enlightenment is indeed analogous to Emersonian
transcendentalism, a philosophy in which an individual is taught to discipline the
self and look within, for divinity resides not only in nature but in human beings.

But there are certain differences between Zen and Emerson. Fascinated by the
mysticism of the East, Emerson adapted to his own poetical use many allusions

to Eastern religions. From time to time, however, one is surprised to find in his essays an aversion to Buddhism. This "remorseless Buddhism," he wrote in his *Journals*, "lies all around, every enterprise, every sentiment, has its ruin in this horrid Infinite which circles us and awaits on dropping into it." Although such a disparaging remark may betray the young Emerson's unfamiliarity with the religion, as Frederic Ives Carpenter has suggested, this passage may also indicate Emerson's aversion to the concept of "nirvana." For Emerson, the association of this Buddhistic enlightenment with an undisciplined state of oblivion to the self and the world is uncongenial to his stoicism and self-reliance (Emerson 318; Carpenter 150). *Satori* in Zen is an enlightenment that transcends time and place, and even the consciousness of self. The African primal outlook on existence, in which a person's consciousness, as Wright explains, corresponds to the spirit of nature, has a closer resemblance to the concept of enlightenment in Zen than it does to Emersonian transcendentalism. To the African mind and to Zen, divinity exists in nature only if the person is intuitively conscious of divinity in the self. To Emerson and Whitman, for example, God exists in nature regardless of whether the person is capable of such intuition.

In Zen, if the enlightened person sees a tree, for instance, the person sees the tree through his or her enlightened eye. The tree is no longer an ordinary tree; it now exists with different meaning. In other words, the tree contains *satori* only when the viewer is enlightened. From a similar point of view, Wright saw in African life a closer relationship between human beings and nature than that between human beings and their social and political environment:

> Africa, with its high rain forest, with its stifling heat and lush vegetation, might well be mankind's queerest laboratory. Here instinct ruled and flowered without being concerned with the nature of the physical structure of the world; man lived without too much effort; there was nothing to distract him from concentrating upon the currents and countercurrents of his heart. He was thus free to project out of himself what he thought he was. Man has lived here in a waking dream, and, to some extent, he still lives here in that dream. (*BP* 159)

Wright's epiphany on the road can be compared to that of Basho (1644–1694), the most revered haiku poet. Basho's life as an artist was that of a wandering bard as recorded in his celebrated diaries and travelogues, the most famous of which is *Oku no Hoso Michi* (*The Narrow Road of Oku*). *Nozarashi Kiko* (*A Travel Account of My Exposure in the Fields*), one of Basho's earlier books of essays, opens with this revealing passage with two haiku:

When I set out on my journey of a thousand leagues I packed no provisions for the road. I clung to the staff of that pilgrim of old who, it is said, "entered the realm of nothingness under the moon after midnight." The voice of the wind sounded cold somehow as I left my tumbledown hut on the river in the eighth moon on the Year of the Rat, 1684.

Nozarashi wo	Bones exposed in a field—
Kokoro ni kaze no	At the thought, how the wind
Shimu mi ka na	Bites into my flesh.
Aki too tose	Autumn—this makes ten years;
Kaette Edo wo	Now I really mean Edo
Sasu kokyoo	When I speak of "home."
	(Keene 81)

The first haiku conveys a sense of *wabi* because the image of his bones suggests poverty and eternity. Although Basho has fallen of fatigue and hardship on his journey, he has reached a higher state of mind. The expression of *wabi* in this verse is characterized by the feelings of agedness, leanness, and coldness. Basho's attachment to art rather than to provision on his travel is shown in this haiku:

Michi nobe no	Mallow flower
Mukuge wa uma ni	By the side of the road—
Kuwarekeri	Devoured by my horse.
	(Keene 85)

That the art of haiku comes from a human being's affinity with nature is also explained by Basho in his travelogue *Oi no Kobumi* (*Manuscript in My Knapsack*):

One and the same thing runs through the waka of Saigyo, the renga of Sogi, the paintings of Sesshu, the tea ceremony of Rikyu. What is common to all these arts is their following nature and making a friend of the four seasons. Nothing the artist sees but is flowers, nothing he thinks of but is the moon. When what a man sees is not flowers, he is no better than a barbarian. When what he thinks in his heart is not the moon, he belongs to the same species as the birds and beasts. I say, free yourselves from the barbarian, remove yourself from the birds and beasts; follow nature and return to nature! (Keene 93)

Basho, like Wright, not only had great confidence in his art, but he also believed that, though the form of haiku differs from that of any other art, the essence of haiku remains the same.

Wright's discussion of the African concept of life is also suggestive of Zen's emphasis on transcending the dualism of life and death. Zen master Dogen (1200–

1254), whose work *Shobogenzo* is known in Japan for his practical application rather than his theory of Zen doctrine observed that since life and death are beyond human control, there is no need to avoid them. Dogen's teaching is a refutation of the assumption that life and death are entirely separate entities as are seasons (Kurebayashi 121–29). The funeral service Wright saw in an Ashanti tribe showed him that "the 'dead' live side by side with the living; they eat, breathe, laugh, hate, love, and continue doing in the world of ghostly shadows exactly what they had been doing in the world of flesh and blood" (*BP* 213), a portrayal of life and death reminiscent of Philip Freneau's "Indian Burial."

Wright was moreover fascinated by the African reverence for the nonhuman living, a primal African attitude which corresponds to the Buddhist belief. He thus observed:

> The pre-Christian African was impressed with the littleness of himself and he walked the earth warily, lest he disturb the presence of invisible gods. When he wanted to disrupt the terrible majesty of the ocean in order to fish, he first made sacrifices to its crashing and rolling waves; he dared not cut down a tree without first propitiating its spirit so that it would not haunt him; he loved his fragile life and he was convinced that the tree loved its life also. (*BP* 261–62)

The concept of unity, continuity, and infinity underlying that of life and death is what the Akan religion and Buddhism share. Interviewed by *L'Express* in 1955 shortly after the publication of *Black Power*, Wright responded to a question, "Why do you write?" He replies, "The accident of race and color has placed me on both sides: the Western World and its enemies. If my writing has any aim, it is to try to reveal that which is human on both sides, to affirm the essential unity of man on earth" (*Conversations* 163). At the time when Wright was among the Ashanti, he was not consciously aware of an affinity between the two religions, but as he later read Blyth's explanation of Zen and its influence upon haiku, he found both religious philosophies fundamentally alike. Indeed, his reading of the African mind conforms to both religions in their common belief that humankind is not at the center of the universe. It is this revelatory and emulating relationship nature holds for human beings that makes the African primal outlook akin to Zen Buddhism.

II

With this frame of mind Wright attended the Bandung Conference in Jakarta, Indonesia, in 1954 and then wrote *The Color Curtain*. The narrative structure of the book, however, suggests that this nonfiction work was intended as a travelogue. Unlike a typical travelogue, which describes a journey from home to elsewhere, Wright's travel begins not in America but in Europe and ends in Asia. Living in Paris as an exile, Wright traveled to Madrid, Spain, by train and then from Madrid to Jakarta by plane with brief stops at Cairo, Egypt; Karachi, Pakistan; Calcutta, India, and then Bangkok, Thailand. Much of the initial narrative consists of planned interviews he conducted on the train and plane with a variety of fellow travelers, intellectuals of diverse cultural backgrounds, including a young anti-racist Dutch woman; a young Indonesian-born Dutch female journalist; a dark-skinned twenty-six-year-old daughter of an Irish Catholic mother and an Indian Moslem father; a male, middle-aged, married, Westernized, Indonesian educator, whom Wright dubs "the H. L. Mencken of Indonesia"; a male, single, restless Indonesian student of political science; and a young male Pakistani journalist educated by Christian missionaries (*CC* 53).

What distinguishes *The Color Curtain* from Wright's other works of nonfiction and fiction such as *Black Boy* and *Uncle Tom's Children*, respectively, is the multiculturalism that underlies his discourse in it. While Wright's observations and analyses deal with diversity in culture and religion, his overall vision is unified in terms of race. The international travelers and participants at the Bandung Conference, as a reviewer of the book points out, "found in the very fact of being nonwhite a basis of unity and, in relation to that fact, the events of history and the problems of the present and of the future were discussed" (Logue 351). Because Wright in *The Color Curtain* is concerned with cultural diversity as well as with racial unity, his observations at the conference have a direct corollary with his comments on and reactions to American racial issues in his other books. The Bandung Conference thus taught Wright that the progress of nonwhite people in Asia and Africa would come about through the peaceful coexistence of diverse cultures, and through the scientific and technological assistance the West was to give to the East. Such a lesson makes a strong allusion to Wright's observations on American racial issues. The advancement of racially-oppressed people in the United States, Wright seems to imply, should be achieved through mutual respect for diverse cultural heritages and through the assistance society is obligated to give the educationally and economically disadvantaged.

Just as the close relationship and friendship with Kwame Nkrumah had provided him with enormous insight into Africa, the dialogues among the Asian leaders and intellectuals whom he heard at the Bandung Conference enabled him to understand various Asian cultures. Above all, in *The Color Curtain* he is impressed by the Westernized elite of Asia and Africa, who are able to look at their cultures from both Eastern and Western points of view. In the introductory section of *Black Power* Wright describes himself as a member of the Westernized elite. He describes himself in *The Color Curtain* as a nonwhite individual who is educated in the West. Such an intellectual has the vantage of being able to see "both worlds from another, and third, point of view" (Baldwin 47). In his African journey, Wright came to realize that the African American, like himself, is the product of neither Africa nor America but of both cultures. Just as he urges African Americans not to return to Africa, he urges Westernized Asians not to go back to their religions and cultures. In his eyes, the new Asian leaders play the role of a bridge between the East and the West.

There are some differences in ideology between *The Color Curtain* and *Black Power.* Interestingly, reviews of *The Color Curtain* were more favorable than those of *Black Power,* since in *The Color Curtain* Wright takes a less anti-colonial and more pro-Western stance. Furthermore, he is decidedly anti-Communist, admonishing the elite of the Third World against sympathizing with world Communism. In *The New York Times Book Review,* Tillman Durdin, himself an elite of Indonesia, concurred with Wright's conclusion: the crucial question facing Asians is whether Asia will be dominated by Communism or by democracy (Durdin 1). As Wright recognizes in *The Color Curtain* that the emerging nations in Asia were anti-Communist, he observes in *Black Power* that Africa was decidedly anti-colonialist. Realizing that building a new African culture must be accomplished by building self-confidence, he pleads with Nkrumah "to find your *own* paths, your *own* values.... Above all, feel free to *improvise!*" To overcome the "stagnancy of tribalism," Africa must establish a new social discipline based on pride and confidence. Wright thus maintains: "AFRICAN LIFE MUST BE MILITARIZED." If such a militant tactic is construed as Communist or Fascist, Wright has faith that an African leader like Nkrumah will not become a dictator. Arming Africa, as Wright says, must be "not for war, but for peace; not for destruction, but for service; not for aggression, but for production; not for despotism, but to free minds from mumbo-jumbo" (*BP* 346–47).

Wright in *Black Power* argues, as Edward Margolies has noted, that the Western influences on Africa have "all but debilitated once-flourishing civilizations" (Margolies 46). It is, therefore, understandable that the new Africa is anti-colonialist in principle and militaristic in tactic. In *The Color Curtain,* on the other hand, Wright observes that Asian democracy and Communist China are politically at war and that the only way in which new Asian cultures can surpass their adversary is through the help of Western science and industry. That he took an anti-Communist stance in *The Color Curtain* was prophetic, for not only has Communism failed to influence the Third World but the Soviet Union has collapsed in recent years. It is also prophetic that he regarded the problems of Asia and Africa as "beyond left and right" (*CC* 11). The Third World, in his view, was confronted with more profound issues like colonialism, racialism, and war or peace—on which both left and right could and did agree.

At the outset of the book Wright's wife questions him about his qualifications for writing such a book. He replies:

> I don't know. But I feel that my life has given me some keys to what they would say or do. I'm an American Negro; as such, I've had a burden of race consciousness. So have these people. I worked in my youth as a common laborer, and I've a class consciousness. So have these people. I grew up in the Methodist and Seventh Day Adventist churches and I saw and observed religion in my childhood; and these people are religious. I was a member of the Communist Party for twelve years and I know something of the politics and psychology of rebellion. These people have had as their daily existence such politics. These emotions are my instruments. They are emotions, but I'm conscious of them as emotions. I want to use these emotions to try to find out what these people think and feel and why. (*CC* 13)

Wright's emphasis on the emotions that underlie the burden of his race consciousness echoes what Wright told Horace Cayton, a sociologist who intimately knew Wright's method of writing. "I feel," Cayton quotes him as saying, "that literature ought to be a sharp instrument to reveal something important about mankind, about living, about life whether among whites or blacks." To Wright, what moves and conditions the reader is the author's expression of emotions side by side with his portrayal of facts of life. "I try to float these facts," he says, "on a sea of emotion, to drive them home with some degree of artistic power, as much as humanly possible, to the level of seriousness which characterizes science" (Cayton, *Twice* 263). Unlike a typical literary naturalist such as Zola, Wright does not hesitate to express emotions side by side with his portrayal of social facts.

In *Black Power*, his emotions are expressed on several different levels. When he viewed the Gold Coast, he did so as a Western intellectual, an African American, an exile in Paris, a man of New York and Chicago, and a southerner. "As a Negro," as Russell C. Brignano has noted, "he approached Africa, as it unfolded before him, with attitudes and emotions different from those of a white Westerner" (91). In *The Color Curtain* as in *Black Power*, Wright approached Asia with the same point of view and feeling. As *Black Boy* tells more about the young Wright than about the South, *The Color Curtain* reveals more about the mature Richard Wright than about the Bandung Conference.

Among the characteristics of the Third World, multiculturalism is what unites Wright's vision of that world with his feelings about his own country. While attending the conference, he was keenly aware that Indonesians were anxious to annihilate the Dutch colonial culture but were uncertain as to what kind of culture was best for their nation. The informant who provided Wright with this sentiment reminded him that Indonesia consists of "several" cultures—Muslim, Christian missionary, overseas Chinese, and Polynesian. To this informant and other Westernized Asian attendees of the conference, Indonesian culture emerged as a challenge to the traditional concept of race and culture. The Asian masses, as this informant pointed out, used to think that "some vague, metaphysical principle in nature had decreed that Africa was for the blacks, China for the yellows, Europe for the whites, etc." "It was amazing," Wright remarks parenthetically, "how widespread this feeling was in Asia and Europe, but less in Asia than in Europe." He learned that the uneducated Asians took their racial and cultural environments for granted and believed that "nature had ordained the present arrangement." At the same time he realized that those Westernized Asians "who had been shaken up, as it were, by war, racial prejudice, or religious persecution, had become awakened and felt that the world belonged to all of those who lived in it" (*CC* 37).

Wright also learned that this perspective on multiculturalism could be put into action by a politician like President Sukarno of Indonesia. Asians, as Wright saw, did not fall victim to their cultural environment; they were instead taking advantage of their diversity in religion and race. "Sukarno," Wright argues, "was not evoking these twin demons; he was not trying to create them; he was trying to organize them." On the one hand, Asian leaders were deeply religious men, products of the mystical cultures; on the other, the Third World populations had been subjugated on the assumption that they were racially inferior. To defend their cultures from colonialism, Asian leaders tried to generate a racial consciousness which was "slowly blended with a defensive religious feeling." The Bandung Conference showed Wright that the double consciousness of race and religion "had combined into one: *a racial and religious system of identification manifesting itself in an emotional nationalism which was now leaping state boundaries and melting and merging, one into the other*" (121).

The key to the prosperity of the new nations in Asia is its leaders' insight in creating harmony out of diversity in their cultural legacy. Above all, as Wright was convinced, the Asian leaders were flexible and pragmatic in adopting democracy and capitalism. They readily admitted that Asia as a whole was handicapped with antiquated technology and work ethics. Paula Snelling, a reviewer of *The Color Curtain* who had lived in Indonesia, found Wright's account of "the myth of white superiority upon Asia" illuminating, even though she admitted that his knowledge of the philosophical and cultural history of these people was inadequate (39–40). What the Asian elite, Wright, and Snelling shared is a vision of harmony and prosperity that prevailed in Asia after World War II.

White Man, Listen!, a work of nonfiction that appeared a year after *The Color Curtain*, expresses much the same view as does *The Color Curtain*. The new leaders of the Third World, as Wright portrays them, "stand poised, nervous, straining at the leash, ready to go, with no weight of the dead past clouding their minds, no fears of foolish customs benumbing their consciousness, eager to build industrial civilizations" (*WML* 63). Wright considers Jawaharlal Nehru of India, for instance, exemplary of the Asian and African elite. For Nehru, India is "a halfway house between East and West" (*CC* 142). Wright admires Nehru because Nehru's thinking is autonomous: his greatness "consists of his being what his country is: part East, part West. If one day Nehru says that the perplexities facing Asia are moral, then he is acting in a Western manner; if the next day he says that the world is gripped by a power struggle, he is looking upon life as an Asian" (141).

Nehru's role as a bridge between East and West can also be attributed to other leaders of the Third World. Dr. Mohammed Natsir, a former prime minister of Indonesia and a staunch Muslim, believed that Islam had made his country neutral in the battle between Communism and capitalism. "There will be no need for Communism in Moslem countries," he told Wright. "Pan-Islam will represent a world force, socialistic in nature, keeping a middle ground between Communism and Capitalism." Social and economic progress for a country like Indonesia was possible not only because its leaders were knowledgeable about diverse cultures and ideologies but also because they had unwavering faith and confidence in their legacy. In short, Wright calls Natsir "more pro-Islam than anti-Communist or pro-Capitalist" (107).

Among the Asian and African elite, Wright found Carlos P. Romulo, a member of the Philippine cabinet and chairman of the Philippine delegation to the Bandung Conference, the most pro-Western. In keeping with Romulo's ideas, Wright argued that the West had the moral obligation to assist the East for its technological and economic development. Wright was remarkably impressed by Romulo's speech to the Asian and African delegates at the conference. Romulo, while criticizing the West for having fostered racism, acknowledged its positive influences on the East. He reminded the Third World representatives that it was

Western political thought that had given Asia and Africa their "basic ideas of political freedom, justice and equity." He maintained that it was Western science that after World War II had "exploded the mythology of race." Romulo's idea of cooperation between the East and the West, based upon a secular and rational thought and feeling on the part of the Asian and African elite, warranted "the West's assuming the moral right to interfere." To Wright, the elite of the Third World were "more Western than the West in most cases.... And those two bases of Eastern and Western rationalism must become one!" If the spirit of coexistence and coprosperity should fail at this point of human history, "the tenuous Asian-African secular, rational attitudes will become flooded, drowned in irrational tides of racial and religious passions." The final message Wright received at the conference was that the development of Asian and African cultures would be accompanied by peace rather than war, which characterized Marxism, and that the development would be toward "a rapid industrialization" rather than "a static past" (186–87).

The effects of multiculturalism on the Third World also bear a strong resemblance to those on African American life. "All intelligent Asians," as an Indonesian educator declared, "now know that the Western white man is praying for us to fight among ourselves, and that we'll never do." In his view, Western people, admitting that colonialism had failed, were attempting to reconquer that world by dividing the people of the Third World. "Fighting among ourselves," he says, "is the white man's only chance of getting back. We're closing ranks. The white man will be disappointed" (58). Solidarity among the oppressed, particularly among African Americans, is the most powerful weapon against racism, as Wright shows in "Fire and Cloud" when the Reverend Taylor succeeds in uniting his congregation. With the stoicism and endurance buttressed by his racial and religious consciousness, Taylor succeeds in leading the poor and the oppressed to freedom.

Another affinity between colonialism in the Third World and racism in America can be seen in the appeal Marxism had to nonwhite people. "I agree with Nehru," a Pakistani journalist maintained. "Colonialism and not Communism is the main danger. Get rid of colonies and you'll not have a trend toward Communism." Reminding Wright that Russia was a colonial state before she became the Soviet Union, a Marxist state, he argued that the American fear of world Communism was "shortsighted and unhistorical." He considered Marxists' friendly posture toward Asia understandable and realistic, for a Marxist, a leftist, was ideologically opposed to a colonialist, a rightist. "But," he concluded, "we would have risen without the Communists" (58). Much of Wright's early fiction demonstrates that

African American intellectuals in the depression years were strongly attracted to Marxist philosophy. *Black Boy*, for example, includes an episode in which the young Wright wondered why he could not eat when he was hungry and "why some people had enough food and others did not" (26). The purpose of Chou En-lai of Communist China in attending the Bandung Conference was to promote the understanding that Marxism was a revolutionary call addressed to socially- and economically-oppressed people everywhere. Chou En-lai's appeal, as Wright saw, won sympathy from the leaders of the Third World partly because the Chinese were racially akin to the people of that world. In America, on the other hand, it was the Depression of the 1930s, an economic environment, that made an African American intellectual like Wright fascinated by Marxism. The Reverend Taylor's freedom march, as "Fire and Cloud" indicates, is triumphant primarily because the African Americans form an alliance with the workers, the economically oppressed.

What the victims of colonialism and racism have in common is a sense of insecurity. In the Third World, as in America, the psychic growth of the people has been stunted by the dictatorial policies of the rulers. Sukarno's keynote speech makes it clear that the people of the Third World are "living in a world of fear." Sukarno emphasizes: "The life of man today is corroded and made bitter by fear. Fear of the future, fear of the hydrogen bomb, fear of ideologies. Perhaps this fear is a greater danger than the danger itself, because it is fear which drives men to act foolishly, to act thoughtlessly, to act dangerously" (119). This psychological state of Asians and Africans strongly resembles that of African Americans. The anxiety an African American man feels in a white-dominated society is vividly described in Book 1 of *Native Son* entitled "Fear." Wright poignantly shows that Bigger Thomas the hero hangs psychologically suspended in a no-man's-land, neither in the white world of rich people he sees in the movie *The Gay Woman* nor in the world of African natives depicted in *Trader Horn*.

The colonial policy is to deprive the natives of autonomy and self-determination, and this oppressive policy has created anxiety and fear in their minds. "For many generations," Sukarno underscores, "our peoples have been the voiceless ones in the world. We have been the unregarded, the peoples for whom decisions were made by others whose interests were paramount, the peoples who lived in poverty and humiliation" (*CC* 119). What Sukarno says about the people of the Third World indeed echoes what Wright reports in *12 Million Black Voices*. The lack of individuality among African Americans in the South, as Wright shows, has taken a heavy toll on the African American character. The oppressive system, in his analysis, "created new types of behavior and new patterns of psychological reaction, welding us together into a separate unity with common characteristics of our own" (12; 14). What Wright calls "the steady impact of the plantation system" also affected the education of African American children. In many southern states, the white authorities edited the textbooks that African American children were allowed to use, automatically deleting any references to government, constitution, voting, citizenship, and civil rights. The school authorities uniformly stated that such foreign languages as French, Spanish, and Latin were not suitable for African American children to learn. This provincial policy is reminiscent of the famous scene in the *Adventures of Huckleberry Finn* in which Jim cannot understand why a Frenchman cannot speak English. Huck thus fails to convince Jim that there are languages other than English and cultures other than English and American (Twain 79). In *12 Million Black Voices*, Wright reports that white men "become angry when they think that we desire to learn more than they want us to" (64).

Just as the racist tradition was upheld in depriving African American citizens of education, colonialism persisted in indoctrinating natives with Eurocentrism. Before the people of the Third World can move from a colonial state to an independent state, they must establish a sense of confidence not only in their tradition and culture but also in their ability to industrialize. The first part of the Bandung communiqué, therefore, stresses the economic development of Asians and Africans. The swiftest way for them to rid themselves of their feelings of inferiority was through development of their industries. "When the day comes," as Wright notes, "that Asian and African raw materials are processed in Asia and Africa" by themselves for their benefit, "the supremacy of the Western world, economic, cultural, and political, will have been broken once and for all on this earth" (*CC* 171). The Pakistani journalist, mentioned earlier, told Wright that the Asian elite "knew in his heart that the West had been irrevocably triumphant in its destruction of his culture, but he insisted that when he embraced a new way of life he was going to do so on his own terms, with no monitoring or overlordship from Westerners" (61).

What this Asian intellectual advocates is a new awareness among Asians and Africans that a reorganization of economic and industrial power was not sufficient in itself and that a sense of autonomy and confidence must come from the Third World, not from the West. Like *The Color Curtain, 12 Million Black Voices* is intended not only as a report on the progress of African Americans from a subjugating environment in the South to an industrial society in the North, but also as a history of how the northward movement of African Americans led to an increase in their self-esteem and, above all, an independent vision. Wright told Irving Howe, one of the most distinguished liberal critics of our time, that "only through struggle could men with black skins, and for that matter, all the oppressed of the world, achieve their humanity" (Howe 109).

To Wright, freedom for African Americans can become a reality only when all of them acquire independent vision as outsiders. No matter how courageous Silas, the prosperous African American farmer in "Long Black Song," may appear, his fight against the racial oppressors makes little impact on African American liberation as a whole because his rebellion is motivated by a private matter. African Americans' emancipation from the rural South, Wright warns, must be accompanied by the vision of the outsider. "Negroes, as they enter our culture," Ely Houston, the New York District Attorney in *The Outsider*, says, speaking as Wright's mouthpiece, "are going to inherit the problems we have, but with a difference. They are outsiders and they are going to *know* that they have these problems. They are going to be self-conscious; they are going to be gifted with a double vision, for, being Negroes, they are going to be both *inside* and *outside* of our culture at the same time" (*Outsider* 129).

The achievement of independent vision, which Wright considers imperative for African Americans, is also what characterizes the new Asians and Africans. Wright thus found at the Bandung Conference that the harbingers of the Third World were not only well educated in Western culture and philosophy but also proud of their history and tradition. He indeed envisioned "THE WESTERN-IZED AND TRAGIC ELITE OF ASIA, AFRICA, AND THE WEST INDIES" as "men who carry on their frail but indefatigable shoulders the best of two worlds" (*WML* v).

Their double vision is what enables them to acquire the basic ideas of democracy and freedom from the West but reject the inhuman aspects of capitalism: greed and materialism. Buttressed by the spirit of their tradition, they are able to sustain some of the fundamental values of humanism: peace, loyalty, love, and kinship, the values Wright initially witnessed while traveling in Africa. At the end of his agonizing career in exile, his African and Asian journeys yielded him a primal, Zen-like vision of human existence. In these travelogues he tries to give an admonition, as he does in many of his haiku, that only by paying nature the utmost attention can human beings truly see themselves.

Richard Wright's Passage to Indonesia

The Travel Writer/Narrator as Participant/Observer of
Anti-Colonial Imperatives in *The Color Curtain*

Virginia Whatley Smith

It was the kind of meeting that no anthropologist, no sociologist, no political scientist would ever have dreamed of staging; it was too simple, too elementary, cutting through the outer layers of disparate social and political and cultural facts down to the bare brute residues of human existence: races and religions and continents.

Richard Wright, The Color Curtain

The leap from Richard Wright's six-month assignment in New York as a paid reporter for the Communist *Daily Worker*, June 8–December 28, 1937, to his three-week stint in Indonesia at the Bandung Conference as a self-employed writer and temporary press reporter, April 10–May 5, 1955, is an eighteen-year period that embraces the multiple, professional guises that he would assume on his way to international acclaim as a writer of fiction, nonfiction, and specifically narratives of travel. It was owing to Wright's previous experience as a journalist, his present literary stature, and his proposed trip to Asia in 1941 that Carl Murphy, President of the Afro-American Newspapers, solicited Wright again as a field reporter for his syndication. The Asian trip never bore fruition, but the fact that Wright was even entertaining the idea of traveling abroad to Asia indexes the global mindset of the author who now was internationally renowned for his novel *Native Son* (1940) and its dramatized version due to appear on Broadway in March 1941. The book was published by Harper & Row on March 1, 1940 and "sold 200,000 copies in under three weeks. Wright suddenly found himself famous; he was called the 'sepia Steinbeck'" (Fabre, *UQ* 180). Wright had already traveled outside the United States to Mexico during his honeymoon in 1940, and perhaps this trip emboldened him more to look beyond America's borders. Murphy in January 1941 asks Wright to consider factors of race, color, and difference—issues that would interest an American audience. But, despite his stature, Wright himself was still experiencing the negative aspects of America's own racism and incidents denying him basic human rights and privileges of citizenship. Conditions became so intolerable that they impelled Wright permanently to seek freedom of expression abroad by becoming an exile in Paris, France, in 1946.

Still, Murphy's request for Wright to file news articles on how Asian people or various residents in Asia agree or disagree on matters of race and color reprises data-gathering strategies in journalistic writing that correspond to Wright's own approach to writing which had been influenced by his studies of the social and behavioral sciences. Already known as a social determinist through his fictions and nonfictions of the 1940s, he would continue to integrate such ideas in his nonfictional travel accounts of the 1950s. As far back as the early 1930s when Wright had become a member of the John Reed Club of Communist Party in Chicago, Illinois, he was drawn to the proletarian style of exposing social disparities. The young Communist writer enhanced his ninth-grade education through self study, especially of the social sciences, and developed a penchant for investigating, observing, and interpreting racially different subjects, specifically blacks and whites, and presenting contrasts, implicit or explicit, between the "strange" and the "familiar"customs of each group that would ultimately cause conflicts. Revealing hegemony and particularly the subordinate, powerless ranks of blacks to whites would become Wright's forte. This disparity between the races he probed in his literary writings as well as in over two hundred articles that he wrote for the Communist *Daily Worker* in New York (Davis, *RW* 5–19). His expertise on how social factors influence human behavior is why Murphy, in 1941, asks Wright to probe into racial/ ethnic differences between non-American and American peoples, and to recount how the physical appearances and habits of foreigners, Asians in this case, would appear to ordinary, domestically-bound citizens. The average American, black or white, would not be venturing abroad too quickly because of the ongoing, World

War II conflicts between America, Japan, and Germany. Even later, the post-World War II hostility towards Japan and the immediate Cold War struggles for world dominion between the United States and Russia would deter the heartiest American from straying abroad in this recovery period from human genocide.

But the desire to traverse the "strange," destabilized, foreign soil versus the inclination to embrace the comfort or discomfort of "home," America the "familiar" country of Wright's birthplace, is exactly what sets Wright the global traveler apart from the average American, especially Negro American. Wright occupied a different plateau as one of America's foremost writers in the 1940s that subsequently placed the world at his fingertips, especially with the foreign translations and/or reprints of *Native Son*, his other short story collection *Uncle Tom's Children* (1938), his photographic text *12 Million Black Voices: A Folk History of the Negro in the United States* (1941), and then his autobiography *Black Boy: A Record of Childhood and Youth* (1945). Wright's exile in 1946 also broadened his vision of the globe from his new "adopted home" of France, and served as a capstone for his unconstrained travels to Haiti, Jamaica, and South America between 1949 and 1951 for the filming of *Native Son*. His trip to continental Africa in the 1950s for the researching of his first travel book *Black Power* (1954) made Wright an authority on African affairs. Asia was next on his agenda.

The Color Curtain: A Report on the Bandung Conference (1956) is Wright's Asian travel book delineating the author's passage into the "unfamiliar" world of Indonesia in April 1955 for the purpose of eyewitnessing, assessing, data gathering, and participating in a conference that brought together global leaders of twenty-nine Asian and black African countries. The work is a nonfictional text presented to his readers as a report, an exemplum of Wright's journalistic skills; however, *The Color Curtain* exceeds that narrow, generic label. It was John A. Davis of the Council on Race and Caste who later says in his letter to Wright dated November 17, 1956 that the field definitely had "lost an important social scientist" ("Letter"). Davis expresses his comment to Wright in this 1950s time frame from having noted Wright's acknowledgement of the role of the social sciences in his writing of *Black Power* (267) and *The Color Curtain* as well as from having heard Wright's public comments in speeches before group meetings and conferences in Paris affiliated with Pan-Africanist organizations and the American Society of African Culture of which Davis was an active member. In any case, whether Wright is producing texts or giving public speeches, his activities and travels in this mid-1950s period indicate the author's continued practice of synthesizing his literary and scientific knowledge in his writings, except his subject matter is now directed on a global scale beyond

America. While the remark which Wright expresses in *The Color Curtain* is that "no anthropologist, no sociologist, no political scientist would ever have dreamed of staging" a meeting of "the human race," his "report" on the Bandung Conference is the author's re-staging of that arena in print to illuminate his expanding consciousness as a global humanist. His period text *White Man, Listen!* (1957) containing supplementary remarks about Wright's Asian-African travels also affirms the author's position. For this very reason of Wright's being situated in a global space during this 1950s time frame, *The Color Curtain* transcends its mere typology as a journalistic account. Rather, it links that aspect of writing associated with the arts and humanities to the many other humanistic and scientific disciplines and fields which Wright adopts and integrates into his travel narratives, and that ultimately define his expression of the style as "eclectic." This natural fluidity of the genre known as travel writing associated with the branches of English literature and anthropology is why Wright the author/producer of the travel text presents his nonfictional, alter ego as a self-taught writer, reporter, and social scientist who is gathering, assessing, and interpreting his fieldwork data like an ethnographer. As such, the materials which Wright presents to his reader by means of his multiple guises as the travel writer/narrator and participant/observer of the text are all thematically unified to function as an anti-colonial imperative by Asiatic and African nations to their former oppressors and still-perceived nemeses of Western imperialists.

I
The Travel Writer/Narrator as Participant/Observer

Richard Wright's passage to Indonesia that resulted in his publication of *The Color Curtain* (1956) is remarked by his multiple roles which need to be identified in order for the reader of his travel account to grasp the text's unity by form and content as a travel narrative. On the one hand, he is the travel writer/narrator of and participant/observer in the "story time" framework of the text; on the other hand, he is the author/producer of his fieldwork experiences after cessation of the travel experience. These differentiations affect the reader's comprehension of how Wright's travel accounts are constituted, and particularly, how the finished product of *The Color Curtain* has been shaped by third-party members of Wright's literary agent and publishing house staffs.

In defining travel literature, I. S. MacLaren notes that its form includes "the decasyllabic couplet, the discontinuous field note, the journal, the diary, the nar-

rative, the report, the letter, the history, the ethnography, the novel, and the combination of them all" (qtd in Blunt 20). Added to this list of forms, fields, disciplines, and genres which MacLaren describes as travel literature is the field of
communication studies, and its specific branch of journalism which also is associated with the term "report." Richard Wright makes a similar argument in *The
Color Curtain*, for the role which he assumes as a press reporter, and which is indexed
also by the work's subtitle *Report on the Bandung Conference*, does not negate the field
of journalism as an aspect of travel literature. The opening scene of *The Color
Curtain* places Wright at home in his apartment in Paris during the December 1954
Christmas-to-New Year seasonal break when he learns of the upcoming Bandung
Conference by means of a newspaper headline. In many of his fictions such as
Native Son (1940), *The Outsider* (1953), and the 1934 posthumous novel *Lawd Today*
(1963), Wright had or has demonstrated his prior skills as a journalist by utilizing
newspaper headlines as a stock, rhetorical trope. In his application for a Guggenheim Fellowship dated October 11, 1937, Wright had stamped his form with a statement that he lacked formal training and had become a journalist through self
study ("Guggenheim"). He was writing in the late 1930s and early 1940s when documentary expressions—photographic texts, newspapers, periodicals, fiction and
nonfiction, et cetera—were intrinsic tools of proletarian writers, and Wright was
no exception in integrating his training in journalism with his literature. Now in
this 1950s home setting of *The Color Curtain*, Wright uses one of the devices of
journalism as a rhetorical strategy to start the action. He is drawn to a newspaper
headline announcing the international meeting of brown, yellow, and black leaders
from twenty-nine Asiatic and black African nations recently freed from Western
colonial rule. Not only is this prospective assemblage an "unimaginable" feat to
Wright—this scenario of a shocked protagonist again being a stock rhetorical
trope from the 1930s–but also is the idea that these "colored" leaders would boldly
announce that their common ground is "race and religion." This blatant pronouncement to the white Western world attains, in the mind of Wright, the plateau
of the "yet still unimaginable," the surreal behavior of people of color whom
Wright knows have only been decolonized in the last decade (Stott 47). This "at-
home" scene where Wright inserts irony into his character's portrait for the conception of the global meeting as unbelieveable to him, a sophisticated, global traveler, is paradoxical.

   Thus, Wright signals to his reader on the first page of *The Color Curtain* that
the work is a journalistic narrative. By his inclusion of the rhetorical tropes of a
newspaper headline, a reader's response of disbelief, and irony, Wright immedi-

ately infuses devices from journalistic writing. This staged opening scene nor his eventual donning of the title of "press reporter" in order to attend the Bandung Conference, however, do not disqualify the field of journalism and its narrative forms and techniques from being defined as an expression of literature, and specifically travel literature in terms of this essay. In *The Politics and Poetics of Journalistic Narrative*, Phyllis Frus argues for reconsideration of journalistic writing as an aspect of literary expression. Frus says of her own study:

> This is a book about both journalism and fiction, specifically about the relationship between the two narrative modes over the course of the twentieth century. By "journalism" I mean writing that appears in periodicals; I also include book-length nonfiction which tells of recent events but which may not have appeared first in a magazine.... Some of my examples are conventionally called "nonfiction novels" or true-life novels; others, especially those published since the 1980s, are not.... I use the term in its broadest sense to mean "writing about newsworthy subjects." Because writers make whatever they are interested in as "news" to others, they in effect make their subjects journalistic by writing about them. (ix)

Here, Frus defines journalism to mean "true-life" stories which encompass both nonfictional and fictional works in periodicals and book-length nonfiction novels as well. The point is that her definitions complement Wright's; similarly, he integrates nonfictional accounts into his fiction or vice versa in order to bring convincing, "true-life," "newsworthy" subject matter to his audience. An example is his incorporating of a news account of the "real-life" Nixon murder case in Chicago as substance for the fatalistic character portrayal of Bigger Thomas, the hero of *Native Son* (xxviii; 260). Now in the 1950s, the "true" account forms the central focus of Wright's narratives of travel. The prospect of Wright providing keen insight into the habits and thoughts of a foreign people forms the basis of Murphy's proposed assignment for Wright in 1941, and, similarly, forms the substance of his interests in writing "true-life" stories about his travels in this mid-century era.

The Color Curtain is, on the one hand, arguably a journalistic account, for Wright's assuming the role of a press reporter was the only way that he was able to attend the global meeting of twenty-nine "colored" leaders of the world since Wright held no such position of rulership over a country (nor other newspaper men and women for that matter). The Paris apartment scene depicts Wright in conversation with his wife following his discovery of this incredible conference in the newspapers. It is here that Wright the seasoned travel writer, the author of *Black Power* (1954/1956) delineating his first, nonfictional narrative of travel about his ten-week experience of investigating Kwame Nkrumah's Gold Coast and the country's drive for independence; the author of a travel book on Spain in progress who has just completed his second data-gathering trip (August 15–September 10, 1954 and November 8–December 17, 1954); and the author, now on a holiday respite prior to his third and concluding field trip to Spain (February 20–April 10, 1955), asserts his determination to attend this conference under any guise (11). Wright even provides a rationale for his being in attendance based upon reasons of "race and religion." But Wright, one must keep in mind, is not just anybody. Implicit in Wright's "power" to scale barriers of foreign entry is his international acclaim as a writer and spokesperson for oppressed "colored" people worldwide. He can identify with these recent decolonized subjects. Says Wright to his wife:

> ...I feel that my life has given me some keys to what they would say or do. I'm an American Negro; as such, I've had a burden of race consciousness. So have these people. I worked in my youth as a common laborer, and I've a class consciousness. So have these people. I grew up in the Methodist and Seventh Day Adventist churches and I saw and observed religion in my childhood; and these people are religious. I was a member of the Communist Party for twelve years and I know something of the politics and psychology of rebellion. These people have had as their daily existence such politics. These emotions are my instruments. They are emotions, but I'm conscious of them as emotions. I want to use these emotions to try to find out what these people think and feel and why. (13)

Again juxtaposing his stock tropes of reveal/conceal codes, Wright embeds these present/absent markers in his statement. Explicit in Wright's comparison of "his life" to "their lives," the brown, black, and yellow people oppressed by Western imperialism, for instance, is his attachment of a personal meaning to his emotional response. He has authority to understand and to speak about the conference based upon his own "lived"experiences which he has specified in his seven points of birthright, class status, religious expression, or political affiliation, et cetera. This personal matrix along with professional concerns is why Wright subsequently applies for a visa with the Indonesian embassy and attends the Bandung Conference as a newspaper reporter, because he identifies with these newly empowered, colored human subjects at odds with white, Western imperialism.

In defining journalistic writing as literature, Frus addresses the groundswell of arguments separating journalism, a branch of communication studies, from literature, a branch of English language and literature studies. The professional and academic perspectives of these branches as different kinds of writing index attitudes also expressed by Wright's literary agent and publishing house staffs who ultimately influenced the form, and thus the definition, of Wright's nonfictional accounts, especially *The Color Curtain*. Says Frus on the arguments separating factual/documentary writing from creative/literary expressions in terms of her own book: "The story I tell in the chapters that follow traces the separation of journalism and fiction as narrative categories (via such oppositions as 'nonfiction' versus 'literature,' 'factual' versus 'literary,' 'real' versus 'invented'), and the various ways writers and texts on the border have muddled these neat distinctions and questioned their basis" (xvii). This same "muddlement" between "factual" versus "literary" textual representations is invested in misconceptions about Wright's nonfictional texts as not being exemplary of travel literature. One cause of the confused thinking is the major change which occurred in Wright's relationship with his long-term publishing house of Harper & Row in the 1950s. Edward Aswell, Wright's longtime publisher and friend, moved to McGraw-Hill. Another reason is that Harper & Row turned down Wright's Bandung book, and Paul Reynolds, Wright's long-time literary agent and friend, hastily placed the work with World Publishers whose editors were William Targ and Donald Friede. To complicate matters, Wright also had to deal with Innes Rose, his London agent affiliated with John A. Farquharson, Ltd., which served as an intermediary firm for negotiating the British productions of *Black Power* and *The Color Curtain* with Dennis Dobson, Ltd., a London publishing house. The Dobson, Ltd. edition of *The Color Curtain* (1956) was typeset and reprinted from the American edition issued by World Publishers. This former publication (herewith declared the "base text" for this essay) is slightly longer than the American edition because Dobson has included six photographs in the London version, as did the company also for their publication of Wright's first travel book *Black Power* (1954). While the pagination differs, the contents of both the American and English editions of *The Color Curtain* remain the same and consist of five important divisions delineated as "I. Bandung: Beyond Left and Right"; "II. Race and Religion at Bandung"; "III. Communism at Bandung"; "IV. Racial Shame at Bandung"; and "V. The Western World at Bandung."

The production of *The Color Curtain* was not accomplished without Wright's having to make some typical compromises during the editorial processes owing to suggestions of and/or power plays by Donald Friede, William Targ, Innes Rose, and Paul Reynolds or subordinates working for them. Once Wright returned to Paris, France, from Jakarta, Indonesia, after May 5, 1955, he immediately began work to produce his narrative in its final form. A triangulation of voices pertaining to the production of the text, its revisions, the author's contractual agreements and fees, and publishers's sales and promotion campaigns for *The Color Curtain* emerge from the disparate files of Paul Reynolds, the World Publishing Company, and John Farquharson, Ltd. The letters and notes associated with these correspondents are housed in the Yale Collection of American Literature, Beinecke

Rare Book and Manuscript Collection, Yale University. Wright's personal letters initiating contact are absent owing to their being held by his estate; however, the scope of the agent/publishing house letters, which often are responding to Wright's inquiries or remarks, tell a story themselves of why a reader might presume that *The Color Curtain* is merely a journalistic "report" rather than a narrative of travel. One issue, first, is the matter of photographs since Wright was an avid photographer (see also cover photograph of Wright armed with camera). During each of his travels in the 1950s, Wright took hundreds of pictures which were left out of the American editions of his texts. Oliver G. Swan of Paul Reynolds & Son, in a letter to Wright dated May 26, 1954, tells the author that Harpers does not find it cost effective to include Wright's photographs in *Black Power*. While they plan to include a cover photograph of Nkrumah and a map in the front matter, they feel that pictures are more appropriate in a *"conventional travel book"* but not Wright's book ("Letter"; emphasis mine).

A similar anti-photograph, anti-travel narrative refrain occurs in the correspondence to Wright from his literary agent dated April 5, 1956 pertaining to *Pagan Spain*. Paul Reynolds tells Wright that he is transmitting the original manuscript as of this date, and also remarks that photographs would not be helpful for this book since it *"isn't a travel book"* ("Letters"; emphasis mine). And what happened to *The Color Curtain* in this conversation about photographs and definitions of the genre of Wright's travel books? The answers lie in the files of John A. Farquharson, Ltd. The bulk of letters from Innes Rose and his affiliates to Wright provide light on their role in defining Wright's literature. It is evident from statements made by Reynolds to Wright that Wright did not like Innes Rose, was very angry with the latter, and was considering dropping Rose and company quickly were it not for the wisdom of Reynold to advise Wright to calm his temper and to placate Rose until negotiations for all of his nonfictional and fictional books were settled. To illustrate some of the confusions created by Dobson that lent to Wright's frustrations, George Greenfield of Farquharson, Ltd. tells Wright in a letter dated July 26, 1955 that Dobson plans to publish three books by Wright inclusive of *Black Power*, his unnamed Asian book, and an untitled novel. But apparently in response to Wright's letter of July 18, 1955, Greenfield sends a contradictory message in his letter to Wright dated August 5, 1955. Regarding Dobson's overdue contracts, Greenfield assures Wright that they are waiting on Mr. Sandelson's decision as to whether Dobson will be publishing the Bandung book and "Savage Holiday," Wright's new novel ("Letters").

There is a noticeable distinction here in the mindset of Farquharson personnel which is that agents do not attempt to define Wright's travel books or the fictions for him; in particular, they only refer to the Bandung book as a work of nonfiction. This publishing house, moreover, is where valuation of Wright's photographs takes place. Even though Greenfield goes on to account for Dobson's bad image of being lethargic and remiss in paying debts or authorial fees owing to their financial problems, and that Dobson's liquidated firm was now under control of Putnams and a Mr. Sandelson, it is Dobson who takes both *Black Power* and the Bandung book and also asks for Wright's photographs. In a letter of January 9, 1956 to Wright, Innes Rose relates two points raised by Dobson on these two London editions in progress. Rose points out that Dobson is concerned about costs, but would like to use Wright's photographs to illustrate the Asian book if they are as "first rate" as those for *Black Power.* Dobson also wants to know if Wright has strong feelings about including the preface written by Gunnar Myrdal in *Black Power* ("Letters"). Wright's fortitude as a writer, text producer, and contract negotiator is at question here, but according to his actions that were corroborated in interviews with Ellen Wright in 1992, Wright maintained strict control over his texts even though he made concessions. In a letter of January 13, 1956 to Wright, Innes Rose confirms Wright's authorial power when, in a conciliatory vein, he indicates that he will convey Wright's comments about the "preface and photographs to Dobson." He also encourages Wright to proceed in developing his prints since Dobson would most likely want to see them. Rose additionally illuminates how Wright protected the integrity of his texts. Rose comments in this same letter that Dobson is typesetting from the American proofs and assures Wright that even the most minor changes in the American edition would automatically be reprinted in the London edition.

What proves to be a major argument in terms of *The Color Curtain*'s being a travel book, despite Reynolds's point of view, is Rose's remarks to Wright in his letter of February 16, 1956. He thanks Wright for the package of photographs enclosed with his letter of 11 February and relays to Wright that Dobson should pay him "£3" or "approximately 3,000 francs" to cover expenses ("Letters"). Unlike Harpers and World who eliminated the pictures because of costs or their own preconceived ideas of what defines a narrative of travel, Dobson, contrarily, sees their merit in enhancing reception of the works. In the Dobson edition, the publisher includes six of Wright's photographs which are located between pages 70–71. There are also 44 other film negatives in Wright's manuscript files at the Beinecke

Library ("Film Negatives"). Since photographs not only define news accounts by journalists but also modern and contemporary travel literature by amateurs and professionals dating as far back as the perfection of photography in 1888, Wright correlates journalism to travel writing. This correspondence is especially discernible to Wright's readers if they use the London editions published by Dennis Dobson, Ltd. Photographs were not inordinate to Wright's other nonfictional text of the 1940s, either, for he had submitted a personal example and also acquired reprints of photographs taken by field photographers working for the Farm Security Administration for inclusion in his 1941 photographic text *12 Million Black Voices* which Wright co-produced with Edwin Rosskam (104). In this work, Wright designed his version of a photographic text by synthesizing aspects of this genre with that of the slave narrative, thereby creating an "eclectic" neo-slave narrative inclusive of pictures. He, moreover, integrates features from the fields of literature, sociology, psychology, and history, to name a few, to create his unique narrative. This photo text and the "Foreword" which Wright produced for *Black Metropolis* (1945), the famous study co-produced by Chicago sociologists St. Clair Drake and Horace R. Cayton, early validated Wright's credentials as a self-taught social scientist (Smith, "Image" 2–5). What Dobson's inclusion of Wright's photographs in *Black Power* and *The Color Curtain* does is to corroborate Wright's narratives as "eclectic" travel accounts, for the author in the 1950s does not abandon his tendency to draw upon multiple disciplines and fields to create a form that is purely "Wrightean." This interdisciplinary technique includes *The Color Curtain* with its obvious overarching frame of journalistic writing, but which, simultaneously, merely illuminates one aspect of Wright's "eclectic" travel account about his trip to Indonesia.

Wright, for instance, asks the paramount questions of "Who, What, Where, When, Why, and How" germane to journalistic writing, but these key rhetorical devices, too, are closely related to travel writing. In scene after scene throughout *The Color Curtain*, Wright insinuates the range of questions into his text. The "Who" question is Wright's rarest interrogatory form, but one occurs in the sequence in Jakarta when Wright is picked up at the airport and chauffered to town by Mochtar Lubis, editor of the *Indonesian Raya*, "an independent socialist daily" (see page 60). Wright asks, "Who puts out the story that the country is almost in the hands of Communists?" Lubis replies, "There are people who were once here and they want to come back" (87). During the flight from Madrid to Jakarta when Palestinians board the plane at Cairo, Egypt, Wright asks of one one member, "What are these?" The man answers, "Photos of Arab refugees driven by Jews out of their homes!" (66). Going on a 10:00 p.m. stroll with Mochtar Lubis, Mr. P., the engineer with whom Wright lodges for a week in Jakarta, and Mr. P.'s wife, Wright notices young school children on the streets at such a late hour. He asks, "Where are those children going this time of night?" He is told by Mrs. P. that they are going "To school... We don't have enough schools, not enough teachers. So these children are going to the night shift." Wright also asks in this same scene, "When was your Republic proclaimed?" and Mr. P. replies, "In August 1945" (90). A young Japanese reporter boards the plane at Calcutta and expresses his interest in African affairs. Wright asks, "Why?" and the man replies, "We know nothing about Africa in Japan" (69–70). And to a young Indonesian student educated in Holland who boards the plane at Baghdad, Wright says "How did you enjoy your stay in Holland?" The young man replies, "I didn't." And Wright surmises to himself, "He was anti-Western, all right" (68). The "What" question is Wright's favorite interrogatory frame. Moreover, Wright opens *The Color Curtain* on the rhetorical device of a question, and closes the text on the same paradigm. After reading the headline announcing the Bandung Conference and noting the racial identity of prospective leaders, Wright says to himself, "What is this?" (9). At the ending of the work when he is summing up his conclusions about the Bandung Conference and the silent but pervasive threat to the West posed by Communist Red China, Wright asks: "Is this secular, rational base of thought and feeling in the Western world broad and secure enough to warrant the West's assuming the moral right to interfere *sans* narrow, selfish political motives? My answer is, Yes" (185). The author both asks and answers questions himself as well as allows interview subjects to speak directly.

Donald Friede and company at World were very cautious in their negotiations for revisions with Wright, for the publishing house was quite interested in having Wright commit his future books with them. Already they had suggested one huge cut and revision of the opening scene that would affect the reader's conception of the text as solely a journalistic account. In a letter of July 18, 1955, Donald Friede relays to Paul Reynolds that he and Bill Targ were impressed with portions of Wright's Asian book, but had already concluded that it would not be a "runaway best seller." It would, however, make a vast contribution to the public's "understanding of a very important subject." He then proceeds to critique Wright's Bandung book, and indicates to Reynolds that he and Targ felt that the opening was "wrong" and the ending in need of strengthening. Preferably, Friede says, Wright should start the text at page 71 where he is sitting in a Spanish cafe. The conversation taking place would provide a striking contrast between totalitarian and democratic rules. However, this suggested reshifting of materials raises questions about what to do with the first 70 pages. Friede goes on to remark that he and Targ felt that the present opening format was not effective ("Letters"). Here, Friede is objecting to Wright's impositioning of 120 questions in these opening pages as well as the author's pre-conference interviews with European-based Asians (Questionnaire). Friede felt that this section was too orchestrated. Although Wright's four interview subjects had come from dissimilar backgrounds, the reader would still sense that they had been preselected rather than randomly chosen. Apparently Wright does not like Friede's comments, nor does he change his mind. It is William Targ who rushes in as peacemaker when he communicates by letter to Wright on August 1, 1955 that he had heard of Wright's reactions to their comments from Paul Reynolds. And in the next paragraph, Targ, attempting to placate Wright, assures the author that they would be able to reach an amicable agreement, even though Wright may not totally agree with them. Going back to Friede's letter of July 18, 1955, it is evident that Wright conceded to make two revisions to his satisfaction. As per Friede's suggestion, he deleted pages 61–70 of the manuscript which concerns the religious festival of Semana Santa in Spain, and that more clearly connects how Wright's research endeavors for his Bandung project overlap with his Spanish travel book project (Friede, "Letters"; Wright, "Semana Santa"). For his new opening in Part I entitled "Bandung: Beyond Left and Right," Wright foregrounds the Parisian apartment scene of discovery, quickly moves to the Spanish cafe scene seven pages later, and then proceeds to augment his four interviews of Parisian-based Asians by a fifth.

Pages 9 to 65 are Wright's sanctioned revisions; at page 65, he boards the plane at Madrid for Jakarta. However, Friede and company got their way on the title and subtitle for the work. In his letter to Wright of August 31, 1955, Friede indicates that he and his staff had not enthusiastically responded to Wright's suggested title of "The Human Race Speaking," a phrase from his text. He then coaxes Wright to think of a title that would describe the "mass of humanity represented by Bandung" and who constitute the majority of the world's population. In another letter to Wright dated September 13, 1955, Friede indicates that he and his staff had decided that "The Color Curtain" was the best title, and "A Report on the Bandung Conference" the appropriate subtitle. While Wright seems to have queried on September 10th if they had entertained his other titles (not identified), he seems to have lost this battle. However, Wright held to his remark criticizing Adam Clayton Powell although he removed the parenthetical frames (152), and also retained the scene of his discussion with the American woman who did not understand the purpose of her black female roomate's using of liquid sterno to heat her pressing combs (158). The World editors had feared these scenes would be construed as libelous or ridiculous. Indeed, Friede and company moved with caution on procedural matters pertaining to the conclusion of the text's production, namely, some minor issues and small changes relating to copy editing, galley states, the book jacket design, the back jacket, the short biographical sketch written by Wright, and the "Foreword" written by Gunnar Myrdal. Besides Wright, World took extra precautions not to offend Gunnar Myrdal when they made a slight emendation to his "Foreword." According to Friede's letter of October 4, 1955 to Wright, they took the liberty to add the adverb "heavily" to Myrdal's opening line: "This book does not pretend to be a [heavily] documented analysis of the Bandung Conference . . . ("Letters"; "Foreword" 7). Addition of the adverb is both appropriate and accurate, for it speaks to the research habits of journalists, creative writers, and social scientists and the amount of proof that they gather to support their claims.

Throughout *The Color Curtain*—whether it be the Dobson or World edition— Wright provides his reader with documented evidence by integrating an assemblage of field data into his text. He records first-person interviews; on-site speeches and excerpts from printed copies; scenes of his dialogue with others or his sole meditations; extracts from books; excerpts from multiple newspapers; and photographs of participants. His text is not heavily documented, as World Publishers was quick to emphasize, but his statements are corroborated by facts intrinsic to nonfictional works, "true-life" accounts, or case studies. But Wright's insertion of these kinds of factual data into his 1950s narratives of travel is not inordinate; it is the norm. In the Dobson edition of *Black Power*, for instance, he has integrated 30 photographs throughout the text; inserted legal data on fines to Africans who commit adultery (114); an African newspaper account of a death (187); and a letter by the United Gold Coast Missionary Alliance dated July 5, 1952 (190), and so forth. He also closes *Black Power* on an epistolary note as rendered by his letter of advice to Kwame Nkrumah (342). The tendency to provide documentary evidence in *Black Power* and *The Color Curtain* are rhetorical strategies carried over from Wright's days as a proletarian writer in the 1930s and 1940s when documentary texts such as James Agee and Walker Evans's photographic text of *Let Us Now Praise Famous Men* (1941) brought the genre to its peak (Smith, "Image" 3), and to which Wright added his statement with *12 Million Black Voices* (1941). Now in his travel accounts he does the same. Readers will find Wright's integration of the Falangist Española, the catechism on behavior for young girls and women in *Pagan Spain* (58), and multiple excerpts from books integrated into the draft of Wright's fourth travel account on "French West Africa" that never bore fruition ("FWA"; see also final essay, this collection). What all this documentary evidence means is that Wright is always searching for the "truth," and inserts "true-life" evidence as proof in his nonfictional and fictional texts to support his claims.

The Color Curtain, thus, is a journalistic account, but only a segment of the overarching form under which it assists in defining Richard Wright's "eclectic" narrative of travel that links the humanities fields of communication studies and English literature to the social and behavioral science fields of history, sociology, psychology, and anthropology to travel writing. And being that Wright mixes kinds of literature in his works, it is not surprising that he utilizes dramatic scenes as a key device to lend authenticity to the idea or argument that he is presenting. In returning to complete his fieldwork in Spain, for instance, he includes a scene at a cafe involving his final meeting with his Spanish friend:

> "When are you leaving us?" my Spanish friend asked.
> "Tomorrow," I said.
> "You are returning to Paris?"
> "No. I'm going to the Orient."
> "Really? Where?"
> "Indonesia."
> "Why are you going there?"
> "On the eighteenth of April there is a great conference taking place."
> "What conference?"
> I stared at my friend in disbelief. (15–16)

Wright again portrays his character as expressing incredulity. But this time, it is, as Donald Friede well pointed out, to contrast the difference between "truth" being available in a free state versus being quashed in a totalitarian or Fascist country like Spain. His Spanish friend lets Wright know that Franco the dictator does not allow such news of revolutions or independence movements to be published in Spanish newspapers in order to keep the people ignorant and contained.

In the opening scene of *The Color Curtain*, Wright cites the social science fields which also inform travel writing. Reflecting on Burma, India, Indonesia, Ceylon, and Pakistan, all religious countries and the five nations sponsoring the Bandung Conference, Wright surmises: "This smacked of something new, something beyond Left and Right. Looked at in terms of history, these nations represented *races* and *religions*, vague but potent forces" (11). Wright refers to the field of history by two modes in his text: by way of an individual's personal history or by means of a na-

tion's history. In musing over his pre-field interviews of Asian subjects, Wright provides the background of number five, a journalist from Pakistan: "His father was
educated in the United States and returned to Pakistan with a heightened political consciousness; so, as a young boy, he breathed an atmosphere of political dis-
cussions that raged in his home. He learned early that he was a member of a subject
nation and race. While still in his teens, he participated in the liberation of his
country, but he has not served any time as a political prisoner. He refused to serve
in the British Army" (55). During his walk about Jakarta with Lubis and Mr. and
Mrs. P., Wright inquires how the present government came to power. Mr. P. responds: "That's a little complicated. . . . On the 18th of August, 1945, after the
Republic had been proclaimed, our Independence Preparatory Committee designated Sukarno as President of the Republic and Hatta as Vice-President. . . . This
committee was composed of outstanding leaders in all fields of Indonesian life.
After full sovereignty was gained, the following bodies were welded into a House
of Representatives. . . ." Wright concludes that Indonesia is a "baby country" (91).

Wright's infusion of sociological information regarding the city of Jakarta's
organization and structure also is an aspect of his literature of travel. Being driven
by Lubis through the city of Jakarta on the morning of his arrival, Wright notes
its correlations to African society:

> Jakarta is a vast, sprawling city, disordered, bustling, overcrowded. Wide ornate boulevards
> alternate with districts called *kampongs*, the equivalent of the African compound. These *kam-*
> *pongs* were formerly villages and the rapidly growing city swallowed them up; now Indone-
> sian peasants still live in them within the modern city, following the ways and the manners
> of their forefathers, oblivious of the rage of alien ideology that circles about them. The
> Chinese section was a nightmare, overflowing with shops, stores, warehouses, and restau-
> rants. (34)

Wright inserts indigenous terms and explains their foreign meanings to his readers, but at the same time, he contrasts the symbiotic worlds of the ancient and
modern within Jakarta's social structures.

Psychology is also a province of Wright's intellectual domain, and it is a primary tool for his depiction of his "second self" as the travel writer/narrator and
participant/observer of *The Color Curtain*. For example, in the opening apartment
scene, he infuses allusions to his knowledge of psychology and specifically the
development of ego-identity in the socialization of a child in his formative years
when Wright provides his wife with the seven reasons why "my life has given me
some keys to what they [the twenty-nine nation leaders of the Bandung Confer-
ence] would say or do." The first reason which Wright supplies alludes to psy-

chology when he states by indirection that "I'm an American Negro." Both his citizenship and race speak to Wright's socialization process and ego-identity formation as a child born in the Deep South state of Mississippi in 1908, and his formative years from ages four to twelve being marred by poverty, family fragmentation, abandonment, rootlessness, and white fear and white violence, to name a few (*BB* 4; 15; 31; 63; 109; Erickson 28). The last reason that Wright provides directly names the field of psychology as his mode of assessment when Wright says: "I was a member of the Communist Party for twelve years and I know something of the politics and psychology of rebellion. The people have as their daily existence such politics. These emotions are my instruments. They are emotions, but I'm conscious of them as emotions. I want to use these emotions to try to find out what these people think and feel and why" (13). And the psychological implications and emotional strains affiliated with oppression from Western imperialism Wright does provide from the perspective of the "observed subject," the interviewee or subject under his gaze, and from his own point of view as the "observing object" assessing his subjects and data (Foucault, *Archaeology* 52–53). For example, among his five interviewees, Wright identifies subject number three as Mr. X, a Westernized Asian. In summing up his conclusions, Wright examines his reactions to the subject during his musings on the train to Madrid: "I felt there must have been a factor of Asian skepticism in that man's outlook. Compassion for man was the keynote in that man's outlook." Mr. X's "disdainful skepticism toward Democracy" surprises Wright, and the author reports that he "jokingly dubbed him the H. L. Mencken of Indonesia. . . ." Further along, Wright shows his capacity to understand the psychology of Mr. X's thinking. Wright surmises, "He took the view that, in the long run, the impact of the West upon the East would undoubtedly be entered upon the credit side of the historical ledger. I was inclined to agree with him." But this authorial agreement is shortlived, for Wright follows up his affirmation with the statement, "But that was not what the individual Asian colonial victim felt about that Western impact while he was undergoing his torturous 'liberation' from his irrational customs and traditions, his superstition and folklore" (45–46).

With his interview of subject number four, a twenty-year-old "full-bloodied Indonesian" and student of political science whom Wright dubs as his "basic Asian," Wright the travel writer/narrator indulges in psychological discourse again in his description of the young man's ego formation: "Personal relations were not important factors to him; his affective identifications were with nations, movements, religions, cultures, races. . . . Personal insults meant nothing; only when those aims in which he fondly believed were maligned or threatened did he react with passion" (53).

After completing his assessment of all interview subjects, Wright plunges into pure psychological discourse to describe the thought process and emotional behavior of "the [typical] Asian" whose portrait has emerged from these five studies: "Rendered psychologically uncertain as to motive, the uprooted Easterner did everything self-consciously, watching himself, as it were. Behavior was spontaneous only when passionate action lifted him to the plane of self-forgetfulness." In addition, "He felt that history now coincided with his feelings, for he knew that what he did was now making history; he might be right or wrong, but what he did would count historically for good or ill." And lastly, "A sort of depersonalization took place in his thinking, and buttressed his personality toward an attitude of irresponsibility. Worlds of infinite possibility opened up before the eyes of the new, young Asians and Africans and they felt as gods" (115). The terms of "Psychologically," "behavior," "feelings," "depersonalization," "personality" rendered in Wright's discourse define the image of Wright's typical Asian subject. Today, his language in post-colonial theory would be considered biased. In fact, Mary Louise Pratt in her essay on "Scratches on the Face of the Country; or, What Mr. Barrow Saw in the Land of the Bushmen" examines similar ethnocentric language intrinsic to Western discourse on Self/Other dichotomies of difference as used by John Barrow in his *Accounts of Travels into the Interior of Southern Africa in the Years 1797 and 1798*. She observes in one of Barrow's statements about the natives that "Any reader recognizes here a very familiar, widespread, and stable form of 'othering.' The people to be othered are homogenized into a collective 'they,' which is distilled even further into an iconic 'he' (the standardized adult male specimen). This abstracted 'he'/'they' is the subject of verbs in a timeless present tense, which characterizes anything 'he' is or does not as a particular historical event but as an instance of a pregiven custom or trait" (139). Similarly, Wright uses the collective "he"/"they" referents in his language as far back as *12 Million Black Voices* (1941) and his representation of the collective experience of "the Negro" (30) while other documentary writers were focusing on "the Indian," "the poor white," et cetera. Now in *The Color Curtain* (1956), he uses deictic phrases again for his collective representation of "the Asian" whose image the author has assembled from the remarks of his five Asian interview subjects. There is also clear gender bias in Wright's term, for Wright's typical Asian is expressed in masculine discourse as a "he" although one of his subjects is a woman (29). But Wright, it has to be recalled, is writing in the timeless present tense historically rooted in biased Western patriarchal discourse owing to his own socialization as a Westernized American Negro who is responding to language used by white male, dominant writers of the thirties and now writers of the fifties. In fact, Wright's travel writings of the 1950s and his self-portraits in the texts as the unifying "I" travel writer/narrator and participant/observer foreshadow post-colonial theories and concepts of ethnography and travel writing in the 1990s.

MacLaren in the 1990s conceives of ethnography as an aspect of travel literature owing to current reconceptions of this sub-branch of anthropology as being adaptable to any field or discipline. Preceding him, Wright in the 1950s demonstrates how that adaptability works in his configuration of the travel book as an "eclectic" account by his integrating the disparate humanities fields of English literature and communication studies with the social and behavioral science fields of history, sociology, and psychology into his work. All of these fields Wright intermingles in order to complement the anthropological sub-branch of ethnography which he appropriates to define his role as the participant/observer of the text. Already in the opening scene, he has declared that the gathering of twenty-nine "colored" Asiatic and African leaders was a meeting that "no anthropologist . . . would ever have dreamed of staging" (11). Yet, this is exactly what he "re-stages" in *The Color Curtain*. Historian and cultural critic Michel Foucault has done much to influence medical, social scientific, and literary thinking in his study of the positions of power in his multiplicity of works inclusive of *The Archaeology of Knowledge*. His examinations of hegemonic relations in their descending ranks of power from the "observing object," the above-ranking institution or individual who casts its or his gaze below on the "observed subject," the individual (prisoner, mental patient, et cetera) under study, has done much to influence all fields, including the prevailing popularity of anthropology and its interrogation of novel writing (52–53). For instance, E. Valentine Daniel and Jeffrey M. Peck remark in their "Introduction" to *Culture and Context* how literary studies have become married to anthropological studies: "The presence of the literary in anthropology is best described as 'uncanny'—a nonscientific drive lodged in the heart of a putative science, a presence both desired and dreaded, a Freudian *unheimlich*. For literary study, anthropology has for the most served merely as a source of the esoteric in theory and example. About fifteen years ago, the two fields found deeper significance in each other, which resulted in a flurry of publications heightening this awareness" (1). For Wright, his purpose in studying anthropology has not been an esoteric exercise; rather, each of his texts, whether fiction or nonfiction, has been generated for a wide audience, and especially a white audience, to give them a wake-up call.

His warning to the white West at the conclusion of *The Color Curtain,* and his appended collection of essays entitled *White Man, Listen!* with its candid racial title concluding with an exclamation mark, indicate that he is not writing to assuage the consciences of the private sector or a select few. He corrected that misconception early in his career after publication of *Uncle Tom's Children* (1938) when he engaged the sympathies of a wide, public white audience whose reaction to his short story collection was that of inaction. Wright states: "I found that I had written a book which even bankers' daughters could read and weep over and feel good about it" (*NS* xxvii). In *The Color Curtain,* Wright again is writing to shock his white audience into awareness about the ills of Western imperialism, and he uses the tools of anthropology to accomplish his goal.

In going on to explain "From an Anthropologist's Point of View: The Literary" merits of the merger of the oppositional fields of literature and anthropology owing to flaws historically rooted in anthropological studies, E. Valentine Daniel remarks that "The atonement an anthropologist is capable of making is at best an atonement *between* self and Other, almost never an at-one-ment *with* the Other." And in expanding his views about the anthropologist's mission to learn about the Other, he makes some cogent points relative to Wright's position as a literary ethnographer. Says Daniel:

> Getting to know the Other has been anthropology's *raison d'être.* This Other has existed for anthropology in two modes. The first concerns another people, the second another form. The form in question goes by the popular appellation of the day, "the text." My emphasis in this introduction will be on the form that sustains the notion of the text, the literary. To appreciate anthropology's encounter with the literary, we need to briefly review anthropology's engagement with its other Other, another people. The Other as a people has borne various names throughout anthropology's brief history: primitives, natives, traditional peoples, tribes, and ethnic groups, to mention but a few. In short, anthropology has been enamoured by that which is foreign to it. (2)

Just as Carl Murphy in 1941 had expressed to Wright that the purpose of his role as a journalist would be to know the foreign Asian subject, Daniel in 1996 is reiterating that same mission of knowing the "Other" in anthropological studies. Daniel simply uses current terminology. At the same time, the "otherness" applies to relationships of oppositional fields; in this case, the relationship of anthropology to literature, as much a disciplinary "Other" to anthropologists as journalism has been to literature according to Frus's statements.

"The text," to recall Daniel's term, is Richard Wright's travel account of *The Color Curtain,* a work of literature that engages anthropological methodologies to illuminate "the Asian," and sometimes "the African" conceived as the Other to Westerners. These, "The despised, the insulted, the hurt, the dispossessed—in short, the underdogs of the human race" who were meeting in Bandung are the subjects under the gaze of Wright the ethnographic participant/observer before, during, and after the Bandung Conference in April 1955 (*CC* 10). He depicts his position as the "observing object" of the "observed subject" throughout his travel narrative, but unlike Foucault's description, he holds no nation-state position of power; instead, "words," the tools of his literary trade as well as for the journalist or social scientist, are his weapons of power. For example, Wright demonstrates his skills as a keen "observer" of and "participant" in the Bandung Conference in his section IV, entitled "Racial Shame at Bandung." Readers locate his observing eye when Wright states: "As I watched the dark-faced delegates work at the conference, I saw a strange thing happen. Before Bandung, most of these men had been strangers, and on the first day they were constrained with one another, bristling with charge and countercharge against America and/or Russia. But, as the days passed, they slowly cooled off, and another and different mood set in. What was happening? As they came to know one another better, their fear and distrust evaporated" (149). Within this racially-charged climate, Wright also acts the role of conference participant as he engages in exchanges, a highlight being one with Nehru. In one scene, Wright shows that he is as much of a participant in the conference as the distinguished leaders, and also illustrates how his opinion is balanced equally with that of Nehru's (152–53). And in this capacity of participant/observer, Wright easily blends in with the people of color. He had discovered this very early while doing a preliminary test of his questionnaire in Europe, and then thrown his instrument away after the fifth interview. He had sought "reactions" to his questionnaire of 68 points from "two typical Westerners living in Paris" who had warned Wright that "few Asians would know what the questions were about." Wright was skeptical, but also learned of his naiveté. He states: "I had reasoned that if I, an American Negro, had thought of them [the questions], then an Asian, meeting the West from the 'outside,' so to speak, must surely have thought of them more. How naive I had been! Little had I suspected that I would have to do no questioning at all, that all I had to do was to show up and the Asians would gush, erupt, and spill out more than they knew. I had used the questionnaire five times, then I had thrown it away" (21).

In this excerpt, Wright draws in factors of identity formation that occurs between and among people of color because of their common experiences of suffering racial discrimination from Western colonial powers. In *The Outsider*, he had drawn up definitions of "outsider" and "insider" and expressed their distinctions in the remarks made by Ely Houston, the hunchback attorney, to Cross Damon (129). In reprising these terms in *The Color Curtain,* Wright assumes that since he had thought up these questions on socio-political and religious issues, surely, he surmises, these Asians would do so. But he learns that he had misjudged his subject on two points. First, Wright inserts the trope of the "outsider-within," his term now repopularized in 1990s cultural studies (Merton 7; Collins, "Learning" 15). Wright assumes that the indigenous Asian subject who is foreign to Western culture would more easily be able to discern these socio-political disparities by bringing their "insider's" perspective to the multiple problems, since he, a racially-victimized American Negro who has suffered equally, had thought about these questions. How wrong he was! All he had to do was to show up as a Western man of color, and they would "gush, erupt, and spill out more than they knew" (21).

What Wright reveals here, and what also becomes a formal dynamic during the Bandung Conference, is that people of color tend to talk freely between and among themselves when they know that they are occupying a "safe haven" free of white, Western intervention or threat (Collins, *BFT* 95). Wright reports that the Western papers launched a "press tirade" against the conference when they learned that the "sponsoring powers had not invited any white Western powers to attend" (*CC* 72). However, white European and American journalists were in attendance, and their presence caused discomfort for the "colored" participants. Wright reports: "On many occasions I found that the moment a European or a white American entered a room in which I was talking to Indonesians, a sense of constraint and awkwardness at once came over the Indonesians, and the conversation would veer quickly from intimate descriptions of their personal feelings toward general topics" (162). The presence of a white Westerner tended to mute their tongues which they had wielded freely in their insular "safe haven" spaces.

A second point that Wright's false assumptions about his Asian survey reveals is that Wright, the travel writer/narrator portrays himself as endowed with an enlarged "ego." Wright presents himself countless times as the controlling consciousness of the text, and also as a superintellectual and visionary acutely perceptive of world affairs and Western threats more than anyone else. But this image of the hero as a self-absorbed, introspective superintellectual is a feature recursive from Wright's involvements with French existentialists, and then his fictionalized representation of that philosophical discourse in the characterization of his hero Cross Damon in Wright's 1953 novel *The Outsider.* Now in this same time period Wright is inserting that image of the introspective, self-absorbed, narrator/visionary in his self-reflexive nonfictions, starting with *Black Power,* repeating in *The Color Curtain,* and eventually manifesting itself as the full-blown self-absorbed, egocentric existentialist, global humanist, and Western Man of Color in *White Man, Listen!* And this image of an existentialist, global humanist derives from Wright's Afro-Asian experiences (*WML* xvi-xvii). For example, Wright delineates the four goals of the conference during his reading of the newspaper headlines in the opening apartment scene. Their aim for item "d." is "to view the position of Asia and Africa and their people in the world of today and the contribution they can make to the promotion of world peace and co-operation" (11). This statement is the humanist platform beginning with and emerging from the twenty-nine nation conference, and the Bandung communiqué that they distribute at the conclusion of the meeting is what Wright intreprets overall as a "Last Call of Westernized Asians to the Moral Conscience of the West!" In Wright's summation, he notes particularly the humanist goals, stating: "On the plane of human rights and self-determination, the communiqué endorsed the principles of human rights as set forth in the Charter of the United Nations; ...." (170–71). This conference statement was adopted as an article of the constitution developed by the African, French African, and African American members of the "world congress of black writers, artists, and intellectuals" held in Paris, France, September 19–22, 1956 of which Wright played a major role as a charter member and designer of their bylaws (*WML* 22; Wright, "Conference"). This Bandung communiqué additionally provides the rationale as to why the members of the Bandung Conference eventually vote for "nonalignment" or of not forming a unified block against the West. Their immediate goals are to open rather than close doors and to promote humanistic causes and good will despite the West's counter activities towards them.

Very early, Wright constructs his role as the unifying figuration in the travel account to reflect his indebtedness to the genre of autobiography because it pertains to the self-life-writing of an individual, including the travel writer in various fields. This "I" central character Wright illuminates countlessly in his representation of his "second self" as the superintellectual visionary, travel writer/narrator and participant/observer of the text. For example, one reason why Wright's role is so pronounced in the travel account, besides the autobiographical genre's commanding of this foregrounding, is owing to the role of Wright's editors at World. It was Friede's argument in his letter to Paul Reynolds dated July 18, 1955 that it would be impossible for Wright to list the direct responses to his 120 or 68 questions to his interview subjects ("Letter"). Wright, in fact, horizontally rather than vertically lists his 68 questions to save space. But this suggestion or objection of Friede is why Wright increasingly begins to summarize the remarks of his interview subjects in indirect discourse, thereby diminishing their direct comments and thus their stage presences. And by the time the reader encounters Wright's meditations or "reactions" after the second interview, it is clear to the audience that Wright is really the subject of the narrative of travel. The data ends up being filtered through Wright's consciousness and presented through his eyes; as a result, it is still presented from a limited point of view since Wright selects interview subjects, scenes or events, and excerpts of books, newspaper accounts, speeches, and legal accounts for the reader's consumption. This slanted perspective of the author is also remarked in Wright's statement at the front matter of the text. Another scene illuminating Wright's egocentrism occurs on his flight to Jakarta when the plane is aflutter with the chatter of newspapermen on board. Wright thinks: "To them Bandung was a contest of personalities. I soon realized that American newsmen had at least two grave disabilities in trying to grasp what was happening" (71). While praising their stature as being from some of the most prestigious news agencies in the world, Wright sees that the American newsmen were especially dense in their understandings of the mindset of Third World people because the newsmen were ignorant of racial history and philosophy from the "colored" perspective.

As the travel writer/narrator, central intelligence, and participant/observer of the text, Wright incorporates the usual kinds of rhetorical frames associated with travel writing that make *The Color Curtain* also a standard representation of its form. For instance, Wright inserts the trope of "home" and illustrates its different meanings. Rosemary Marangoly George in *The Politics of Home: Postcolonial Relocations and Twentieth-Century Fiction* defines "home" as "a desire that is fulfilled or denied in varying measure to the subjects (both the fictional characters and reader) constructed in the narrative. As such, 'home' moves along several axes, and yet is usually represented as fixed, rooted, stable—the very antithesis of travel" (12). Wright inserts this trope of "fixed home" versus "temporary field home" when he opens the text on the statement: "In order to spend Christmas with my family, I'd returned to Paris from a long, tiring trip in Spain where I'd been gathering material for a book" (9). The exact locale is unstated, but "fixed home" refers to 14 rue Monsieur le Prince, Paris, the site of his "adopted home" in exile. This setting contrasts to the "temporary home," the "field home" in Spain from whence he had just returned from research activities. Ethnographer James Clifford also provides new conceptions of the field home in his essay on "Traveling Cultures." Clifford remarks:

It may help to view 'the field' as both a methodological ideal and a concrete *place* of professional activity. Since the 1920s, a certain kind of research experience, participant observation, has been normatively conceived as a sort of mini-immigration. The field is a home away from home, a place of dwelling. This dwelling includes work and growth, the development of both personal and "cultural" competence. Ethnographers, typically, are travelers who like to stay and dig in (for a time), who like to make a second home/workplace. Unlike other travelers who prefer to pass through a series of locations, most anthropologists are homebodies abroad. The field as spatial practice is thus a specific style, quality, and duration of dwelling. (99)

Wright both affirms and resists Clifford's past and contemporary definitions of the ethnographer's relationship to his field home. For instance, seven pages later, Wright inserts a "white space" designating a change of scenery or event as he often does in his works. He identifies his new "away from home" location to his reader, stating: "I was ready to fly to Bandung, to fly from the old world of Spain to the new world of Asia. . . . My work in Spain was over and I was sitting in a cafe with a Spanish friend . . ." (15). The reader has no sense of time passing when Wright left his "fixed home" for his "field home" or how he got there; moreover, the reader does not know how long Wright had been in Spain. He actually spent December 17, 1954–February 20, 1955 at his fixed home in Paris, and then spent February 20–April 10, 1955 at various transient field dwellings in Spain (Fabre, *UQ* 412). But one cause of confusion derives from Friede's insistence in his letter of July 18, 1955 to Paul Reynolds that Wright must cut the Semana Santa religious festival sequence which identifies Wright's location as being in Seville according to entries in his daily journal from April 3–6, 1955 ("Letter"; "Semana Santa"). Four days later, Wright departs Madrid by air for Indonesia on April 10th, and, unlike his transient existence from one city to another during his three field trips to Spain, Wright "digs in" and stays somewhat, fixed during his Asian field trip. Although not always specified in *The Color Curtain*, he stays three weeks instead of one (April 10–May 5, 1955), and resides April 12th to 17th first in Tugu at the home of Mochtar Lubis in the outskirts of Jakarta, and then in Jakarta proper with Mr. and Mrs. P. at their private dwelling. During week two at the mountainous site of Bandung, Wright stays at the Hotel Van Hengel from April 17th to 25th. He returns to Jarkarta and stays an additional week, April 25th–May 5th, in order to learn more about the country. It is assumed that he resided with his same hosts. During this time, he records in his notes on "Return from Paradise" (Bandung) that he found himself inundated with requests from art, literary, and divinity groups to give speeches, the text of which later became recorded in *White Man, Listen!* as "Negro literature and industrialization." These lectures were also covered by the local English and Indonesian presses ("Return to Paradise"; Fabre 420).

The uncertainty of Space or Time is a normative rhetorical device in Wright's fictions and nonfictions. The certainty/uncertainty of natural versus mechanical

Time Wright had associated early in his fictions with agrarian life in the Deep South and the way that peasant Negroes could tell time by the rising and setting of the sun. In *The Color Curtain,* Wright intermixes these diurnal references with direct/indirect remarks about seasons, climate, or sporadic dates to illustrate his work habits or work experiences in the field. For example, his modes of transportation remark about passing Time. He takes the night express from Seville to Madrid (April 9th). This is a one-day trip in which Wright meditates about his five interviews and his own conclusions over fifty-seven pages, but periodically interrupts his thoughts with statements such as "I lifted my eyes from my notes and, to the rocking of the train, I reflected" (26); "The express pounded on into the night as I poured over my notes" (29); "It was nine o'clock; in the corridor of the train, the bell sounded for dinner" (36); "After dinner back in my compartment, I resumed perusing my notes" (39); and "In the morning light I stared at the tilting olive groves on the Spanish mountainside" (54). He provides his reader with no clue about his time of arrival except that it is "morning," and he never tells his audience how he gets to Madrid's airport.

Time becomes interminable once Wright boards the plane for his two-day flight to Jakarta. He tells his reader that he boards a TWA constellation bound for Rome on Easter Sunday (April 10, 1955) that connects with a KLM plane bound for Cairo, Egypt. Time passes from day to night as Wright's plane travels through the "hot night...high over Africa" which becomes specific when it lands over a "far-flung lake of shimmering lights" to take on passengers at Cairo. The twilight of dawn breaks the journey on April 11th just before Wright's plane lands at Bagdad, Turkey, and then he reports moving into the Timelessness of airborne Time. "High up in the skies of Asia," he starts to "lose track of time; day skies alternated with night skies and [Wright] cat-napped when [he] could" (69). After stops at Karachi, Pakistan, nighttime juxtaposes with dawn as the plane next stops at Calcutta, India. Wright reports feeling groggy from lack of sleep and takes a "Nembutal" that enables him to doze until the morning of a day two stop at Bangkok, Thailand. He balances looking "high over the jungles of Malaya" with the chattering of passengers (80). His reviewing of prior news accounts by biased Western papers takes Wright through the remainder of the flight when he lands on the afternoon of April 12th in Jakarta.

At the field site, Wright travels by car or walks about on foot. Always he is observing and assessing his subjects, the Indonesian peoples, his hosts, nation leaders, or other newspapersmen. He is greeted by Mochtar Lubis and driven through town to Lubis's suburban home, and then a week later, driven by Lubis to the mountainous conference site of Bandung. By car in Jakarta, Wright is struck by something that looks like a three-wheeled tricycle, which he learns is Indonesia's human transportation system or "Indonesian taxicab." The famous canals built by the Dutch pale in beauty when Wright also sees a man defecating, children urinating, women washing clothes, and a child brushing his teeth all in the same vicinity of the river (82). Despite the presence of rustic technology such as the water system, sanitation facilities, or poor air conditioning in the humid climate and tropical heat, Wright is struck more by the rapidity and veracity of the human communication system. Just talking with Lubis in the car, Wright reflects: "It was strange, but, in this age of swift communication, one had to travel thousands of miles to get a set of straight, simple facts" (87). Wright never mentions his mode of transportation from Jakarta, but his notes indicate that he took passage on the *Willem Ruys* to Naples on May 5, 1955, and it is assumed that he flew home to Paris from there ("Notes on Bandung").

Certain political information also is omitted by Wright, but he compensates by highlighting it in another way. He is granted visa clearance by the Indonesian embassy and picks up his press card, valid until May 5th, at the Ministry of Information once he arrives in Jakarta. The four stamps by the Minister of Information, the Minister of Defence, the Minister of Justice, and Central State Police Service indicate the legal hurdles that he, and other outsiders, had to surpass in order to gain clearance. But Wright chooses to focus on the presence of military force at the conference where flags of all twenty nations greet participants; where sirens announcing the arrival and departure of dignitaries scream constantly; and where security to enter or leave is tightly enforced by armed policemen at all times. And when Wright announces that he entered the press gallery on the morning of April 18th, he does not mention that he had to be seated by 8:30 a.m. in order to be on time for President Sukarno's opening speech ("Inaugural Invitation").

II
The Travel Writer/Narrator's Message of Anti-Colonial Imperatives from the East

The volatile remarks about the "life line of imperialism" spoken by President Sukarno of Indonesia during his inaugural address to participants of the Bandung Conference strike at the core of why twenty-nine Asiatic and African leaders have converged upon the tiny island of Indonesia, the country that first broke free of Western colonial control seemingly hours after the closure of World War II (*CC* 137). His words complement Wright's observations in the opening scene at his

Paris apartment that "no political scientist" would have dreamed of staging such a yellow, brown, and black threat to the West. With these words, Wright brings in the trope of political discourse that also defines *The Color Curtain* as a narrative of travel. The Western world previously had drawn a global "lifeline" of colonial control around its "colored" subjects, and imposed laws to keep them "unfree," but these Eastern subjects had broken free and declared their emancipations in various proclamations between 1945 and 1955. Their political acts of resistance had not been provoked without undue cause, which Wright illustrates to his reader by means of facts which he has gathered or by way of statements from the liberated subjects which he has recorded. In linking these grievances together thematically as a cause-effect argument, Wright the travel writer/narrator as participant/observer illustrates that the main message emitting from these Asian-African revolutionaries is that of an anti-colonial imperative from the East to the West.

Taking Indonesia as an example, Wright, throughout his narrative, countless times reinforces the fact that this post-colonial nation had suffered under 350 years of colonial rule. How can that be, one asks, for the time period just barely precedes 1619 when the first African slaves arrived in Jamestown, Virginia? Thomas Kerstiens in *The New Elite in Asia and Africa: A Comparative Study of Indonesia and Ghana* (1966) provides answers where Wright leaves gaps. From Kerstiens's remarks, one can construe Indonesia's history as being divided into three phases: the pre-colonial period until 1500; the colonial phase, 1500–1945; and post-colonial period, 1945–1966 (the end of Kerstiens's study). According to Kerstiens, Indonesia forms the largest group of islands in the world (1,498,562 square kilometers). Together with the Philippine Islands, it comprises the Malay Archipelago which itself encompasses two regions—the Asiatic and the Australian. Wright shows his familiarity with Indonesia's geographical features when he asks Lubis during his ride from the airport about the size of the "archipelago," and learns that it is made up of "fifteen thousand [islands], but only three thousand are inhabited." In proportion, the archipelago is equivalent to the "size of the United States" (*CC* 83). Continues Kerstiens, the equator "passes through the middle of the Archipelago, cutting the big islands of Sumatra, Kalimantan (Borneo), the Sulawesi (Celebres), and Halmaheira." Most of these "islands belong to the great equatorial forest belt" which accounts for Wright's complaints about the humidity and the tropical sun, and notation about Bandung's mountainous location.

In terms of indigenous peoples and the wealth of early society, Kerstiens states that Indonesia "was always a melting pot in pre-colonial times" because of its attraction to Chinese and Roman traders seeking its rich resources of silk, precious stones, spices, gold, and ivory, to name a few (30). Wright confirms that these claims still existed in 1955. During his ride into Jakarta with Lubis, Wright learns that Indonesia's natural resources make the nation "potentially the third richest on earth" (*CC* 83). Trade, in some respects, influenced religion. Between the fifth and fourteenth centuries, "there was Brahmanism and Buddhism of the Mahayana type, imported from India" which led to development of a Hindu-Javanese religion once the Hindu religion was introduced from India. This latter group also introduced Islam into Indonesia, says Kerstiens, and it very quickly "spread over the whole of Indonesia, with the exception of Bali" (33). Hence, the blending of religion with politics forms Indonesia's common ground with its Asiatic neighbors because of their kinships owing to pre-colonial trading and importation of Asiatic religions. This bonding based upon common religions accounts for the majority presence and voice of Asiatics rather than Africans reported by Wright as active in the Bandung Conference.

European traders came to Indonesia in the sixteenth century, reports Kerstiens, and found a "population of high cultural standards." It was an agricultural society built around the concept of the village as a "closed unit," with its inhabitants therein being governed by a chief. On his ride into town, Wright notices how sediments of ancient village society still existed alongside Jakarta's modern culture. The Dutch were aware of Indonesia in early colonial times, but acted as observers, choosing initially to obtain Indonesian products from the Portuguese who arrived in the country in 1512. But the Dutch defeated both the Asians and the Portuguese in gaining rulership of the country once the formal Dutch East India Trading Company (the "Verenigde Nederlandse Geoctroyeerde Oostindische Compagnie or V.O.I.C.") was sanctioned by Dutch law in 1602 (37–38). This early occupation by the Dutch is why Wright and other persons whom he interviews in Europe, during informal conversations in flight, or within formal settings in Indonesia, consistently date the country's oppression under a European sovereign as a period of 350 years. The V.O.I.C. came to symbolize the perniciousness of Dutch and thus Western sovereignty in Indonesia. With their isolationist habits of establishing their own colonies separate from the natives and restricting their inter-social contacts to the slaves in their homes, the Dutch early established dichotomies of difference between themselves and the native Indonesians correlating with hegemonic relationships of self/Other; Westerner/Easterner; dominant/subordinate; white/ non-white; master/slave power, et cetera (41).

The strong hand of colonial power enforcing these relationships of the powerful to the powerless occurred in the nineteenth century when the Dutch introduced their policies of direct and indirect rule in sync with other Western powers over their colonies. Kerstiens points out three factors making this successful: (1) industrialization taking place in Europe (i.e., invention of cotton mills, sugar refineries, et cetera, in England; introduction of the steamship making global travel more accessible; and the opening of the Suez Canal); (2) the European's partitioning of the globe and expanding of their disparate empires; and (3) the European's development of social philosophies governing their subjugated peoples (43–44). Specifically to impose the latter in Indonesia, the Dutch devised two forms of governance: direct and indirect rule. Explains Kerstiens: "Under a system of direct rule we understand a system whereby political administrative authority is handed down from the mother country directly to the people in the subjugated territories along proper channels which are directly controlled by the colonial power. This means that from the lowest loci of power, the village head, to the Governor General, a system of civil servants is introduced which is directly in the service of the colonial power." In terms of indirect rule, Kerstiens states: "Indirect rule is the system whereby the sovereign power recognizes the existence of a political elite as constituted by tradition. It leaves this system untouched at the lower echelons but it puts political advisors next to them at the middle and higher levels, to ensure that the policy of colonial power is being carried out. Such a system obviously disrupts much less the indigenous society and is easier to put into practice" (44–45). Both Dutch policies were tried in Indonesia under different Governor-Generals, but it was Van den Bosch's 1830 decree of *Cultuurstelsel* (forced system of cultivation) in which the Dutch government became "sole possessor of all the land and the population only the 'renters,'" thereby requiring crop farming in which renters were mandated to "cultivate an export crop of one-fifth of their land." This law proved to be effective. The Dutch treasury subsequently flourished from Indonesian export products of coffee, tobacco, sugar, pepper, et cetera (47). This system of forced labor and crop-lien mortgaging compares to descriptions of neo-slave, economic conditions imposed by whites which Du Bois describes in Chapters VII and VIII in *The Souls of Black Folks* (1903) as occurring in the Cotton Kingdom of South Georgia (91; 111). Moreover, Wright revoices Du Bois and represents this neo-slave system in pictures and words as still being present in Mississippi in 1941 in Parts 1 and 2 of *12 Million Black Voices* (1941 [10; 30]). Having been born in this same agrarian climate in 1908 but in Natchez, Mississippi, where the same system of white control of the Cotton Kingdom and its neo-slave policies still existed, Wright could identity with the "forced labor" conditions imposed by the Dutch upon the Indonesians.

Van den Bosch's system of government was typical of how indirect rule set up distinct ranks of power based upon color between the white colonial rulers and the colored Indonesian subjects. Kerstiens lists eight socio-political positions from lowest to highest ("a"–"h") that lent authority. At the bottom scale were the four native ranks classified as the Indonesian political elite: "(a) Village head; (b) Sub-district officer (*Assistant Wedena*) comprising about 20 villages; (c) District officers (*Wedena*); and (d) Regent—head of township." At the top in progressive rank were the four positions of power held by the Dutch civil servants: "(e) Assistant Resident (leading an area comprising several regencies); (f) Resident; (g) Governor—head of province; and (h) Governor-General" (48). While there were periodic changes in colonial policies over the next 115 years, Van den Bosch's system set the rules in motion that would keep the Indonesians "unfree." To insure their subjugations, the Dutch, like their fellow European imperialists of the French, English, Germans, and Portuguese, devised social policies in 1850 that would divide Indonesians against each other because of class systems. In his section "Social Change: The European Elite: Native 'Bourgeoisie' Western-Educated Elite," Kerstiens provides information that presents the problems of the Indonesians, other Asiatics, and Africans which caused their revolt against colonial systems instilling their inferiorities as the Other to Europeans. The Dutch socially constructed the image of the Indonesian as that of a dependent like that of a child in relation to his parents, and, as a result of these policies of 1850, even felt some "social responsibility towards the dependent people," one being that of education (55). Kerstiens reminds us that in pre-colonial Indonesian society, there were three classes: the *Prijaji* (political elite); the free farmers, and the slaves. In the nineteenth century, these classes changed, he says, because slavery was abolished or nearly gone, the *Prijaji* remained intact, and a new class was borne of "the white man" owing to more European migrations to the colonies, here meaning Indonesia. The whites discovered that they lived better; even the poorest one in Europe lived in some state of opulence with a large house staffed by Indonesian servants. With this influx of whites and their self-perceived, increased social standings over the indigenous Indonesians, the Dutch instilled "race" as a factor in class division, one reason now being cases of miscegenation and births from mixed-race relationships. By 1900, according to Kerstiens, a "social stratification of different classes" existed in Indonesia. By rank from the highest to the lowest, these included: "I. The European whites; II. The half whites (Singo's, which included Arabs and Chinese as well); III. The *Prijaji* class (two divisions—the elderly, hierarchal, more conservative branch and the younger, more Western component); IV. The Indonesian bourgeoisie; and V. The Indonesian peasant class" (58–59).

To insure social construction of the subjugated Indonesian as the inferior Other, the Dutch developed a vocabulary of imperatives for whites to use in their verbal encounters with the natives. Wright dramatizes such one-sided power relations. He remarks upon locating a "little book" of "elementary Malay" entitled *Bahasa Indonesia* initially compiled by a Dutch author, S. Van der Molen, adapted into English by Harry F. Cemach, and published by a Dutch press, W. van Hoeve at The Hague in 1949. It gives Wright "insight into how the Dutch created racial conditioning in Indonesia, just what the nature of Dutch and Indonesian relations were." And he surmises how the poorest white in Europe transplanted to the colony of Indonesia came to feel superior to them. Says Wright: "Whether the author knew it or not, he was writing a book to instruct an army of invaders how to demean, intimidate, and break the spirit of an enemy people in a conquered, occupied country.... All sentences were rendered in terms of flat orders, commands; an exclamation point usually followed each sentence, implying that one actually shouted one's orders." He provides samples of these imperatives as would be spoken in their English equivalents for his reader's insight. Lessons pertain to typical behavioral patterns of Indonesians when authority must be imposed. For instance, lesson 7 pertains to relations with menial servants where the white Dutch enslaver, male or female, would give such orders as "Gardener, sweep the garden!"; "Make a new broom!"; or "Babu, wash the clothes!" Lesson 13 entitled "Hold the Thief!" and relating to what Wright perceives as the "humanity of the Indonesian" could pertain to any peasant or member of the political elite. Typical statements or questions are: "Didn't you close the window last night?"; "All the silver is gone"; "During the night there was a thief"; or "He was arrested by the police." The masterpiece of degradation which could pertain to a servant or a member of the political elite is lesson 24 entitled "The Master Is Cross" presented in forms of questions, statements, and orders: "Who is it?"; "Why are you running about here?"; "You must stay over there!"; "You are stupid"; "Are you ashamed?"; "I think you are lying"; or "Don't talk nonsense!" (154–55).

These racially-biased, Dutch-mandated class distinctions and derogatory forms of address to differentiate the superior positions of the white Dutch colonialists from the inferior ranks of their "colored" Indonesian subjects are the factors motivating Wright's construction of his 68-point questionnaire. He excavates specific socio-political laws governing the rank and/or class positions of Indonesians on matters of their labor and wages, purity or non-purity of blood lines, qualifications for or levels of education, or position of office in a separatist society favoring the rulership of the powerful Dutch over the powerless Indonesians. Thus Wright's selectivity of five pure or mixed-race European-based Asians as interview subjects, and his specificity of the conference conveners and participants as representations of the "Asian and African elite," signify upon Kerstiens's findings and bespeak the thoroughness of Wright's background readings, collection of data, and presentation of his research materials in *The Color Curtain* in his role as a humanist/social scientist author of a narrative of travel. The imperatives reflect the psycho-social success of the Dutch imperialists in instilling a sense of self-loathing into the Indonesian's psyche for being their "Other." At the same time, the Dutch set up rewards endorsing the Indonesians as humans according to their successful mastery of a particular Western rite. Education, whether informal or formal, is an example, for the closer an Indonesian mastered the ways of the white West, the more he or she would appear "civilized" and thus acceptable to the Dutch. Needless to say, these issues of "identity" caused confusion in the mind of the Indonesian which Wright eventually dubbed as the "Frog Perspective" in *White Man, Listen!* This definition Wright had worked out during his lectures on "Negro literature and industrialization" before the Bandung Conference, during his observations and musings at the conference, and after it. His premise is clearly grounded in Freudian psychology based upon attraction and repulsion. Says Wright, "This is a phrase I've borrowed from Nietzsche to describe someone looking from below upward, a sense of someone who feels himself lower than others." Moreover, "A certain degree of hate combined with love (ambivalence) is always involved in this looking from below upward and the object against which the subject is measuring himself undergoes constant changes. He loves the object because he would like to resemble it; he hates the object because his chances of resembling it are remote, slight" (6). The author applies this Frog concept of attraction/repulsion to explain the "reactions" to "whiteness" felt by "Asians, Africans, Americans, or West Indians" whom Wright had just completed investigating or exploring in his various fictions, narratives of travel, or prose pieces. The five Asian interview subjects, the young Dutch-educated student on the plane, Mr. and Mrs. P., now living in Jakarta housing formerly occupied by the Dutch, Indonesian elite political leaders of Sukarno and company, and the population in general all must have become confused and suffered identity crises.

These Dutch imperatives of social conduct explain why the Indonesians would go "Dutch crazy," says Wright, and feel reactions of "anger" upon seeing a Dutch face. The commands also signify the effect of psychological warping over 350 years of oppression resulting in the revolution on August 17, 1945, the day Indonesian citizens mandated the end of Dutch colonial rule and became a republic. Wright uses two terms in his lecture essay on "Negro literature" presented in Jakarta and later recorded in *White Man, Listen!* that explain the rationale behind the Indonesian's uprising. He says: "Entity, men integrated with their culture; and identity, men who are at odds with their culture, striving for personal identification" (75). Wright takes standard Western definitions and gives them reverse meanings, which is a feature typical in his writings and travel literature as well. The Indonesians in colonial times were forced involuntarily or willfully tried to emulate the representation of "entity" to Western eyes. But owing to contradictory messages from the Dutch, despite strides of Indonesians to leap Western hurdles and even become educated, they never surpassed their statuses as "the Other" because of their brown skins. This is why the trope of "identity" in Wright's definition signifies the meaning of the revolution of 1945—Indonesians at odds with their white, Western culture, and now striving for their own personal, re-identifications.

Indeed, Wright has been alluding to Kerstiens's data of Indonesia's pre-colonial, colonial, and post-colonial histories all along in his volumes of questions, musings of responses, and interpretations of "history." In fact, Wright's summation of the events leading up to Indonesia's declaration of emancipation from colonial rule on August 17, 1945 correlates with Kerstiens's analysis of the set of historical and political circumstances causing Indonesia's drive for nationalism. His statement occurs after Wright had finished analyzing seventeen newspaper accounts of the West's responses to the Bandung Conference which he gathered between December 1954 and April 1955 while he was "at home" or in the "field." Says Wright, "It should be remembered that these quotations fit into a real, concrete, historical context." And he surmises that America, "leader of the West" after World War II when "Western Europe" was "prostrate from Hitlerian domination," had proceeded to launch "a campaign, the intensity of which it did not appreciate, to frighten the men of the Kremlin, and month after month that campaign kept up, flooding the world on all levels of communication." Wright then points to America's naiveté in underestimating how its concept of proaction had led to the Third World's concept of reaction. The author then cites how America had thus fostered precisely "the very thing it sought to defeat...an organization of Asia and Africa around a Communist cell on a global scale: BANDUNG....The dialogue of events had reached a pitch that involved the totality of man on earth" (80).

The Bandung Conference of 1955 transcends the narrow limits of Indonesia's personal problems with the Dutch on matters of entity/identity formations. It, in fact, assumes global proportions and global dynamics as an anti-colonial imperative by the East to the West. Wright's above summation turns again to psychological discourse, for he continually remarks upon what the combinations of deprivation and fear will do to the oppressed. He, in fact, is alluding to the activities of the "superego" defined by Freud as the "third aspect of the personality structures to develop." It has two functions "based upon built-in reinforcement processes: (1) to reward individuals for acceptable moral behavior and (2) to punish actions that are not socially sanctioned, by creating guilt" (Feshbach/Weiner 81–82). The Asiatics and Africans have experienced the moral disfavor of the West in their consistent disobedient behaviors of uprisings against the Western master. But Wright also touches upon resistance theory in his analysis as he had worked it out in *Native Son* as the "Bigger Thomas Syndrome" and discerned it in the natures of Asians and Africans from his travels. He says in *White Man, Listen!*, "In almost every instance of colonial revolt, the white Westerner has had absolutely no inkling of the revolt until it burst over his head, so carefully hidden had the rebels kept their feelings and attitudes" (21). The West created, as Sukarno had already stated, precisely what it had sought to defeat—a monster of negative unity as signified by the brown, yellow, and black leaders of former Western colonies banding together. They had tried the two stages of first the physical and then the ideological resistances to oppression as Edward Said identifies in his chapter "Themes and Resistance" in *Culture and Imperialism* (209). This latter tactic had made them "free" by way of their proclamations, although the problems of nationbuilding without assistance from the West become the next stage of self-reliance as Wright points out consistently as the internal problems, circa 1955, still afflicting Indonesia in its modernization efforts. This is why he poses the question to his interview subjects as to whether they believe Indonesia should become more industrialized. But Indonesia, like its Asiatic and African neighbors, must formulate another strategy in its stridency against and paradoxical dependence upon the West in this mid-1950s time frame. This is why they eventually choose the strategy of nonalignment in order not to negate their chances of becoming industrialized like the West by means of its superior technology.

Ultimately, the Bandung communiqué devised and issued by the participants on the last day of the conference is their greatest tool of resistance. It is an imperative formulated as a "Last Call . . . to . . . the West!" to develop humanist concerns, and one so important that Wright punctuates its urgency by boldfacing the warning and ending it with an exclamation mark (170). In their knowledge of their options to choose between two vying superpowers—American democracy or Russian Communism—as their paths to modernization and industrialization of their countries, the conferees also know that their human exclamation mark is Chou En-lai of Red China. Throughout his coverage of the conference, Wright incorporates the trope of fear in his language to describe the psychological reactions of the conveners towards each other, towards the West, and most importantly, towards Red China. From the time of his European-based interviews to the time he boards the plane, attends the Bandung Conference, and engages in post-conference activities in Indonesia, Wright magnifies the fear extant between and among the Asiatic and African peoples. Even during the platform speeches of nation leaders or their delegates, he notes a strain of anxiety undergirding the speeches of Abdel Nasser of Egypt; Nkrumah's representative of Kojo Botsio, Minister of State, the Gold Coast; Prince Wan of Thailand; Mohammed Fadhil al-Jamali of Iraq; the Chairman of the Ethiopian Delegation; and Sami Solli, Prime Minister of Lebanon. Only at the speech of Tatsumosuke Takasaki, the principal Japanese delegate, does Wright notice a "level of the rational" returning to their thinking. Chou En-lai, however, overshadows everyone by his understatement. Instead of using the conference to vent his hostilities against the United States over Formosa, he turns the matter into an "at home" issue. And by choosing a nonconfrontational line of alliance, Chou En-lai, according to Wright, decides to "identify himself with those millions with whom not many Western nations wanted or would accept identification." Among his brief remarks, Chou En-lai says, "The majority of the Asian and African countries and peoples have suffered and still are suffering from the calamities under colonialism. This is acknowledged by all of us. If we seek common ground in doing away with the sufferings and calamities under colonialism, it will be very easy for us to have mutual understanding and respect, mutual sympathy and support, instead of mutual suspicion and fear, mutual exclusion and antagonism" (134–36). These are the reasons that Chou En-lai concludes his remarks by stating, "Red China has agreed to support the four goals of the conference and has chosen not to make any other proposals." Moreover, he does not attempt to subvert their religious beliefs although Chou points out that Communists are atheists. Says Wright, "Chou was most anxious to join this Asian-African church and was willing to pay for his membership." And he concludes of Chou's "master stroke" of nonconfrontational persuasion: "Hence, Chou En-lai, by promising to behave, had built a bridgehead that had found foundations not only in Asia but extended even into tribal black Africa" (134–37). It is the leader of Red China who represents simultaneously an option for the East and threat to the West by his connections to the Soviet Union and Russian Communism, the nation and philosophy antithetical to the democratic principles of its vying superpower of America. But it is Wright who adds the exclamation point of alarm in his last call to the "superego" or moral conscience of the West in *The Color Curtain*.

It is Wright who warns that Chou En-lai is Asia and Africa's anti-colonial imperative. This linguistic marker Wright affixes visually to the cover of *White Man, Listen!* in his effort to awaken the West's attention to humanistic principles of world peace.

Richard Wright made some prophetic observations in his narrative of travel that would influence the nature of post-colonial studies in the 1990s. During production of the text and his correspondences with Wright, Paul Reynolds in his letter of July 6, 1955 to Wright again grapples with Wright's charges of America as being a colonial power and Wright's perception as being "anti-American" ("Letters"). Several times Wright is heard making qualifying statements of "I'm not anti-Western" such as the instance of his comment to Lubis during their drive into Jakarta (85). At the same time, he, by indirection, condemns the West and/or America, a case being his summation of the newspaper headlines. Nonetheless, Wright's comments stem from his recognition of America's participation in colonial practices of oppression by importation and enslavement of millions of Africans. In his lecture on "industrialization" in Jakarta that becomes his second essay in *White Man, Listen!*, Wright predicts future changes in the academy on theoretical concepts of imperialism. He says:

> Today, as the tide of white domination of the land mass of Asia and Africa recedes, there lies exposed to view a procession of shattered cultures, disintegrated societies, and a writhing sweep of more aggressive, irrational religion than the world has known for centuries. And, as scientific research, partially freed from the blight of colonial control, advances, we are witnessing the rise of a new genre of academic literature dealing with colonial and post-colonial facts from a wider angle of vision than ever possible before. The personality distortions of hundreds of millions of black, brown, and yellow people that are being revealed by this literature are confounding and will necessitate drastic alteration of our past evaluations of colonial rule. (5)

So true are his words, for in corroborating Wright's predictions, we hear Ashcroft, Griffiths, and Tiffin in their "Introduction" to *The Empire Strikes Back: Theory and Practice in Post-Colonial Literatures* (1989) miming:

> So the literatures of African countries, Australia, Bangladesh, Canada, Caribbean countries, India, Malaysia, Malta, New Zealand, Pakistan, Singapore, South Pacific Island countries, and Sri Lanka are all post-colonial literatures. The literature of the USA should also be placed in this category. Perhaps because of its current position of power, and the neo-colonizing role it has played, its post-colonial nature has not been generally recognized. But its relationship with the metropolitan centre as it evolved over the last two centuries has been paradigmatic for post-colonial literatures everywhere. (2)

Without mentioning Wright's foregrounding of these post-colonial studies, they confirm Wright's astute predictions in the 1950's. Moreover, they now "Wright," to use a pun, the wrongful charges made to Wright of being "anti-American" because of his advanced thoughts in theorizing the frames of post-colonial literature. In fact, Ashcroft and company go on to define the common grounds for these literatures, stating: "What each of these literatures has in common beyond their special and distinct regional characteristics is that they emerged in their present form out of the experience of colonization and asserted themselves by foregrounding the tension with the imperial power, and by emphasizing their differences from the assumptions of the imperial centre. It is this which makes them distinctly post-colonial" (2). And this Wright does in his post-colonial narratives of travel, *Black Power* (1954) and *The Color Curtain* (1956). To come would be *White Man, Listen!* (1957), his addendum to these first two, and his fourth planned but unpublished post-colonial travel account of "French West Africa" (c. 1959). By Spain's lead role in instituting colonial rule in Africa and the Americas, *Pagan Spain*, by default, would be considered a post-colonial text in today's context. Wright's account also is considered a travel book of oppression because of Spain's "at home," historical practices of imperialism towards and discrimination against the non-Catholic, non-Fascist Other, meaning the Jews and Protestants. *The Color Curtain* thus invites these intertextual analyses of Wrightean tropes defining his literatures of travel. He integrates the fields of literature, journalism, history, sociology, psychology, and anthropology to construct a text delineating his role as the travel writer/narrator and participant/observer of the Bandung Conference. As such, he is the eyewitness to history and prophetic voice of Asiatic and African relations to the West that define the genre of travel literature as well as the direction of post-colonial studies today.

Richard Wright with Two Spanish Youths, Spain (c. 1954–55)

Essays on *Pagan Spain* (1957)

Richard Wright as Traveler/Ethnographer

The Conundrums of *Pagan Spain*

John Lowe

Ethnography is moving into areas long occupied by sociology, the novel, or avant-garde cultural critique.

James Clifford, 1986

I'm inclined to feel that I ought not to work right now on a novel. This does not mean that I'm giving up writing fiction, but, really, there are so many more exciting and interesting things happening now in the world that I feel sort of dodging them if I don't say something about them.

Richard Wright, 1954

"What does the ethnographer do?"—he writes.

Clifford Geertz, 1973

When Richard Wright's meditation on Spanish life and culture was published in 1957, everyone—including Wright and his publisher—expected it to be controversial. As Richard Strout, one of the early reviewers aptly put it, "There are so many ways of misunderstanding this vivid book of travel-journalism that it is likely to kick up a controversy—a Negro writing about whites, a man of Protestant background appalled by the degradation of a quasi Church-state, an expatriate drawing upon his native land for occasional comparisons, an ex-radical describing Franco's Falange." Strout hastened to add, however, that "Wright is a citizen of the world writing compassionately about Spain's poverty and self-hatred and fanaticism. He uses a terse, lucid dramatic style like Hemingway's" (Strout, n.p.).

Although literary critics found the book interesting, Catholic and Protestant reviewers alike objected to Wright's thesis—that an apparently obsessively Christian country was actually pagan—and to his insistent focus on the many sexual symbols in Spanish life in general and Spanish Catholicism in particular. These kind of objections had more to do with the repressive mores of the time than with the accuracy of Wright's reading.[1]

No doubt there was an underlying racist resentment too, that an African American, a former Communist and an expatriate, dared to challenge the integrity of one of Europe's most fabled and ancient cultures. There was more acceptance of Wright reporting on events in Ghana in an earlier book, *Black Power* (1954).

In light of the response it eventually received, it is interesting that the opening pages of *Pagan Spain* offer no hint of either an anthropological field trip or a Freudian hegira. Indeed, one gets the impression that Wright's initial Spanish sojourn (there were three in all) was somewhat whimsical, or alternately, merely the fulfillment of Gertrude Stein's deathbed encomium to "see Spain." As Wright begins the narrative, he is alone in his car, "in torrid August," near the Spanish border: "I was under the blue skies of the Midi. . . . To my right stretched the flat, green fields . . . to my left lay a sweep of sand beyond which the Mediterranean heaved and sparkled. I was alone. I had no commitments. Seated in my car, I held the steering wheel in my hands" (1). This statement ingeniously establishes Wright in both a cosmic moment of destiny (the four elements, air, earth, water and fire converge in an otherwise bleak landscape), and in a pose that suggests both choice-at-the-crossroads and a tabula-rasa. Wright frequently employed this metaphor to express his stance and identity, claiming he had no race except that which was forced upon him, no country except the one he had to belong to, and so had no traditions. "I'm free. I have only the future" (17). This implied a kind of detachment: "I'm a rootless man. . . . I do not hanker after, and seem not to need, as many emotional attachments, sustaining roots, or idealistic allegiances as most people. . . . I like and even cherish the state of abandonment, of aloneness. . . . I can make myself at home almost anywhere on this earth, and can, if I've a mind to . . . easily sink myself into the most alien and widely differing environments" (*WML* xxix).

As we can see, Wright carefully sets himself up here as the perfect type of participant/observer, the ideal "seeing man." Indeed, one of the reviewers of *Pagan Spain*, Raymond Carr, asked a crucial question at the start of his reading: "Who best understands a country? Is it the social anthropologist, with his professionally *blank mind*, his notebooks and his two years' penal residence? Is it the historian who has devoted his life to wresting truth from other minds? Or is it the sensitive tourist? There is something to be said for the claims of the non-professional" [my emphasis] (Carr n.p.).

Wright, always a man at the crossroads of various disciplines, fits all of these categories, in one way or another. Unfortunately, our natural preoccupation with his literary masterpieces has kept us from a full understanding of his contributions to nonfiction. As Paul Gilroy has recently asserted, Wright was dedicated to an examination of the idea of the "Negro" in western culture, and saw from the start that the "double-consciousness" (Wright himself preferred the term "double vision") he and other investigators of African descent had could be an invaluable tool in deconstructing the conundrums of the western psyche, thereby making Wright a member of what Gilroy calls the "international movement" (161).

Wright's close connection with leading sociologists had made him highly aware of contemporary modes of investigating culture. He had extensive contact with the professional interpreters of culture of the "Chicago school," such as Robert Park, William Issac Thomas, Ernest Burgess, and Louis Wirth. The latter two used realist and proletarian literature to illustrate sociological principles. Wright shared their interest in employing scholarly research for didactic purposes in his fiction, and had no difficulty extending this approach to the kind of writing he proposed to do in Spain. His work in Africa researching *Black Power* and his 1955 trip to the Bandung Conference of the Free Countries of the Third World eased him further toward a more participatory and anthropologically focused reading of cultures. The writing of *Pagan Spain* from its inception situated itself amid a set of changing and experimental approaches to political thought, scholarly research, philosophy, oppression, world liberation, and culture.

The Shaping of a Literary Ethnographer

An understanding of the impulses behind *Pagan Spain* must proceed from the events that preceded Wright's Spanish hegira. Accordingly, this essay investigates the various conundrums suggested by Strout's remarks, focusing on the ethnographic aspects of Wright's reading of Spanish culture. Wright will be compared here to Zora Neale Hurston, his usual adversary, whose training in anthropology equipped her to observe and interpret cultures, and not only her own; her book *Tell My Horse*, like *Pagan Spain*, limns the contours of foreign cultures.

At the same time, Wright's book definitely still fits certain parameters of travel writing; what follows here links him to that tradition and its curious history, which often has intertwined with ethnography. My speculations employ the recent work of Mary Louise Pratt, who investigates the ideological and even imperial aspects of such writing in the European tradition, which Wright "inherited," although in certain respects he appears to be confronting it. This latter claim is tested here through a brief digest of ethnographic aspects of Wright's preceding fiction, and the techniques of two non-fictional books that preceded *Pagan Spain*, *Black Power*, and *The Color Curtain*. Finally, I situate Wright's unusual project with the discourse recently mounted on "Writing Cultures" by James Clifford and others. Throughout this discussion, I will demonstrate a shift in his perspective to one we would today identify with that of the participant-observer anthropologist.

How does Wright set this up? He creates a leading role for himself in the narrative at the outset, isolating himself on the stage, and making us privy to his paranoia and fear, providing impetus for this from his Mississippi background. Apparently random things he notices set the stage for thematics to follow. A military man he gives a ride to seems intent on arresting him, setting up the menace of Franco's men. Then, in the first village he sees, shimmering in the heat, "every dog in Spain seemed in heat; canine copulation was everywhere" (6), initiating a thematic of almost bestial sexuality that permeates the book. Virtually all landscapes and cities are made to fit this personal mood of paranoia and disjuncture; Barcelona, normally described as lovely, now has "bleak suburbs," "tiny, dirty streets" and overall presents the image of a noisy, "garishly modern" city. Still, Wright makes poetry from the urban landscapes more often than in the villages, as in this passage, which is strongly personal, but quite useful in backing up the claims he is making elsewhere in the text: "We drank *cafe con leche* and the liquid looked green under the neon lights. We then set out down a narrow, smelly alleyway; from opened windows above my head poured harsh sounds of flamenco music, handclapping, stomping, and the wild, melancholy twanging of guitars" (19). Always, Wright the narrator is struck by harsh contrasts. "A barefoot girl in a ragged black dress knelt [in a church] at the side of a fashionable-dressed woman whose lips were rouged, whose neck was roped with pearls, and whose fingers sparkled with diamonds" (9).

By adopting this stance, and fleshing it out with exotic detail, Wright ironically echoed many techniques employed by his sometimes nemesis, Zora Neale Hurston, in her path-breaking *Mules and Men* (1935), which has recently been praised and dissected as an early example of participatory observation. Both texts depend for their effect on the authority of the ethnographer, which is manifest in his/her firsthand experience of the culture. Hurston and Wright go "South" to investigate exotic cultures, he to "pagan" Spain, she to the rough venues of Polk County and its sawmill camps; both string together conversations and experiences to give a narrative flow to the material and a high degree of involvement on the reader's part, as Richard and Zora continue their investigations. Hurston, however, is looking for folklore, while Wright, the sociologist, seeks what an earlier time would call "lifelets," or life stories. Also at play in each book is the movement of the speaking participant toward the subject. In this regard, Hurston and Wright were ahead of their times in anthropological/sociological circles; personal narrative has since become a conventional part of ethnographies. Usually this approach manifests itself in the opening chapter of a study, wherein the participant/observer moves to the site of research, learns the language, and grapples with the initial difficulties of access, acceptance, and entry into the culture. Indeed, as Mary Louise Pratt has observed, these scenes are frequently the "most memorable segments of an ethnographic work," as in Evans-Pritchard's classic 1940 study, *The Nuer* (Pratt 31). In an essay on field work, Pratt goes over the history of ethnography and demonstrates a trend toward the personally involved anthropological narrative, and away from the comparatively bloodless accumulation of data that once prevailed as the correct approach (Pratt, "Fieldwork" 31).

Similarly, Richard Wright never saw any point in writing *anything*—fiction, nonfiction, whatever—that wasn't based on personal perception: "the artist must bow to the monitor of his own imagination: must be led by the sovereignty of his own impressions and perceptions; must be guided by the tyranny of what troubles and concerns him personally. There is no other true path" (qtd in Fabre, *World* 67).

The Script of Cultural Immersion

Wright begins *Pagan Spain* with a series of misunderstandings that he has about the intentions of various military figures he encounters on the road, sequences that reveal his paranoia but also his inept use of Spanish and his tendency to "misread" cultural signs. This sets the stage for his "growth" as cultural interpreter and central consciousness, as he stoically presses on in his search for meaning.

In one of the book's key early scenes, Wright meets two Barcelona "boys" (actually, young men in their twenties, André and Miguel) who take him to a *pensión*, and later introduce him to their families; first, however, they show him their church:

"I was a stranger and they were taking me into their Christian fellowship even before they knew my name, their solicitude cutting across class and racial lines.... We paused before a vast basin of white marble. 'That is where the first Indians that Columbus brought from America were baptized,' the taller boy informed me. It was beginning to make sense; I was a heathen and these devout boys were graciously coming to my rescue" (8–9). But as the book develops, the opposite seems the case; Wright, the missionary from the West, has come to diagnose Spain's pagan/heathen illness and suggest a cure. As an American, he stands in for the Indian; also like the Indian, he will see Spain from the viewpoint of a stranger, and he too will be "baptized," but with cultural understanding rather than religion.

Thus Wright initiates a long series of revelations that course with life because they find intimate expression in his individual understanding and in his actions and reactions as participant-observer. Again, this echoes Hurston; in their studies of different cultures, Hurston and Wright seem to understand intuitively, no doubt because of their experience as novelists, that any narrative, but especially those dedicated to journeys and exploration, profits from a central consciousness who knits together the speaking voice of the book and the events that take place in it. Further, both of them saw how a central component of the society he/she was exploring could operate as a catalyst for the reader: a sexual dynamic. John Dorst has recently demonstrated how a kind of "erotic code" operates throughout *Mules and Men*, as Zora's success in gathering tales increasingly relates to her sensual appeal in the community. Although Wright's emphasis on the carnal is very different, the sexual nature of many of the tales he hears—particularly from women—has the same kind of effect in *Pagan Spain*. Early on, André and Miguel, desperately seeking outlets for their bursting sexuality, but also determined to honor the virginity of "good girls," become metaphoric of larger issues of repression and anarchy that Wright repeatedly raises as characteristic of Spain. They introduce him to both a "professional virgin" (André's fiancé) and to prostitutes. It is no exaggeration to say that Wright's ethnography proceeds along psycho-sexual lines more often than not, informing every subject he opens.

Prior to the kind of writing Hurston did in *Mules*, ethnographers usually followed "the rules," epitomized in many ways by the pioneering work of Hurston's mentor, Franz Boas, who practiced a documentary kind of reportage that sacrificed personal involvement in favor of detached, objectified description. Should one wish, a second, more personal account could be written later. And we should remember that Hurston had written a dry-as-dust compilation of her folklore material, sans her own role, and published it in *The Journal of American Folklore* (1931); her dissatisfaction with it led to *Mules and Men.*

Mary Louise Pratt has outlined how this practice of dual texts long character-ized ethnography. Such figures as David Maybury-Lewis, Jean-Paul Dumont, Napoleon Chagnon, and Paul Rabinow all published formal ethnographies, and then, as a subgenre, a personal narrative that accompanied the first one. As Pratt notes, until recently it was the formal text that counted professionally, while the personal narratives were deemed "self-indulgent, trivial, or heretical," often pro-ducing "disciplining" reviews by peers (Pratt, "Fieldwork" 31). For Pratt, personal narratives have persisted because they "mediate a contradiction within the discipline between personal and scientific authority, a contradiction that has become espe-cially acute since the advent of fieldwork as a methodological norm." Many mod-ern ethnographers now combine personal narrative and objectified description in one book; this was preceded in various types of travel writing, as early as the six-teenth century. Pratt has urged ethnographers eager to create more innovative kinds of reportage to examine modes outside the discipline that mediate the gap between objectivity and subjectivity. I would add that examples within the literary tradition which are not, strictly speaking, travel documents or ethnography—for instance Melville's *Journal Up the Straits* (1857), or a more hybrid form like John Gunther's various books, including *Inside Africa* (1955), which Wright wrote a review of but never published—could be of service here, not to mention Zora Neale Hurston's work, which Pratt inexplicably does not consider.

Although many critics expressed surprise (sometimes bordering on incredulity) that the "Negro writer," as Wright was usually labeled, was turning out travel lit-erature, his accounts of his experiences were actually part and parcel of his long stated goal: his mission as a writer, he felt, was "to create a new life by intensifying the sensibilities and to work towards world understanding by improving living con-ditions" (qtd in Fabre, *UQ* 203). Wright had been moving toward his role as hu-manist "citizen of the world" for some time, especially after his break with the Communist Party, his self-imposed exile in France, and his eventual frustration with French existentialist circles. All these and other events had involved him in multi-cultural, interdisciplinary research, debate, and meditation, which made him eager to test new theories in the "laboratories" of different cultures. A trip to Haiti in 1950 inspired a set of notes that reveals a plan to write an impassioned travelogue, one that would analyze that country's history and current situation, especially its poverty and youth cultures (Fabre 351–352).

Moreover, Wright was increasingly disturbed by Cold-War events in the United States, especially as McCarthy began his ascendancy in the senate. Right-wing American tourists in France were negatively effecting the racial climate for black expatriates. Consequently, Wright helped found the French-American Fellowship (FAF) to promote friendship and to combat racism; more specifically, they sought to "urge the spread of the principles of fundamental education among the non-industrial peoples of the world; to lend encouragement and support to all minorities and exploited groups in their aspirations and struggles for freedom ... [to expose] all those mental habits which tend to solidify racial, class, social, religious, and national divisions between men" (qtd in Fabre, 358). Wright served as President of the FAF, which disbanded in 1951 when funds diminished. Still, the group had done what it had set out to do and had helped solidify Wright's purpose of expanding his interests to a larger domain. For him, the issue of freedom in Mississippi and the South had become, as he told an interviewer, the "problem of freedom in the Western world, the problem of Africa and Asia" (qtd in Fabre, *UQ* 364).

Writing his existentialist novel, *The Outsider* (1953), gave fictional expression to these new perspectives, in its concentration on profound moral and philosophical problems that pertained to all people; *Pagan Spain* and the other "travel" books Wright produced in the 1950s were logical developments of this novel. Indeed, James W. Ivy, the perceptive reviewer of *Pagan Spain* for *Crisis* magazine, noted "What Mr. Wright lacks in erudition he makes up for in intuitive understanding of a people who have a psychological affinity in many ways with American Negroes" (314), while the reviewer in *Christian Century* applauded Wright's appellation of Spaniards as "white negroes" (preceding Norman Mailer's use of this term), as justified by the similar position of Spaniards to that of "people of his color in our southern states" ("Bishop," n. p.). Wright himself, on the opening page of *Pagan Spain*, declares "God knows, totalitarian governments and ways of life were no mysteries to me. I had been born under an absolutistic racist regime in Mississippi; I had lived and worked for twelve years under the political dictatorship of the communist party of the United States; and I had spent a year of my life under the police terror of Peron in Buenos Aires" (1).

I would add a caveat to these claims, however; it seems to me, for all the affinities that Wright located between African Americans and Spaniards, that he would draw a sharp distinction as well. In *The Outsider* (speaking through the character Cross Damon) he posited that what "makes one man a Fascist and another a Communist might be found in the degree to which they are integrated with their culture. The more alienated a man is, the more he'd lean toward Communism ..."

(364). Damon doesn't finish the sentence, but the implication is that if a man is overly integrated in his culture—as was true of Spaniards obsessed with the myths and rituals of the Church, gender, and so on—it is more likely he will support fascism.

In keeping with this idea that the Church operated as a powerful prop of the Franco government, another interesting aspect of Wright's fix on Spain is his fascination with the plight of Protestants. Even though he had long ago given up on organized religion, his rigorous Protestant upbringing surged to the fore as he confronted the legacy of the Spanish Roman Church and its record of persecution. On the one hand, his profound knowledge of the Bible dictated that he would constantly fail to find biblical precedent for many fundamentals of Catholic faith and practice (the prominent display of relics, for instance, offended him). As if to remind the reader of his religious background, he tells a character who exclaims over Wright's biblical learning, "I was weaned on it" (43). Simultaneously, Wright is never more the researcher, never more the anthropological myth-critic than when he is debunking Catholic holy places. After visiting the shrine of the Black Virgin with his friend Pardo, who works for the Vatican, Wright gives a lengthy lecture on the ancient avatars of Virgin-worship, concluding that "That statue is one of the ways in which the Church can accept sex, the most prevalent, powerful, emotional, and factual experience in human life. Man senses that if there is anything at all really divine or superhuman in us, it is linked to, all with, and comes through sex, and is inescapably bound up with sex. In worshiping the Black Virgin, men and women are worshiping the female principle in life, just as they have always done" (65).

On the other hand, Wright would also state, "I am an American Negro with a background of psychological suffering stemming from my previous position as a member of a persecuted racial minority. What drew my attention to the emotional plight of the Protestants in Spain was the undeniable and uncanny psychological affinities that they held in common with American Negroes, Jews, and other oppressed minorities" (138). The specter of McCarthy in the United States and what Wright saw as the increasingly evident impotence of French existentialism to act against world injustice made him especially attentive to the plight of the Spanish Protestants, and also caused him to see a connection with the structures of oppression he had noted previously, in a very different context, in Africa.

Consequently, Wright loses no opportunity to underline the menace of imprisonment, even torture, in scene after scene, and not just that inflicted on Protestants. He himself falls victim to a police scam, and at several points fears he's being watched and about to be arrested. The man who had entitled an entire book of *Native Son* "Fear" knew how to use it to spice ethnography too. This is, however, in contradistinction, a kind of counterpoint to intimate exchanges with his informants, and with often quite detailed descriptions of daily life. In many of the examples cited above, we see Wright functioning as any ethnographer must. As Vincent Crapanzano puts it, such an investigator "must render the foreign familiar and preserve its very foreignness at one and the same time. The translator accomplishes this through style, the ethnographer through the coupling of a presentation that asserts the foreign and an interpretation that makes it all familiar...he must make use of all the persuasive devices at his disposal to convince his readers of *the* truth of his message" (Crapanzano, 52).

But we may go further with our definitions of contemporary ethnography. According to James Clifford, ethnographic writing is determined in at least six ways: "(1) contextually (it draws from and creates meaningful social milieux); (2) rhetorically (it uses and is used by expressive conventions); (3) institutionally (one writes within, and against, specific traditions, disciplines, audiences); (4) generically (an ethnography is usually distinguishable from a novel or a travel account); (5) politically (the authority to represent cultural realities is unequally shared at times contested); (6) historically (all the above conventions and constraints are changing)" (Clifford and Marcus, 6).

Because it seems to me that Wright satisfies all these requirements in *Pagan Spain*, he was, through his synthesis of travel reportage and ethnographic observation, pioneering a new, hybrid kind of literary/scientific work that has now become a field of endeavor in its own right. *Pagan Spain*, however, did not emerge suddenly. Many of Wright's preceding works, both fiction and non-fiction, had been moving in these directions for some time. As Lynn Weiss has shown, Wright was writing on the Spanish Civil War in the thirties, and began thinking of Spain through the lens of the Communist Party he then served. At the same time, he took pride in the role of the Afro-Americans who had fought there in the Abraham Lincoln Brigade (Weiss 213). I cannot rehearse here all of those steps, or even the long trip Wright made to the Gold Coast in 1953, but the book that came out of that trip, *Black Power* (1954), was an important precursor for *Pagan Spain*. The results of ten weeks of intensive and determinedly independent efforts to explore the social realities of an emerging nation, from the turbulent coastal cities to the hidden interior hamlets, *Black Power* marked an important turning point in Wright's quest for identity, and produced a new stance toward his mission as both a man and a writer. Just in terms of approach and technique, Wright's use of native informants, books, newspapers, government publications, interviews, photographs, and residence amid the people he was studying demonstrate him moving closer to the model of anthropological research he would refine further in the writing of *Pagan Spain*.

Writing *Black Power* deeply conflicted Wright; life in Africa had paradoxically made him feel profoundly American, yet rekindled his rage against white domination of people of color, both home and abroad. He alternately planned to title his journal of the visit "O My People"; the book that would become *Black Power*, however, at one time bore the title *Stranger in Africa*; at another point, quoting Countee Cullen's magnificent "Heritage," the title was "What is Africa to Me?" (Fabre, *UQ* 401).

Black Power ends with a messianic letter to Kwame Nkrumah, the leader of the people, self-consciously written in the manner of Whitman; as such, it functions both as a heartfelt formula for resistance to Western imperialism, and on a deeper level, as a tacit admission of his own separation from African society. Wright had in fact been deeply disturbed by the differences he felt as an American and a Westerner in a largely animist, non-Western culture, and in his notes admitted, "I'm of African descent and I'm in the midst of Africans, yet I cannot tell what they are thinking or feeling." Still, he told Nkrumah:

> While roaming at random through the compounds, market places, villages, and cities of your country, I felt an odd kind of at-homeness, a solidarity that stemmed not from ties of blood or race, or from my being of African descent, but from the quality of deep hope and suffering embedded in the lives of your people, from the hard facts of oppression that cut across time, space, and culture. I must confess that I, an American Negro, was filled with consternation at what Europe had done.... In defending their subjugation of Africa, they contend that Africa has no culture, no history, no background.... I'm not impressed by these gentlemen. (342–343)

Wright sees grounds for hope, but is worried by Africa's failure to counter tribal culture's effacement of the individual. For Wright, revolution demanded "egos that are stout, hard, sharply defined; there is too much cloudiness in the African's mentality, a kind of sodden vagueness that makes for lack of confidence" (343). The source for this was a "gummy tribalism" coupled with a "psychological legacy of imperialism" (344). And yet, while preaching against the West, Wright ends by extolling America's heroic past: "Your fight has been fought before. I am an American and my country too was once a colony of England" (351).

Wright has recently been praised (if briefly) by Mary Louise Pratt for his attempt in *Black Power* to resist the domineering stance of most "seeing men" (as she calls traditional Western travel writers). Pratt claims that Wright, describing at one point the overpowering sensations of the African night, "is trying to represent an experience of ignorance, disorientation, incomprehension, self-dissolution which does not give rise to terror or madness, but rather to a serene receptivity and intense eroticism" (Pratt, *IE* 222). The difference between this stance and the one taken in *Pagan Spain* is striking. In the latter book, Wright seems very much in the mode of the Western traveler in Spain, as many of the early reviewers of the book noted. By this I mean that he disdains much of what he sees, and debases it both by derogatory description, by excluding much of what has always and still does make Spain beautiful and appealing, and by depicting the country as monotonous and paralyzed. On the other hand, in both books he frequently employs an intensely erotic perspective that proves useful in uncovering psychological realities about the respective cultures. Finally, although his posture puts him in congruence with other Western, often Protestant "seeing-men," one must recognize that Wright's emphasis on rationality and morality also springs from his immediate and constant identification with the oppressed peoples of Spain, whose plight so often seems parallel to the downtrodden of America—and not only African Americans, but also Jews, women, immigrants, and memorably, a Catalonian barber who yearns for a separatist nation. Wright's analysis of this anti-Spaniard's paradoxically passionate sense of isolation and Spanish way of stating it—"I am the master of my hunger"—raises parallels with many of Wright's earlier works; indeed, Wright's final, analytical assessment of this man could apply just as well to the defiant Bigger Thomas at the end of *Native Son:* "Proud, sensitive, knowing no practical way out of the morass of his shame and degradation, he had made a monument out of his black defeat" (83).

As these remarks indicate, Wright in *Black Power* and in *Pagan Spain* is more interested in the psychology and reality of everyday life in the Gold Coast and Iberia than in the political situation per se. He seems to have been working toward an assessment of culture along the lines of what Fernand Braudel, working in the tradition of the Annales school and the historians Marc Bloch and Lucien Febvre had already termed, "The Structures of Everyday Life."

Earlier in his career, as noted previously, Wright's prose served the goals and ideals of Communism. By the time he drafted *Pagan Spain*, however, he was writing independently, going far beyond a merely political critique of culture to a more sophisticated sociological/anthropological approach, which he correctly understood as nevertheless inclusive of the political, but of much else as well.

James Clifford has postulated a definition of "ethnographic experience" that may be useful here in understanding Wright's mission in Spain. "Following Dilthey, ethnographic 'experience' can be seen as the building up of a common, meaningful world, drawing on intuitive styles of feeling, perception, and guesswork. This activity makes use of clues, traces, gestures, and scraps of sense prior to the development of stable interpretations. Such piecemeal forms of experience may be classified as aesthetic and/or divinatory" (Clifford 36).

Chicago Sociology and Spanish Applications

The question remains, however; despite the work he did in *Black Power*, was Wright really prepared to write in a hybrid form? This shift in his stance eventually suggested and facilitated a retrieval of methods he had acquired earlier in his career. Carla Cappetti has recently demonstrated how Wright's approach to social, and ultimately, literary problems, was shaped and influenced by the Chicago school of sociologists. William Issac Thomas, the founder of that school, posited "personal life-records, as complete as possible, constitute the *perfect* type of sociological material" (qtd in Cappetti 22). His approach was amplified by the Chicago school to include 1. letters, diaries, court records, records of charities, and 2. life records, preferably "prepared by average or proletarian persons," and 3. extant autobiographies, especially those written in the vernacular (Cappetti 22–23). Wright's determined attempts to interview people from all levels of Spanish society, especially those "furthest down," and his shared belief in personal testimony, speak to his background in Chicago school method, which had deep resonance for a man raised in the communal ambiences of African American Mississippi.

William Issac Thomas saw the inclusion of life stories as a checkmate against the tendencies of the imagination that dramatists and "story writers" would naturally have. At the same time, the Chicago school also prized poetic, evocative writing that was based in objective reporting of actual facts. Wright excelled in such writing: consider the following passage, for instance, describing his entry into a Barcelona bordello: "We pushed through a rattling curtain made of long strings of black beads, flinging aside the strips and hearing them clack and settle into place behind us; we entered an oblong dive whose background was lost in smoke. An unshaven, Greekish face, with an unlighted cigarette stub in its partly-open lips, eyed us coldly from behind a cash register as we moved forward through fumes of tobacco smoke that stung the throat.... Some thirty women of all ages and descriptions and sizes sat at tables and at the long bar, their shiny black purses—the international trademark of their profession—blatantly in evidence" (19–20).

Wright's more important mentor from the Chicago school was Robert Park, who was trained initially as a philosopher. He studied with William James, John Dewey, and others, while working on the side as a court reporter, as a police reporter, and with city newspapers. Ernest Burgess and Louis Wirth, two other important sociologists who influenced Wright's work, used realist and proletarian literature to illustrate sociological principles. Their interest in "Negro" literature provided a special attraction for Wright, along with their belief in the didactic uses of such texts for social progress. Cappetti has diligently explored the various ways in which their intricate connection of sociology, philosophy, literature (especially autobiography), and current events worked in the various courses they taught, and in the influential lectures they gave, and how they created a new theory of American sociology.

For my purposes here, I would like to concentrate on a key pronouncement by Wirth: "If we knew the full life-history of a single individual in his social setting, we would probably know most of what is worth knowing about social life and human nature" (cited in Cappetti 31–32). Wright sought these stories at every level of Spanish society, and seemed particularly interested in women's narratives. He gets his copy of the oft-quoted manual for girls from the 25 year-old Carmen, who seemingly speaks for many single "good girls" when she bitterly cries, "I earn my own living. Yet I can't go out at night. . . . After your mother, father, and the priest get through with you, you can't feel anything else" (16).

Carmen in turn introduces Wright to her brother Carlos, an orange grower who reflects bitterly on the politics of agricultural production. Wright also meets and interviews the bullfighter he had seen perform one afternoon, but seeks out less glamorous figures as well, eventually interviewing a white slave trader. During his subsequent trip, Wright talks with prominent Spanish intellectuals and aristocrats, thereby completing his circuit of all social "types" and "lifelets."

Although we feel his interest in all these characters, he demonstrates particular fascination with Lola, a deranged woman whose family rents Wright a room. Since her illness resulted from seeing her father killed during the Spanish Civil War, she becomes a kind of metaphor for the Spanish "dis-ease," along with her dog Ronnie, who also suffers from abandonment syndrome. Wright had stated in his autobiography that his readings in sociology had made him especially attentive to "the frequency of mental illness" in oppressed blacks (*Hunger* 26). Such "lifelets" helped him paint portraits of societies. One increasingly wonders, however, are these "tales of truth," or is Wright carefully composing an aesthetically managed ethnography? In the passages devoted to Carlos and his orange groves, for instance, the grower tells Wright that Spain's repression is so severe that it's actually a Communist state that endorses Catholicism. As a businessman, he's able to spout statistics for the reader's benefit about agricultural production. The sweeping picture he creates suggests Wright is using him to put forward material his own research provided. This possible "slippage" between realistic telling-it-like-it-is and textbook objectivity and fact occurs more than once in the narrative.

In interacting (in increasingly complicated ways) with the figures before him, Wright embraces yet another tenet of Chicago-school sociology, which looms even larger in American anthropology: participant-observation. Like Park, Wirth, and many anthropologists who have followed these early sociologists, Wright's method is to seek entry into the society, develop relationships and encounters, and then step back to provide analysis. Further, it is always in these peoples' *stories*—both as related from the past and as reflected in their current relation with Wright—that the author/researcher finds a point of departure.

It seems worth noting, however, that Wright repeatedly draws back from these often intense encounters. The travel motif causes this, to a certain extent, as he always leaves to go on to a new locale, a new set of issues and problems. But Wright also takes pains—especially in the potentially explosive area of sexual relations—to avoid total involvement. Nowhere here does he have sex with anyone, although he teases the reader repeatedly with possible encounters, particularly with the many prostitutes who figure in the narrative.

In an attempt to understand the plight of Spain's many victims, Wright considers them from the perspectives of psychology (particularly Freudian) and that of urban sociology, mostly as a result of his work in Chicago. But his sympathy more broadly comes from his oppressed youth in Mississippi, which runs through the book like a hidden underground river. His attentiveness to violence, to the irrational maneuvers of Franco's police state, and the small details that bring this into prominence, recalls much of *Black Boy, American Hunger,* and "The Ethnics of Living Jim Crow." One of the most positive reviewers, writing in the *London Times,* went so far as to declare "He is the American Negro consciously visiting Spain on a mission of inquiry into his own racial and cultural origins. He wants to know what kind of people they were who founded the New World and then, apparently so carelessly, threw it away" ("Red Rag to Spain"). And indeed, Wright signals this very intent in the first chapter, where he visits a church, sees a font, and is informed, "That is where the first Indians that Columbus brought from America were baptized" (*PS* 9). It seems clear that these aspects of his involvement with Spanish culture ultimately led him back imaginatively to Mississippi, the setting of his final, still-underrated masterwork, *The Long Dream*.

Visions of Spanish Women

Wright has often been criticized, especially by feminist critics, of neglecting and/or misreading the stories of women. Many of these critiques, however, ignore Wright's later work, especially *Long Dream*, but including *Pagan Spain*; much of the latter book's purported "preoccupation with sex" (a charge made by several conservative—and I might add, white—reviewers) actually involves a close consideration of the roles dictated to Spanish women. Wright's readings of femininity were influenced by the Chicago school's writings, especially those of William Issac Thomas, the founder of American sociology at the University of Chicago, and like Wright, an immigrant from the South. His important study, *The Unadjusted Girl: With Cases and Standpoint for Behavior Analysis*, focused on seduction, crime, and prostitution, particularly in the cities. As Wright would do in *Pagan Spain*, Thomas illustrates his theories with case studies, and strongly indicates the ultimate fate of his subjects is dictated by social conditions rather than moral degeneracy. Moreover, his strongly comparative, cosmopolitan approach to world cultures would have signaled to Wright a methodology in keeping with the direction of his own interests at the time.

Accordingly, like Thomas, Wright sees through social expectations of Spanish sexual behavior to the underlying interconnection of rigid social foundations. All the women in the book are held accountable to the unrelenting expectation that a Spanish woman will come to her marriage as a virgin. Wright, as many had before him, saw this given prominent social display in the cult of the Virgin, which is ubiquitous in Spanish culture. He pays special attention to the many images of the Virgin carried through the streets during festivals, accompanied by men clad in white robes, masks, and tall pointed hats, all too similar to the garb of the Ku Klux Klan (indeed, Wright specifically notes in the text proper, "Those hooded penitents had been protecting the Virgin, and in the Old American South hooded Ku Kluxers had been protecting 'the purity of white womanhood'" [237]). A picture Wright took of these masked figures (now at Yale) has attached to it the typed note, "In the American South white men march in the regalia shown above to defend 'white womanhood'; in Spain, they wear that regalia to protest the Virgin. In both instances, a vague feeling about 'female purity' provokes men to brutality."[2]

Furthermore, in the text proper, he claims that the white candles the men carry are "flying white drops that were like semen spraying, jutting from the penises of sexually aroused bulls" (236).

Elsewhere in *Pagan Spain*, Wright focuses on the apparent contradiction of massive prostitution in Spain. He snapped several photos of these women; one shows a harsh but well-dressed young woman looking boldly into the lenses, defiant in her stance as she leans against a tree trunk. The typed notation reads "A Spanish streetgirl: desexualized, illiterate, devout, respectful of authority, yearning for something or somebody to serve..." (Figure 1). In fact, Wright shot several of these women in the same pose with the same tree—he seems to have chosen the prettiest woman for the 8x10 blowup, and no doubt liked the inclusion of the tree trunk as a properly phallic signifier.

Wright concludes his musings by admitting the spectacle shows that "all of it, Christianity and Communism, had come from one (and perhaps) unrepeatable historical accident that had been compounded in Rome from Greek science and love of the human personality, from Jewish notions of a One and indivisible God...Roman conceptions of law and order and property, and from a perhaps never-to-be-unravelled amalgamation of Eastern and African religions with their endless Gods who were sacrificed and their virgins who gave birth perennially" (240). I will discuss other images of women in conjunction with other aspects of the book, for their role is so important at every level that it does injury to a sustained consideration of the individual parts of the book to abstract all these passages here.

In Search of the Ethnographer Image: Wright as Scientist/Photographer

Wright's research for this book was both limited and exhaustive. The three trips to Spain—August 15 to September 10, 1954; November 8 to December 17, 1954; and February 20 to early April 1955 (Weiss 215)—while intense and productive, after all only comprise slightly more than three months. More significantly, since he could not speak Spanish, except for rudimentary phrases, one might legitimately ask how he could come away with anything but superficial knowledge of the culture. One of the achievements of the travel book, however, lies in its demonstration of the expressive frequencies humans possess in addition to a native tongue. Scene, gesture, nuance, image, icon, all these and many more contribute to Wright's cavalcade of communicative idioms, which often bridge the seeming chasm of language.

On the other hand, as others have demonstrated, Wright researched Spanish history and culture thoroughly, talked to many Spaniards in English and French, and traveled to virtually every major city and every major region in Spain during the course of his three extended visits. The files at Yale include many letters of introduction Wright had obtained, some in Spanish, others in English, from various Spaniards he knew in Paris and elsewhere. One, from Cuevas de Vera to Ricardo Baeza of Madrid, amuses, in its appeal to "Be an angel and show him 'toreros' and 'intelectuales' who are not the 'dull reactionaries' that he fears" ("Letter").

We should also recall that one of Wright's mentors, Robert Redfield, made studies of the cultures of Spanish speaking peoples in Mexico, and Wright himself spent an idyllic three months in Mexico shortly after his first marriage. He had also lived for a year in the Fascist Argentina of Juan Peron, while shooting the film of *Native Son*. Wright, as mentioned above, had been vitally interested in the Spanish Civil War; eventually he published a review of William Rollins, Jr.'s *The Wall of Men*, a study of that conflict, in *New Masses* in 1938. Even then he was railing about the "deceptions and provocations of the Catholic Church and the fascists" in tandem ("Adventure" 235).

Wright had thus spent a good deal of time pondering the Hispanic temperament, and *Pagan Spain* was a logical outgrowth of that preoccupation. The files at Yale indicate his initial musings on the book, especially in his detailed proposal that he put together on the advice of his agent Paul Reynolds. At that time, the proposed title was "Lonesome Spain," a reflection of Wright's long felt perception of the country as a maverick within Europe. The first sentence of the proposal asserts, "Spain is basically a non-western country, despite the fact that it is a European country and is strongly Catholic" ("Outline–PS" 1). As the document goes on to demonstrate, Wright blames most of Spain's problems on its relation with the Church, which seemingly forgives all sin—"Hence, anarchy is the hallmark of the Spanish temperament. And, amid such anarchy, there must be a strong power to hold society together. That power is Franco and his machine guns." Wright goes on to propose eight sections for the book. The first, "Life After Death" would deal with the huge Paralleto slum in Barcelona, full of Franco's defeated and poverty-stricken enemies, "an urban jungle . . . life lived without any sense of direction save that of animal instinct. Yet they live and derive some strange joy from their living." Part Two was to be "Gods for Sale," a treatment of the Spanish Gypsies; Wright was perhaps drawn to them because of their outsider status in Spain; he reports here, "A Gypsy told me: 'You and me, we the same. . . .'" Part Three, "The Underground Christ," was to deal with the oppression of Spain's 20,000 Protestants.

Here Wright goes into more detail than elsewhere, making it plain that he views Protestants as "white Negroes"—"the problem of the Protestant in Spain is remarkably like that of the American Negro...he never knows at what moment he will be called upon to disclose his religious beliefs....I found them most fearful to talk and that indicates their deep fear. They feel, like American Negroes, that if their problem is known to the authorities, that those authorities will make them suffer for telling of their problems!" ("Outline–*PS*" 3).

Here we may note a shift away from sociological detachment into a more involved anthropological project that might lead to change. Wright increasingly seems preoccupied with uncovering problems not just to provide information but to foment correction. As such, he was remarkably in step with the impulses of contemporary anthropologists; certainly one of the leading figures in this group at the time was Margaret Mead, who proclaimed in the forties, "By insisting upon the systematic interrelationship of different elements of culture, anthropology can warn against any planning which disregards essential components whose relevance may not be immediately apparent to those whose eyes are directed along more special lines. It can provide the underpinning and groundwork for an understanding, which must otherwise remain intuitive, of the importance of certain social trends, of the relevance of certain moves. It can insist upon the necessity of devising psychological-cultural equivalents for traits or practices which social thinking decides should be altered or abolished" (Mead 95). In like manner, *Pagan Spain* reveals Wright evolving a new mode of travel writing, one closely aligned to both the forms and intentions of contemporary modes of ethnography. Integral to both these endeavors is an ideological impulse that plays a central role in all of Wright's work. Cross Damon outlines this program in *The Outsider,* in terms that surely apply to Wright the ethnographer in *Pagan Spain.* "There is one little thing...that a man owes to himself. He can look bravely at this horrible totalitarian reptile and, while doing so, discipline his dread, his fear, and study it coolly, observe every slither and convolution of its sensuous movements and note down with calmness the pertinent facts...he may then be able to call the attention of others around him to the presence and meaning of this reptile and its multitudinous writhings" (367).

Wright had been "inside the serpent's mouth" of totalitarian systems of oppression in the American South, Chicago's slums, the American Communist Party, and fascist Argentina. The descent into Spain's "paganism" seemed to him a final "immersion," one that led to the very roots of man's cultural susceptibility to oppression. Accordingly, Wright repeatedly lapses into a kind of teaching role in the book, trying to get the Spanish to see underlying fundamentals about their culture.

This is nowhere more striking than when he explains to André's family that the use of the word "Ole" at the bullfight is a Moorish term for "God's sake." "They all stood frozen and stared at me with open mouths. They had been uttering the pagan religious phrases of the Moors and had never known it!" (90). This seemingly minor moment in the book is of some import; not only does it offer Wright an opportunity to display this learning, educate the "people," and score points with the reader; it also links him, because of race, with the Moors (both in terms of their rich contributions to Spanish history, and their ultimate banishment and oppression) and with the paganism that he finds so magnetic and yet appalling in Spain, and presumably, within himself, thereby summoning up the specter of the anthropologist "gone native."[3]

In his proposal for section four, "The Love of Death," Wright deals with bullfighting, which he sees as a survival of ancient bull worship, "blatantly a pagan religion." Wright here claims to have acquired a deep knowledge of the sport by associating closely with the bullfighters, and mocks Hemingway's *Death in the Afternoon:* "many bullfighters tell me that Hemingway completely missed the emotional content of the art or game."

Wright followed this with a fifth proposed section, "The World of Catholic Power," which would examine the religious system as one of calculated social control. According to Wright, the Church created irrational, and therefore, dependent men, who would therefore support the State through adherence to the Church. But Wright's final words here make it clear that he isn't interested merely in criticizing the Church, but in demonstrating that "where a dictatorship exists it has roots in the masses of people," whose emotional "paganism" keeps them enslaved.

Significantly, Wright proposed a sixth section, "The Pagan Heritage," which would discuss the roles of the Moor and the Jew in Spanish history. He deals with this, however, in a brief paragraph, and this section was never actually written. He was clearly far more interested in the proposed section seven, "Flamenco, Sex, and Prostitution," which is the longest part of the proposal. Wright comes across here as more than a little Puritanical, but also as a man fascinated by "lost women." He claims, too, that "the degradation of the Spanish woman, has, in an ironical way, lifted her up."

Finally, in the eighth and last section, "Spain in Exile," Wright proposed a treatment of the many Spanish in exile in Paris. As a reading of the published book reveals, however, Wright modified his plan rather substantially. He left out the gypsies, the Spaniards in exile, and much of his projected treatment of the flamenco. Michel Fabre has documented how Wright's publishers also stripped away passages on the Protestants, the entire Valencia Festival section, and parts of Wright's fascinating chapters on Granada, Seville, and Madrid. Fabre feels the book lost much of its local color as a result, and that the criticism of Franco's anti-Protestant policy was also weakened (Fabre, *UQ* 414). In all, over 150 pages were cut. On the other hand, we should also remember that ethnographers often take a similar tack; Renato Rosaldo reminds us that they take great pains to differentiate themselves from tourists on the one hand and from missionaries and officials on the other (Rosaldo 96). Wright would seem to be no exception to this general observation; his omissions along these lines deepened the loss of the material cited by Fabre. Moreover, Wright typed out or had typed out a translation (by whom remains to be seen) of the *Formación Política: Lecciones para Flechas* (*Political Formation: Lessons for the Arrow*), the notorious instruction book for girls that he cites at length in every chapter of *Pagan Spain*. As other commentators have noted (Margolies 39–40; Gayle 248), the manual helps unify and structure the other materials and provides an ironic commentary on the hypocrisy of the Fascists and damning proof of the Church's collusion with Franco's forces.

These quotations have sometimes been criticized as padding that is often irrelevant (Weiss 216). To a certain extent, this view is persuasive; on the other hand, Wright would seem to agree at least in part with Clifford Geertz that culture is best seen "not as complexes of concrete behavior patterns—customs, usages, traditions, habit clusters—as has, by and large, been the case up to now, but as a set of control mechanisms—plans, recipes, rules, instructions (what computer engineers call 'programs')—for the governing of behavior" (44). As such, the manual provides *prima facie* evidence of something Wright detects throughout Spanish society, both before and after Franco: the monumental barriers to individuality heaped up by the accretions of a particular history. We might further speculate that Wright would disagree with Geertz to a point, in that he would have seen the "concrete behavior patterns" Geertz dismisses as in fact auxiliary vehicles for the governance of behavior.

Since sexuality was a major focus of the book, he was excited when he procured a collection of letters belonging to Spanish prostitutes; many had been written by American sailors, some of them African American. As Lynn Weiss notes, these documents were excluded from the published book; for her, this and other changes in the original manuscript which Wright's editors imposed on the project, meant that "In the typescript he is an aggressive detective; in the American text he is little more than a perceptive observer" (215). These terms prove interesting for our purposes, for it pushes Wright, in ethnographic terms, away from the role of scrupulous Chicago-school researcher, toward the role of Pratt's "seeing men." He went to some pains to attend cultural performances and events that mirrored every level of Spanish society, and he took literally hundreds of pictures, which are now at the Beinecke Library of Yale University. He clearly intended the 537-page original manuscript to be lavishly illustrated with these photographs; in fact, the care he took labeling, cropping, and assorting them suggests he might at one time have had in mind a photographic essay along the lines of *12 Million Black Voices*. Aside from the surprisingly powerful effect of the pictures (Wright, after all, was hardly a professional photographer), one is struck by the possibility that the photographic work was surely one of the mechanisms Wright proposed to use to counter his linguistic difficulty with Spanish. Nor are all the photographs his—he purchased many, and also collected postcards, tourist souvenirs, and religious knickknacks for his "Spanish" collection.

The photographs of festivals include some shots that tell us a great deal about Wright's feeling that he was in many ways back in the South. This is particularly true of the elaborate Festival of the Fallas that Wright saw in Valencia in March, 1955. Unfortunately, his account of this experience was cut from the final version of *Pagan Spain*, but his pictures of the event are at Yale. One of the enormous cardboard floats depicts grossly stereotyped African natives in grass skirts—an obese King eating, accompanied by a painfully thin servant who chases flies away (Figure 2). The servant has a bone threaded through his hair, and both of them have exaggerated racial features. On the other hand, this picture is but one half of the complete float/exhibit; right next to the King is a Western business tycoon in formal wear, also obese, also gluttonously eating, also accompanied by a rail-thin servant, this time a proper British butler (Figure 3). The African King sits in front of a grass hut topped by a skull, while the tycoon plops before a nouveau-Norman, overdone mantel, which is surmounted by a parody of modern art. We remember here that Wright had been preoccupied while in Ghana with the thorny problem of Africans selling other Africans into slavery, and of owning slaves. The float would have also appealed to Wright's proletarian sympathies, which to his surprise he found evoked in Ghana, just as they had been in America and France. The fact that he took two pictures of the float to capture its totality is expressive of his fascination.

Perhaps the most interesting group of pictures at Beinecke Library at Yale is a complex of three images that exhibit a fundamental relation to one another. Wright had hired a chair for the Easter processions in Seville; his fixed location serves as a common backdrop for two of these shots, both of which have seated spectators in the foreground. In one, a company of hooded, cone-hatted men, dressed entirely in white (even to white gloves) passes before the camera, dominated by one figure staring at the lens who has one hand at his throat and the other on top of his huge candle/stave (Figure 4). The identical background looms in a second shot of Fascist soldiers passing in review, replete with Nazi-style uniforms, helmets, and weaponry (Figure 5). In the text, Wright comments, "they were doing a modified goosestep. The Church, then the armed State to protect the Church" (236). These two images—of the sacred and secular soldiers—seemingly fuse in a purchased engraving also in the Yale repository, of Santiago Apostol (Saint James), the patron saint of Spain, on a rampant white horse, sword drawn, shield in hand (Figure 6). The horse appears to be trampling on dead and dying Moors, who wear turbans and have dark skin. A shadowy white angel looms behind the equestrian and enhaloed Saint James, blowing on a trumpet (of doom? racial destiny?). Interestingly, both the marching soldiers picture and the engraving of Saint James have the same typed notation attached: "To conquer the infidel was a duty imposed by God." Clearly, Wright had to be horrified and haunted by these images, which in composite, presented him with a sickeningly familiar impression of racist solidarity at every level of a society. We must of course remember, as he no doubt tried to, that the religious processions ostensibly had nothing to do with race—but the expulsion of the Moors, as Wright knew from his research, was fomented by the state and church acting in tandem, just as the ejection of the Jews had been in 1492, under the auspices of the Warrior King and Queen Ferdinand and Isabella. Wright's investigation of the ongoing oppression of gypsies, Protestants, and women by the Franco regime had to be seen as part of a continuum, one that would presumably proceed as the young were indoctrinated into the various rites of oppression; Wright took care, in fact, to photograph a hooded child accompanying the adult maskers, much to the amusement and apparent approval of spectators (several of them women) (Figure 7). A typed notation reads, "Children are the future; they marched also, continuing a great tradition of four hundred years."

Wright, in fact, appended typewritten notations to most of these pictures. One, also attached to the Saint James trampling the Moors, reads "The hooded men were admired." A copy of this picture has appended another notation, which apparently belonged with another picture, but its attachment here is fascinating, since it reads "I was a dark-skinned heathen and these devout boys were coming to my rescue; I was a 'lost' soul in dire need of being saved." Yet another photograph, not included here, depicts a bonfire that apparently reminded Wright all too clearly of the burning of black bodies in the South; his notation reads, "The flames sang with hot fury, soaring as high as the buildings." This wasn't true, as the photograph shows, but one understands the hyperbole.[4]

It is fascinating to note that Wright compiled this photographic research at a time when anthropologists were debating the value of photography in their field. John Collier, Jr., published a piece on this issue in *American Anthropologist* in 1957, and observed that anthropologists to that point had discouraged the use of photography because of their movement "away from the study of the shell of society inward to the emotional, psychic, and intellectual expressions of man. . . . Can other material than the outer form of things be approached through graphic analysis? . . . Photographs also catch many elements of the emotional currents within situations that are involved in a man's reactions to his cultural circumstance" (844). Wright, who had become increasingly fascinated by the interplay of words and images, seems to have been asking these same questions, and the pictures he took in Spain did indeed move into the directions Collier was virtually simultaneously suggesting.[5]

The Corrida as Metaphor

Wright, even more so than Hemingway, saw how profoundly the bullfight reflected the vectors of the Spanish soul. He took over a hundred pictures at the *corrida,* and seemed to be particularly transfixed by the young, sensationally successful matador Chamaco, whom he photographed repeatedly; he also purchased commercial shots. One shows Chamaco in a tiled hallway, looking down holding his cape and hat and looking very boyish. It is signed "Afetuoniminte C. C. Chamaco." A drawn flourish surrounds the name, like a cape around a bull. One of the most spectacular pictures, taken from the stands, depicts Chamaco parading before the crowd after a successful performance, attended by other matadors. A typed notation reads "Chamaco holding the tail and an ear of the slain bull, trotted around the ring to receive his homage" (Figure 8). A review of the contact sheets reveals that Wright constructed this tightly composed shot from a larger one, carefully marking the original in red for cropping. One may easily distinguish which shots he deemed most significant by noting which ones among this group were chosen for 8x10 blowups.

An ordinary family shot is included among those of spectators, perhaps to show that this blood sport was part of the national heritage for everyone, regardless of age, sex, or class. Wright must have been struck, too, by the prevalence of American culture, even here in Seville. Several of his pictures display a poster advertising *El Desfiladero del Cobre* with Ray Milland, McDonald Carey, and Hedy Lamarr. Wright himself seems to have been the object of some curiosity—in several pictures people in the crowd seem to stare at the camera with open mouths and wide eyes.

Wright again and again draws lines of connections between the apparently disparate images that he sees. A purchased color photo, replete with quite a few negatives of same, "La Muerte de Manolete," depicts the famous matador, nude from the waist up, lying in his coffin, clutching a crucifix (Figure 9).[6] At the side is a veiled, weeping woman, while above him rears a huge black bull. A romantic, mysterious night scene, replete with the evening star and mournful cypresses, looms behind the tableau. Two hats—one, seemingly an upturned matador's hat, the other a sombrero, lie on the ground before the coffin. The bull, the dominating figure in the scene, has liquid streaming from its mouth, and appears to have a brand on its haunch suggesting the Alpha and Omega of Christ. A typed notation to the negative reads, "In the photo depicting the death of Manolete, one sees two religions 'co-existing' side by side: Mithraism and Catholicism." Wright had the negative developed and colored at "Tous Travaux Coleur-Tirage sur papier— executes dans nos laborotories Photo-Rico 13, Carrefour de l'Odeon 13. Tel Ode. 28–82 PARIS VI." As he was no doubt aware, the composition of the photograph was strongly reminiscent of various paintings of the deposition from the cross; he had seen many versions of this in his travels through Spain. The weeping woman, whose face is obscured by a mantilla supported by a comb, obviously signifies a secular version of the weeping Madonna; Wright seems to have been fascinated by the various depictions of the Virgin favored by the Spanish, many of them "weeping," and he photographed them again and again. A typed note in the Yale collection reads "In Seville two Virgins reign: Our Lady of Hope in Mararena and in Rriana [this is a typo—it should read "Triana"]. The statues are of wood and are dressed in silk and satin, etc. The tears pasted on the cheeks are of glass. The rings upon the fingers have diamond settings. The robes of the Virgins are changed once a month. It has been known for a man to be killed for slighting one of these Virgins…" (Photos–"*PS*").

The Virgin was the pinnacle of a typology of women; the corresponding one for male images was that of the bullfighter. Wright's fascination with the bullfight no doubt stems from this revelation. As we have seen, in his prospectus for the book, Wright challenged the value of Hemingway's analysis of the bullfight, specifically contrasting that writer's emphasis on "good technical description" with what will be his own interest in the point of view of the bullfighters, and of the

Spanish spectators: "Psychologically, it is more complicated than has been previously thought." Reading *Pagan Spain* one understands that Wright uses bullfighting as a field of synecdoche which relates to others he establishes as literary/social/psychological investigator. These parts suggest the whole, which is Spanish culture. As such, Wright duplicates the famous example of Clifford Geertz, who used the Balinese cockfight as a node wherein one may read important aspects of Balinese culture as a whole. Simultaneously, Wright here and elsewhere uses these cultural nodes and his knowledge of them as "fables of rapport" which signal his attainment of insider knowledge, and thus credibility as a participant-observer. By situating his reading of bullfighting against earlier points made about Spanish culture, Wright establishes the ritual sport as key "text" of that culture, and provides a superb reading, one that therefore spreads backward and forward to validate his other readings of disparate "texts."

Wright seems to have identified with both the bullfighter and the bull. His depictions of the events in the ring demonstrate compassion for the wounded animal, and he relentlessly points out how the bull embodies the male sexual principle, spelling out in graphic detail at one point how the spectators frequently come to kick and dismember the testicles of a dead bull. Tellingly, at another point, Wright himself plays the part of the bull at a party, amid screams of laughter: "I charged, not for the shawl but at Lucile, my head gently colliding with her pelvis. The girl's eyes registered shock; she dropped the shawl and stepped backward. The room exploded with laughter. Pawing the floor with my hind legs, I bellowed: 'RRRRROOOAAR!'" (*PS* 173).

It was no accident that Wright was fascinated by the bullfight. It brought together most of the thematics he had found so striking in Spain in one compact spectacle. Moreover, it illustrated a principle that he had no doubt absorbed from Park, who in talking about the pressures brought on man to conform, had identified the role of sport, play, and art functions: "They permit the individual to purge himself by means of symbolic expression of these wild and suppressed impulses. This is the catharsis of which Aristotle wrote . . . which has been given new and more positive significance by the investigations of Sigmund Freud and the psychoanalysts" (qtd in Cappetti 43). Implicit in Park's philosophy, as Cappetti has noted, is the concept of the sociologist as social physician. Similarly, in *Pagan Spain*, Richard Wright is only momentarily distracted by the glories of Spain's culture; he is preoccupied throughout his study with Spain's various states of disease, relentlessly probing with his pen/scalpel to both the "cancer" and its sources.

Conclusions from Counter-Discourse

I intend to interview these people and let them tell their story.

Richard Wright, 1954

The final section, "The World of Pagan Power" offers a counterpart to the anthropologist's "conclusions" section. Here Wright rehearses and resifts the evidence he has been accumulating for the reader in the previous chapters, and arrives at the conclusion that Spain has less chance of progress than even the post-colonial African states he had investigated earlier, for Spain is mired in a *pre-colonial* state of "paganism"; although everything in Spain is religion, it isn't really a *Christian* religion: "It had never been converted, not to Protestantism, not even to *Catholicism* itself! Somehow the pagan streams of influence flowing from the Goths, the Greeks, the Jews, the Romans, the Iberians, and the Moors lingered strongly and vitally on, flourishing under the draperies of the twentieth century. An early and victorious Catholicism . . . had here in Spain been sucked into the maw of a paganism buried deep in the hearts of the people" (*PS* 193). Wright is well aware, however, that in making such a charge he may be reacting in a "primitive" way himself, out of his own innate Protestant horror. He tries to promote his scientific "objectivity" with the reader by confessing this, and asking "Could I handle their explanations and at the same time stand outside of them? . . . It meant walking a mental tightrope, yet it did not commit me to any creed" (196).

The passage also resonates with a reminder that Spain, like most other European countries, was far from the "pure"/"Aryan" state that racist historians and intellectuals sometimes posited. Here Wright was echoing a refrain that had been established by Franz Boas as early as 1908, who commented at length on the many ethnic strains in Spanish history: "I think we may dismiss the assumption of the existence of a pure type in any part of Europe, and of a process of mongrelization in America . . . [such a process] has taken place for thousands of years in Europe," and especially Spain, where Boas mentions the Basques, "Oriental influences in the Pre-Mycenean period," "Punic influences," "Celtic invasions, Roman colonization, Teutonic invasions, the Moorish conquest . . . the Moors and the Jews" (Boas 321–322).

Wright's methods and conclusions in *Pagan Spain* align him with what ethnographers are now calling "counter-discourses." According to George Marcus, such intellectual work implies an interest in contestatory writing that stems from reaction/opposition to other discourses; frequently these discourses find initial expression among "literati"; on the other hand, such writing may be a search for such responses among the people under study. Marcus calls these "empirically derived counter-discourses" and admits they may be interrelated, and certainly this proves true in *Pagan Spain*. Wright, basing his conclusions on extensive interviews with a broad cross-section of Spaniards, saw his work proceeding in this way. At the same time, the project fit his personal stance of resistance and his ongoing battles against social injustice; he was in both these ways operating in the manner of W. E. B. Du Bois, whose *Black Reconstruction* (1935) offered a powerful "counter-discourse" to the popular (and racist) "history" of post-Civil War America prevalent in his day. Wright had given a concise statement on this subject regarding his purposes in *12 Million Black Voices* (1941), the photo-journalism project he completed with photographer Edwin Rosskum: "To paint the picture of how we live on the tobacco, cane, rice, and cotton plantations is to compete with mighty artists: the movies, the radio, the newspapers, the magazines, and even the Church. They have painted one picture: charming, idyllic, romantic; but we live another: full of the fear of the Lords of the Land, bowing and grinning when we meet white faces, toiling from sun to sun, living in unpainted wooden shacks that sit casually and insecurely upon the red clay" (35). Wright's use of counter-discourse had been perfected by the time he wrote *Pagan Spain*. At the same time, much of the power of his observations stem from the overwhelming evidence he assembles (following Boas's lead) that the problems he uncovers here have existed for centuries and apparently have no solution. As Marcus notes, "the point of finding counter-discourses is to render appropriately complex the cultural analysis embedded in ethnographic description. Thus, in whatever setting individualism is enacted, there is also a process, however masked and submerged, that challenges it" (Marcus 83–84). Accordingly, a monumental sense of paralysis and deadening social repetition casts an awesome pall over the entire book, just as it does in *12 Million Black Voices*.[7]

Pagan Spain also achieves force from the tension Wright creates by co-mingling hard, naturalistic facts and observations, and powerfully charged moments of emotional drama and communion. The latter surges to the fore in the book's most poignant moments. At a party some poor people hold for him in Granada, Wright is asked,

"You will tell the people in America about us?"

"I'll try. I'll do my best."

"What will you tell them?"

"I shall tell them that the people of Spain are suffering."

When the guests accompany him to the train, early that morning, Wright looks into their "naked pleading eyes . . . this love . . . was not for me alone, it was an appeal to that world they had never seen. . . . I took out my fountain pen and waved gently toward them. 'Para usted,' I whispered to them. I put my hand upon my heart" (175). In this moving semiotic sequence, Wright the writer puts a human equation in place of his political and anthropological pronouncements, much in the manner of Margaret Mead or Lévi-Strauss. We may also note here an important aspect of his ethnographic stance. An essential aspect of fieldwork lies in the participant-observer establishing a role in the community. Wright never needs to belabor the point in *Pagan Spain*, for it becomes instantly clear that virtually everyone he talks with desperately wants someone to know the reality of life in Spain. Their "testimony" to the outside world through him may, to be sure, transmit messages they do not sense; they could, in fact, be outraged by Wright's interpretation of their story. Nevertheless, Wright's role, again and again, is that of recorder, of truth-teller. The scene at the train station provides a tender coda to this long line of transactions that is absolutely essential to the ethnographic mission.

Wright's promise to the people also invites an assessment of it on the part of the reader. We all surely feel that Wright kept his promise. As a participant-observer, he narrated a curiously hybrid, innovative travel book, one that attempts therapeutic narrative. By marshalling the tools of sociology, travel writing, psychology, and a deeply personal committed sense of emotional history, Wright was able to pinpoint the sources of the Spanish dis-ease, a malady that has thankfully found new antidotes in our own brighter day.

Figure 1. Spanish Prostitute

Figure 2. Holy Week Parade—African Float

Figure 3. Holy Week Parade—Western Tycoon in Formal Wear

Figure 4. Holy Week: Men in White Hoods and Sheets

Figure 5. Holy Week—Franco's Fascist Soldiers

Figure 6. Holy Week—Santiago Apostol

Figure 7. Holy Week—Children and Men in White Hoods and Sheet

Figure 8. Chamaco the Bullfighter

Figure 9. Death of Manolete

Wright, Hemingway, and the Bullfight

An Aficionado's View

Keneth Kinnamon

O f the three great Latin countries of the Mediterranean, Spain has elicited less attention from North American writers than France or Italy, but the volume of work on Spanish subjects is nevertheless very considerable and the quality is high. Stanley T. Williams even asserts that "for American men of letters the fascination of Spain has in some ways exceeded that of other European countries, hardly excepting England itself" (xx), and his magisterial two-volume work on *The Spanish Background of American Literature* documents the case with substantial treatments of Irving, Ticknor, Prescott, Bryant, Longfellow, Lowell, Harte, and Howells along with briefer accounts of scores of others to 1950. Two of these latter are Gertrude Stein and Ernest Hemingway.

If Professor Williams's study had been published in 1965 instead of 1955, it would certainly have considered Richard Wright's travel book *Pagan Spain* (1957), based on trips he took to that country in 1954 and 1955. And the logical place for such a consideration would have been adjacent to Stein and Hemingway, for there is a clear triangulation of influence among the three with respect to Spain. Although her long residence in Paris may cause us to forget, Stein was deeply attracted to Spain, which she first visited before the turn of the century, seeing her first bullfight before Hemingway was born. Literary results of her exposure to Spain then and later include *Tender Buttons* and *Four Saints in Three Acts.* Her friendship with Pablo Picasso and Juan Gris are well known. Thus, she was in a good position to encourage her young protégé in the twenties and her correspondent and admiring friend in the forties to travel across the Pyrenees and experience what the Spanish call their *fiesta nacional.*

So intensely aware of their debt to Stein were Hemingway and Wright that they acknowledge it on the very first page of their nonfictional and/or travel narratives of Spain. In the second paragraph of *Death in the Afternoon*, Hemingway recalls that "Gertrude Stein talking of bullfights spoke of her admiration of Joselito and showed me some pictures of him in the ring and of herself and Alice Toklas sitting in the first row of the wooden barreras at the bull ring in Valencia with Joselito and his brother Gallo below..." (1–2). In the second paragraph of *Pagan Spain* Wright remembers that Stein,

> ...racked with pain and with only a few days to live, had counseled me (while nervously tugging with her fingers of her right hand at a tuft of hair on her forehead):
> "Dick, you ought to see Spain."
> "Why?" I had asked her.
> "You'll see the past there. You'll see what the Western world is made of. Spain is primitive, but lovely. And the people! There are no people such as the Spanish anywhere. I've spent days in Spain that I'll never forget. See those bullfights, see the wonderful landscape...." (1–2)

Although we do not know whether Wright met Hemingway at the American Writers Congress in New York attended by both in June 1937, we do know that they respected each other's work. In a letter to Charles Scribner in August 1940 responding to the publisher's comments on the manuscript of *For Whom the Bell Tolls*, Hemingway places his own book in the same category as *Native Son* and *The Grapes of Wrath* (Baker 510). For Wright, as for so many other young writers in the thirties and thereafter, Hemingway was central. Edwin Seaver reports that Wright was reading Hemingway while working in the Chicago Post Office early in the decade, and by 1938 Wright was telling interviewers, "I like the work of Hemingway, of course. Who does not?" (Kinnamon and Fabre 10). In an article on the genesis of *Uncle Tom's Children*, Wright wrote of the Chicago Southside Writers Club, in which he was the leading figure: "All of us young writers were influenced by Hemingway.... We liked the simple direct way in which he wrote..." ("How Uncle Tom's Children Grew" 16). And as Edwin Berry Burgum demonstrated more than fifty years ago, Wright's early short stories do indeed show evidence of Hemingway's influence.

Wright owned seven books by Hemingway, including the 1952 English edition of *Death in the Afternoon* (Fabre, *UQ* 70–71). He probably bought it in Paris as preparation for his first trip to Spain, but he may have read it much earlier or at the very least heard about it from his friend Ralph Ellison, a close student of Hemingway's work. In any case, Wright saw his first bullfights in Mexico in 1940, and on his very first Sunday afternoon in Spain, 22 August 1954, he jumped at the chance to renew his acquaintance with the *corrida*. Accepting an invitation to Sunday dinner from one André, a young man Wright meets while asking directions to a *pensión* in Barcelona, Wright goes to an ugly tenement apartment inhabited by the young man and his family. When André mentions that a bullfight will be held that very day, Wright immediately invites the man and his brother-in-law to accompany him to the bullring. In his elation at the prospect of seeing the promising *novillero* Chamaco perform, André snatches a tablecloth from his mother and passes an imaginary bull. From that point on "the talk of bulls and bullfighters swamped a long, heavy luncheon that swam in olive oil" (*PS* 90).

Wright's own talk of bullfighting extends from page 88 to page 114 and from page 127 to page 135 of his travel account of *Pagan Spain*, occupying most of the central section entitled "Death and Exaltation." After a closely observed but emotionally charged account of the crowd, the opening procession, the fight with the first bull, and Chamaco's triumphal circuit of the ring after a superb *faena*, Wright narrates his departure the following day for Madrid, where by prearrangement he meets Harry Whitney, an American bullfighter from Texas. He accompanies Whitney and two Spanish toreros to a *capaea* or informal bullfight in Morata de Tajuña, a village some seventeen miles south of Madrid. A comparison of the bullfighting sections of *Pagan Spain* to Hemingway's full-scale treatment in *Death in the Afternoon* reveals not only Wright's indebtedness to his predecessor but, more importantly, differences indicative of their contrasting artistic temperaments and diverse interpretations of the Spanish ethos.

It is not surprising that Wright writes of the bullfight with *Death in the Afternoon* in mind, for no one who has dealt seriously with the subject in English for the last sixty years has failed to do so. When Wright describes Chamaco's first animal as "a fighting bull, the ever-charging kind, the sort that moved as though he had rails under him to make him come at you like a thundering train" (*PS* 99), the American or English aficionado is likely to recall the first sentence of the fourteenth chapter of Hemingway's taurine classic: "The bullfighter's ideal, what he hopes will always come out of the toril and into the ring is a bull that will charge perfectly straight and will turn by himself at the end of each charge and charge again as though he were on rails" (*Death* 160). Or when one reads Wright's description of the mission of the banderilleros as "planting barbed hooks of steel deep in the center of the mound of knotted muscles on the hump of his monstrous neck, the ultimate object being to wear him down, to tire him and make him lower his defiant head" (*PS* 99), one may think of the corresponding passage in Hemingway: "They are supposed to be placed, two at a time, in the humped muscle at the top of the bull's neck as he charges the man who holds them. They are designed to complete the work of slowing up the bull and regulating the carriage of his head..." (*Death* 96).

But unlike other post-Hemingway writers on the bullfight such as Barnaby Conrad, Tom Lea, John McCormick, James A. Michener, Kenneth Tynan, John Fulton (a matador himself)—experienced aficionados all—Wright made some glaring errors in *Pagan Spain*, including one real howler. As all elementary treatises on bullfighting explain, the spectacle is divided into three major parts. In the first, the fresh animal is passed with capes and then punished from horseback with steel-tipped wooded poles by the picadors. The second part consists of the placement in roughly the same area behind the bull's neck of three pairs of barbed wooden sticks just under a yard long (not two feet, as Wright asserts). This is performed by banderilleros or by the matador himself. The third act of the drama is the *faena* by the matador, a series of passes with the *muleta*, a cloth smaller than the cape, leading up to the moment of truth, when the matador is supposed to go in over the horns with the sword and kill the bull. In his very detailed and in some ways minutely observed account of the first bull, however, Wright reverses the order of the first two parts, so that the banderilleros precede the picadors! This mistake results in great exaggeration of the effect of the banderillas, such as a description of "broad, gleaming patches of scarlet that matted the black, bristly hair of his back" (*PS* 101) after a single pair, and of the muscles behind the neck gushing blood, after the second pair. The descriptions are accurate, but the primary cause of such bleeding is the work of the picadors, which in Wright's version has not yet taken place, and only secondarily and additionally the work of the banderilleros. The effect of this mistake is to exaggerate the bull's suffering and the cruelty of the spectacle, an effect consistent with the overall themes of *Pagan Spain*.

Other mistakes are less significant: confusing the Mexican centavo and the Spanish céntimo; stating that Chamaco received the tail and a hoof as awards for a brilliant *faena* without mentioning the ears, which would have been ceded first; speaking of the bull's "mane" (90) (nonexistent); asserting dubiously that "any man with enough courage to stand perfectly still in front of a bull will not be killed by the bull" (113); rendering the crowd's cry of "bravo, hombre" as the ungrammatical "bravo hombre" (101). A knowledgeable reader concludes that Wright had much to learn about a complex subject. In *Death in the Afternoon*, Hemingway states that "it was much too complicated for my then equipment for writing to deal with and, aside from four very short sketches, I was not able to write anything about it for five years—and I wish I would have waited ten" (3). Wright took extensive notes during his three trips to Spain in 1954 and early 1955, began the actual writing in February of 1956, and sent off the completed manuscript on 1 April 1956. Small wonder that he made mistakes.

Nevertheless, an aficionado finds much to admire in Wright's treatment of the bullfight. For one thing, Wright's focus on the bull rather than the bullfighter is complementary to Hemingway's opposite emphasis. Hemingway does indeed devote chapter eleven of *Death in the Afternoon* to bulls, but he is mainly concerned with physical characteristics, fighting spirit, herd instinct, testing and breeding, the tendency to adopt favorite spots in the ring during the course of a fight. About the bull's appearance and behavior and the effect of these on the spectator Hemingway is remarkably reticent, concentrating instead on the specific problems and opportunities a specific animal presents to a specific matador. Chapter six of *Death in the Afternoon* presents the final preparations for a bullfight in Madrid, the formal procession of the bullfighters into the ring, the display of capes, and the unlocking of the passageway through which the bull will enter the ring. The chapter ends with the words "the door swings open" (62), and the next chapter begins with the following sentence: "At this point it is necessary that you see a bullfight" (63). As anyone who has seen a bullfight knows, the entrance of the animal is one of the most impressive and exciting moments. Even when he is describing specific bullfights, however, with the sole exception of his first *Toronto Star* article on the first he ever saw, Hemingway omits mention of this moment (*The Sun Also Rises* and *Death in the Afternoon*) or passes over it with the utmost brevity: "His second bull came out strong...," "Antonio's first bull came out well...," "Luis Miguel's first bull came out fast and good" (*DS* 73, 116, 155).

No such reticence in Wright's case:

> A huge gate was thrown open by a man who fled to safety. A gaping black hole yawned and all eyes peered expectantly into it. Then out thundered a wild, black, horned beast, his eyes ablaze, his nostrils quivering, his mouth open and flinging foam, his throat emitting a bellow.

He halted for a second, amazed, it seemed, at the spectacle confronting him, then he settled squarely and fearlessly on his four hoofs, ready to lower his head and charge at the least sign of movement, his sharp horns carrying the threat of death, his furious tenacity swollen with a will that would brook no turning aside until all movement about him had been struck down, stilled, and he alone was left lord and master of the bloody field. (96)

Later Wright quotes with apparent approbation a comment by the American bull-fighter Harry Whitney: "Only a few people really understand bullfighting. Hemingway has described the technical side of it, but not the emotional" (128–129). Wright was intensely interested not only in the emotional but the psychological, cultural, and even spiritual dimensions of the spectacle as revelatory of the Spanish national essence:

> It took but thirty seconds of contemplation of that black bundle of bounding fury for my feelings to declare in me the definite conviction that, though that raging bull was indubitably and dangerously real, he was at the same time, a complement of a subjective part of almost everybody in the stadium; he was, though an incontestable and charging beast, a creature of our common fantasy, a projected puppet of our collective hearts and brains, a savage proxy offered by us to ourselves to appease the warring claims that our instincts were heir to....
> *There was no doubt but that this beast had to be killed!* (97)

But the beast that had to be killed was also loved, the object of ambivalent veneration. Wright proceeds to mythologize the bull in a long, extraordinary sentence equally remarkable for the detailed accuracy of its observation and for the soaring style of its prose:

> That starting black hair, that madly slashing tail, that bunched and flexed mountain of neck and shoulder muscles, that almost hog-like distension of the wet and inflated and dripping nostrils, that defiant and careless lack of control of the anal passage, that continuous throbbing of the thin, trembling flanks, that open-mouthed panting that was so rapid that it resembled a prolonged shivering, that ever ready eagerness to attack again and again that was evidenced by those fluid shiftings of his massive and mobile weight from hoof to hoof, those unreserved lunges that sometimes carried him far past the elusive capes and sent him pitching and sprawling into the dirt until his flaring nostrils scooped up sand, that single-mindedness of concentration that would never allow his turning his head away from his enemy, that instinctively imperious pride that told him that he and he alone was right, that superb self-forgetfulness that made him make of his body an expendable projectile to hurl at and annihilate his adversaries, that unheard-of ability to fight on even when rigor mortis was slowly engulfing the tottering limbs, that total and absolute dedication of life to defend life at any cost—all of these qualities made of that murderous leaping monster in that red ring a bull that was obviously something more than a bull. (98)

What more was he, then? Wright answers immediately:

he was a subjective instinct, a careening impulse, a superhuman image to contemplate for an awful hour in the hot sun buttressed by the supporting presence of one's neighbors—something to look at and then forget with a sigh, something to be pushed into the underground of one's feeling till the overmastering need to experience it again would arise. Yes, the mystery and miracle were here: the mystery resided in why the human heart hungered for this strange need; and the miracle was in the heart's finding that a rampaging bull so amply satisfied that need. (98)

The bullfight, then, was a secular equivalent of Spanish Catholicism, itself deriving from peninsular paganism, which Wright discusses at length elsewhere in *Pagan Spain.* Through a *"baptism of emotion"* the bullfight purged the spectators of their guilt and sin in a ritual both violent and ordered, the matador serving as "a kind of lay priest" (99). When Wright remarks to Harry Whitney on the similarity of the torero's costume to a priest's vestment, Whitney responds that "the bullfight has the intensity of religious emotion" (130). As Wright realizes, "in Spain, all things were Spanish" (99).

A major theme of Wright's travel narrative of *Pagan Spain* is the degree to which sexuality pervades Spanish life, including religion, and a major reader response to the book is the degree to which Wright sees sex everywhere in everything. The *corrida de toros* is no exception. The potent bull spends himself in his intimate encounter with the bullfighter-lover: "that proud and insurgent head had to be lowered, that proud lunging had to be calmed" (99). In a successful bullfight, such as Chamaco's in Barcelona, death becomes at the end something almost equivalent to love, as the matador watches the dying animal, "gazing gently, sadly it seemed" into its eyes, his lifted hand a gesture of compassion, perhaps even benediction, as well as triumph (112). At the *capea* to which he accompanies Harry Whitney, Wright witnesses a more overtly sexual spectacle: "The crowd went straight to the dead bull's testicles and began kicking them, stomping them, spitting on them, grinding them under their heels, while their eyes held a glazed and excited look of sadism. They mutilated the testicles of the dead bull for more than ten minutes, until the dead bull's carcass was hauled away" (134). The second of the three bulls received the same treatment, prompting this interpretation of their behavior: "They went straight to the real object on the bull's body that the bull had symbolized for them and poured out the hate and frustration and bewilderment of their troubled and confused consciousness" (135). Here Wright does not allow for different interpretations. Describing the first bull, Wright notes that he was reluctant to charge. Perhaps the second bull had the same defect. The third and final bull did not receive brutal treatment from the crowd, for Wright would surely have mentioned it to confirm his point. A more experienced if less imaginative observer of bullfights might conclude that the third animal was a *toro bravo* which charged readily, eliciting admiration from the crowd, and that the first two were cowardly animals unworthy of bullhood and thus subject to transformation into steers after death. Or perhaps the two bulls were vengefully mutilated because they had killed some of the townsmen in previous *capeas*, a not infrequent occurrence. In the second chapter of *Death in the Afternoon*, Hemingway tells of such a bull. Of the sixteen men and boys killed by this bull, one was a fourteen-year-old gypsy whose brother killed the animal two years later, cut off its testicles, roasted them on an open fire, and, with his sister, ate them.

Hemingway would not have liked *Pagan Spain*. He would probably have classified it as "erectile writing" (*Death* 53), as he did Waldo Frank's *Virgin Spain*. Even the most confirmed Wright apologist is given pause by the inappropriateness of a simile used in the description of the famous religious procession of Holy Week in Seville: "The huge candles rested upon the hips of the penitents and the flickering flames danced above their heads, the molten wax streaming and sparkling in the bright sun, spattering in translucent spots on the dark cobblestones—flying white drops that were like semen spraying, jutting from the penises of sexually aroused bulls" (236). But if Wright is prone to hyperbole, hasty psychologizing, and extravagance, Hemingway's understatement and reticence in the "few practical things to be said" (278) in *Death in the Afternoon* do not address issues of sexuality in relation to the religious impulse that have been present in Western civilization's fascination with bulls from cave drawings to Gilgamesh to Zeus and Europa, Theseus and the Minotaur, right down through Pedro Romero, Frascuelo, Joselito, Juan Belmonte, Manolete, Carlos Arruza to Eloy Cavazos, Ponce, and El Juli. *Death in the Afternoon* will continue to head the required reading list of the English-speaking aficionado, but *Pagan Spain* belongs there, too.

The Good Women, Bad Women, Prostitutes and Slaves of *Pagan Spain*

Richard Wright's Look Beyond the Phallocentric Self

Dennis F. Evans

I wanted to go to Spain, but something was holding me back. The only thing that stood between me and a Spain that beckoned as much as it repelled was a state of mind.

Richard Wright, Pagan Spain

Every native feels himself to be more or less a "foreigner" in his "own and proper" place, and that metaphorical value of the word "foreigner" first leads the citizen to a feeling of discomfort as to his sexual, national, political, professional identity. Next it impels him to identify—sporadically, to be sure, but nonetheless intensely—with the other.

Julia Kristeva, Strangers to Ourselves

Stephen Butterfield's idea that autobiography "lives in the two worlds of history and literature, objective fact and subjective awareness," and that the product of autobiography "asserts that human life has or can be made to have meaning, that our actions count for something worth being remembered, that we are conscious of time, [and] that we not only drift on the current of our circumstances but we fish in the stream and change the direction of the flow" (1), serves to illuminate and define the work of Richard Wright. Wright's fiction is almost universally accepted as being autobiographical in nature; yet, part of this acceptance is the understanding that his works are fictionalized accounts of incidents that occurred in Wright's life and the lives of other people as well. Wright's travel books, however, pose a different problem for literary historicists and critics because, while the genre traditionally dictates the use of a less poeticized style, and a less politicized message, Wright uses the genre as a forum for a highly poetic social and political dialectic. Thus, for a time, Wright's travel texts eluded the gaze of critics because they did not fit the literary molds of either travelogue or fiction comfortably. Our own current ability to critically distance ourselves from Wright's travel books, as well as our ability to be distanced from them due to passage of time, allows us the luxury and liberty to view them now as integral parts of the Wright autobiographical canon—parts that are indicative of the type of autobiography that Butterfield describes. For it is in *Black Power* (1954), *The Color Curtain* (1956), *Pagan Spain* (1957), and *White Man, Listen!* (1957) that Wright finally goes outside of his homeland, his *own* land, in search of himself, "fishing in the stream and changing the direction of its flow"; and it is in these same works that Wright is both surprised and disappointed to discover that he was wrong about how other cultures lived, and how he felt about those cultures. The focus of this paper is on Wright's travel book *Pagan Spain,* and how aspects of that work allow us to expand our understanding of Richard Wright as a writer, and as a human.

Even after Gertrude Stein and several friends' admonishments that he "go to Spain to see what the Western world [was] made of," Richard Wright resisted, claiming Spain to be "the one country of the Western world about which, as though shunning the memory of a bad love affair, [he] did not want to exercise his mind" (1–2). But Wright, himself, was unsure of the reasons why he had not gone, stating: "I had been born under an absolutistic racist regime in Mississippi; I had lived and worked for twelve years under the political dictatorship of the Communist Party of the United States; and I had spent a year of my life under the police terror of Peron in Buenos Aires. So why avoid the reality of life under Franco?" (1). Finally, in the summer of 1954, unable to further justify the prolonged avoidance, Wright went to Spain seeking answers to a question that had interested him all of his life: "How did one live after the death of the hope of freedom?" (2). When we look at much if not all of Wright's other work—from his isolated and angry fictionalized characters such as Bigger Thomas, Jake Jackson, and Cross Damon, to his disillusioned and dissatisfied portrait of African life in *Black Power*—we can see that *Pagan Spain* is merely a continuation of many of the same themes that interested Wright throughout his career: a search for identity and a clear view of his place in the world, combined with his desire to inform and enlighten Westerners, and in particular white Westerners, of the systemic oppression of peoples of color throughout the world.

Yet, *Pagan Spain* is more than a *mere* continuation of these themes for two fundamental reasons. The first reason is that, for only the second time in his career, Wright critically examines the lives of a people he considers to be white.[1] While he witnesses, appreciates, and documents the lives of the people of Spain as being severely oppressed, he does not, however, see them as people of color. The second reason, and one I consider to be more significant, is that, in *Pagan Spain*, Wright gives us his first, and possibly only, sympathetic treatment of women. Several critical and biographical accounts of Wright's life and work indicate clear misogynistic tendencies, and many scholars regard the portrayals of female characters in his works as little more than the objectification and denigration of women.[2] Wright's other travel books tend to show little if any interest in or regard to the roles and status of women. However, in *Pagan Spain*, Wright's report on the treatment of Spanish women—their social, political, and religious indoctrination and subjugation, and their stigmatized, yet, unavoidable participation in prostitution and white slavery—is uncharacteristically empathetic and gives us a view of Wright that is unavailable in any of his other works, both travel and fictional. It is my contention that the unusually harsh and inhumane treatment of Spanish women, by a society that advertised itself to be deeply and morally religious, caused Wright to (for the first time in print, at least) observe, acknowledge, and finally sympathize with the plight of these women.

There are two fundamental strategies Wright uses in his various depictions of female characters, both pertaining to matters of geographic space. One strategy is what I classify as "Wright at Home," where the Bigger Thomases, the Cross Damons, and other various fictionalized heroes of Richard Wright's treat women as "'degraded,' . . . she is whore, cunt, and bitch-the-fallen woman. . . . She is never a real human being. She is stupid, hysterical, emotional, silly, evil, and low-class" (Walker 247). The other strategy involves "Wright as *foreigner*," a concept defined by Julia Kristeva in her book *Strangers to Ourselves*,[3] where Wright and women are themselves foreigners, and they "attempt at all cost [either] to merge into that homogenous texture that knows no other, to identify with it, to vanish into it, to become assimilated. . . . Or else [to] withdraw into isolation, humiliated and offended, conscious of the handicap of never being able to become [a native]" (39).

Generally speaking, in Wright's fiction the authorial characters portray a version of "Wright at Home" writing his "American autobiography" (truly a native son); he is like a man in his favorite chair outwardly projecting his self-confidence and self-assuredness. The level of understanding, and even comfort, of this environment distorts any sensitivity he might possess regarding the status of women.[4] Conversely, in Wright's travelogues—"Wright as *foreigner*," or his "Continental autobiography"—Wright's authorial voice is mindful of the fact that he is not sure of his way home, that he could easily become lost, and that he needs allies. The level of uncertainty and even discomfort of this environment allows him the distance necessary to "see" the various cultural worlds he is visiting in a new and different light. And it is "Wright as *foreigner*," in Spain, that permits him to witness, appreciate, and comment on the doubly horrible oppression women were made to endure.

The book opens with Wright's aforementioned indecisiveness over entering the country and progresses through various episodes and encounters that he has with a diverse sampling of Spanish people. Readers of the book are treated to Wright's characteristically unassuming, yet, descriptive prose as he encounters border guards and bank clerks, and one gets more of a sense that Wright the outsider is on a vacation rather than on an investigative sojourn. Wright, then, quickly moves the narration from standard documentary form into a dialogue between himself and two youths he meets on the streets of Cataluña, and this is the first indication we have that this work is not written in the traditional form of a travelogue, but in a more expressive and inquisitive manner. Utilizing dialogue interspersed among descriptive and interpretive commentaries, Wright begins to establish a dialectic between his own preconceived notions of a Fascistic Spain and the reality of his surroundings: the living, breathing, loving people of Spain. He asks the two boys if they know of a room he might rent, and having been told "yes," he follows them into a church. The boys ask him if he is Catholic and when he replies "no," they express surprise. At first, Wright the non-native is confused as to why they have brought him to a church, but he writes:

> I was a stranger and they were taking me into their Christian fellowship even before they knew my name, their solicitude cutting across class and racial lines.... It was beginning to make sense; I was a heathen and these devout boys were graciously coming to my rescue. In their spontaneous embrace of me they were acting out a role that had been implanted in them since childhood. I was not a stranger, but a "lost" one in dire need of being saved. Yet, there was no condescension in their manner; they acted with a quiet assurance of men who knew that they had the only truth in existence and they were offering it to me.... If

André's and Miguel's reactions were genuine examples of Spanish feeling, then Spain possessed a shy sweetness, an open-handed hospitality that no other people on earth could match. (8–12)

Even as he walks streets that are filled with civil guards carrying machine guns, Wright is struck by the life-loving, peaceful men and women of Spain, and he realizes that there is much more mystery to the Spanish people than he had previously considered.

As Wright begins to describe the two boys in detail, readers become aware of the paradoxical but typical attitudes that Spanish men have for their women.

Both were shy about women. André had a fiancé, but Miguel would not commit himself. To their minds, the feminine half of mankind was divided into two groups: "good" women and "bad" women. "Good" women were women like their mothers, sisters, and sweethearts; "bad" women were the women who could be bought, or who could be slept with for nothing. Since they had to have women and could not have the "good" ones, they frequented the "bad" ones. And since going to bed with either a "good" or a "bad" woman was a sin, it was necessary to be forgiven. Both boys went to confession regularly. (11)

Here, Wright has successfully illuminated the female condition within a traditional patriarchal society, a forced condition. Writing before any of the current radical feminist or womanist theories were in place, Wright portrays André and Miguel's attitudes toward women as being common and acceptable. But, unlike his own descriptions of black women—what Mootry describes as a "collection of bitches and whores"—Wright's description of André and Miguel's beliefs utilizes a tone that suggests a certain ironic awareness of that patriarchal paradox: a polysemousness that simultaneously describes and questions the ethos of the very act. Wright asks the boys how they know when a woman is a "bad woman," to which he gets no real answer, aside from the fact that they "know where to find them," and this further compounds the irrational attitudes that are at work here. The decisions Spanish men make regarding the social status of their women (whether they are "good" or "bad") are often made in relation to notions of place, or *where* these women *are*. Women are regarded, like Wright himself, as foreigners in their own land. Women do not have full access to their homeland; they are kept distanced from it through its laws, education, and economic powers—they are a product of what Michel Foucault describes in *The Use of Pleasure*, a "male ethics, in which women figured only as objects or, at most, as partners that one had best train, educate, and watch over when one had them under one's power, but stay away from them when they are under the power of someone else" (22). Indicative of this male ethics and the tightrope it forces women to walk is Wright's encounter with a young woman named Carmen. Wright arranges a harmless meeting with her, in a public place; yet, she is visibly uncomfortable being seen with him. He asks:

> "Had I been a Spaniard you would not have come?"
>
> "I *couldn't* have come. It's only in an American hotel that I could meet you without a scandal. You don't know what it means to be a girl in Spain."
>
> "And what does it *mean?*"
>
> "I'm supposed to stay home and have babies," she said grimacing.
>
> "Who says you must do that?"
>
> "Tradition," she said. "I wish I were a man; . . . They can do as they like. They are strong. We women are nothing." (16)

Wright could easily identify and sympathize with this condition—this *native foreigner*—because he struggled under the same burdens as a citizen of America. It is only when Wright is able to move outside of his role as *native* to that of *foreigner*, that he is able to begin to appreciate the doubly marginalized position women had to endure. In his role as *foreigner*, Wright, thus, sustains Butterfield's notion of "self" in black autobiography as being "conceived as a member of an oppressed social group, with ties and responsibilities to the other members." It is a conscious political identity, drawing sustenance from the past experience of the group, "giving back the iron of its endurance . . . for the use of the next generation of fighters" (3).

Later in the book, Wright is asked by another American woman to come to her *pensión* and stand guard while she packed her things to leave. Wright is again confused about motives, this time about those surrounding her request. He asks her why she is so frightened of her landlord and she answers with the question:

> "How long have you been in Spain?"
>
> "Just a few days."
>
> "Then you don't know what it means to be a woman alone in Spain," she said.
>
> Holy Moses. Here it is again. I remembered the terror that had come over Carmen's face when I suggested that she meet in a bar. She had reacted as though I had proposed a trip to perdition.
>
> . . . .
>
> "Is it that bad?" I asked.
>
> "You have to see it to believe it," she sighed.
>
> "All right. I'll come with you. I want to see this," I said. "Now what do you want me to do?"
>
> "Nothing. You just stand there. If a man is there, he'll act differently."

There was no doubt in my mind now of her terror. But how could such a thing be? Who had the right to throw gratuitous terror into lonely women? We finished our coffee and headed toward her pension. (72)

Wright is shocked to discover that a woman traveling alone in Spain is often subjected to harassment and ridicule. Having himself experienced the humiliation and indignation of having lived under "Jim Crow" rule in America, Wright is able to understand and empathize with the frustration these women are feeling. His awareness of the rampant phallocentrism as well as his concern for the silent suffering women of Spain grows with each passing page.

When he meets André's family and shares a meal with them, Wright acknowledges the injustice and even the absurdity of the situation without passing judgement. Yet, one is inclined to think that Wright could do no more at this time than to chronicle the events he witnessed as a means of leading up to some kind of future indictment: "Spain being a man's world, we men were served first by André's mother; the women had to wait meekly for their turn. No nonsense here about priority of women, of the mothers of the race, not even if they were certified virgins. The women ate silently with one eye cocked in the direction of their men, ready at a moment's notice to drop their knives and forks and refill the half-empty masculine plates" (90). There is an obvious mocking tone in this passage that causes the reader to think that Wright is witnessing something both horrible and absurd, and that he is making fun of the absurdity while condemning the horrible. His allusions to "the mothers of the race" remaining oppressed even if they were "certified virgins" is sadly, doubly ironic, first for its literal comment on Spanish social conditions, and because of the more accepted notions of Wright's hatred toward his own mother. In the role of *foreigner*, Wright is able to begin a process of understanding that is unavailable to him at home. In Spain he sees phallocentrism staring him in the face—sees how it divides and oppresses—and he understands that, as a foreigner, he must recognize his membership in the group of oppressed and help to affect change. Wright's goal in life was to, like Mencken, use "words as weapons"; in fact, when he was asked "for whom he writes," he replied, "I'd like to hurl words in my novels in order to arouse whites to the fact that there is someone here with us, Negroes, a human presence" (qtd in Charbonnier 224). So it is no great leap of faith to assert that Wright is chronicling these separate but contiguous events as a means of commenting on the state of oppression in which women exist.

I previously suggested that Wright documented these various incidents with women as a means of working his way toward some future indictment of Spanish society. Wright presents the culmination of this effort in the book's penultimate chapter titled "Sex, Flamenco, and Prostitution." It is here that the cyclopean monster is both fully exposed and condemned. He begins the chapter with the bold assertion that "In Spain sex has been converted into a medium of exchange for almost all kinds of commodities and services to a degree that cannot be found in any other European country" (150), and refers to the vast numbers of prostitutes as a "'wall of flesh.'"

Wright contends that women are forced into this commodified position because of a most basic and brutal need: hunger, and more specifically the hunger of their children. He lays the blame for their hunger squarely in the lap of Franco's Falangist government; he places the burden of guilt for their commodified status solely on the shoulders of the Catholic Church. Wright argues that:

> Growing out of this curious intertwining of archaic cultural values and endemic poverty [his indictment of Franco's government] is still another facet that anchors prostitution in the social structure: a religion whose outlook upon the universe almost legitimizes prostitution: The Spanish Catholic concept of sin. Sin exists, so declares this concept. Prostitution is sin, and proof of sin. So prostitution exists. To account for prostitution in economic or political terms is to be guilty of... a mortal sin. (151–52)

Women are taught in the home and by the church—a church that is socially all-pervasive—that they must care for their young; yet they are unable, because of economic hardships, properly to feed these children. But, "if a woman . . . sells her body to feed her hungry children, that in itself is almost a justification of what she is doing" (152). Wright sees these women as victims of the inherent paradox that church and state, both phallocentric organizations, have created for them and forced upon them. In fact, in that same mocking yet disbelieving tone, Wright comments that the phrase "*Para los niños* (for the children) is a slogan among Spanish prostitutes that is almost as prevalent as *Arriba España!* (Spain—Arise!), the slogan of totalitarian Spanish men" (152). The juxtaposition of the feminine giving of the self—a sacrifice made for the children (stereotypically a women's responsibility)—with the masculine imperative to "Arise"—or to project one's self (stereotypically a masculine decision)—allows Wright to begin his condemnation of the phallocentric institutions that are responsible for this hunger that is sin.

Wright brings his condemnation to a boiling point when he suddenly and violently realizes the depth and breadth of the Spanish woman's commodification when he discovers first-hand that these women are being sold into slavery.

> Four girls were at our tables now. The orchestra played and they wriggled their shoulders, rolled their eyes, and snapped their fingers. Most of them were in their twenties. And they kept looking expectantly to me.
> "I you go Africa," a young girl said to me.
> S. bent over with laughter, enjoying my bewilderment....
> "What's the joke," I demanded, nettled.
> "Brother, you would never have thought this would happen to you," he told me.
> "But what's happening to me?"
> "Look, I'm organizing these girls to take them to Africa next week," he explained. "They think that you are the boss. You see, you are *dark*."
> "But—w-what are you going to do with the girls in Africa?" I asked him stammeringly.
> "What the hell do you think? I'm going to put them to work in the houses," he snapped, still laughing.
> It hit me like a ton of rock. *White Slavery*...I was doing a quick laundering job on the moral notions in my brain and the moral feelings of my body. This was white slavery, and how simple and open and jolly it was! The women and girls were begging to go; they were hungry. (184–85)

Here was past and present personified, staring him back in the face, because, while he was not a slave, he was being confronted with the very issue that he had spent all his life trying to understand and rectify—the injustice he had been fighting against—alive and flourishing in the twentieth century. Wright, understandably, uses restraint in his realization of the fact that these women, like the slaves of the American South, were only separated by distance and time from him. As a foreigner, he chose exile to escape the racist hatred that was a product of his own feelings of *foreignness* at home. Yet, in an ironic twist of fate, his going away from America allows him to experience elsewhere and first-hand what he had been witness to all of his life: repressed hatred and the inhumane oppression of slavery. He finds little comfort in the knowledge that Spain has been this way for hundreds of years, as he remarks: "given the conditions, the moral attitude of the Church toward sex, the poverty, the ignorance, this was bound to be. It was all socially determined. The Church could call it sin, but it was something far more awful than that" (186). Here is all Wright can do to condemn the oppression that Spanish men have brought to bear on their women. His statements do not share the searing heat that he exhibits in *Native Son*, and my own contention is that Wright was feeling and fulfilling his role as *foreigner*. Kristeva argues that the foreigner possesses "a secret wound, often unknown to himself, that drives [him] to wandering. Poorly loved, however, he does not acknowledge it: with him, the challenge silences the complaint" (5). I contend that "Wright as foreigner" is a more quiet, less contentious commentator than the *Native Son*. His remarks are caustic in their ironic content and his observations are methods of discovery for himself and for others. For Wright, the inhumane and unjust treatment of Spanish women is so self-evident that he does not need to make his condemnations overly vocal.

Does Wright propose any changes for the Spanish people? Does he think there is hope for the future? I would argue that Wright is optimistic, but guardedly so. Wright's final tribute to the Spanish woman is indicative of this projected hope:

> The daily striving and suffering of Spanish women make what little structure there is to Spanish society, knitting together in a web of care and love what would otherwise be a landscape of senseless anarchy. They are a proud women,...women of easy laughter and easy tears. The mighty maternal instinct of the Spanish woman is the anchor of responsibility that holds the ship of Spanish life steady while the Spanish man babbles abstract nonsense in the countless smoky coffee houses. (188)

And he then proceeds to catalog the diversity of women who bring color, life, and direction to an otherwise bleak environment. Wright recognizes that it is the Spanish man who has caused this suffering, and he realizes that Spanish men have placed Spanish women into their oppressed and marginalized positions. The Spanish woman is damned if she does and damned if she does not, and the Spanish man only sits in a sidewalk café and watches her walk past. Yet, Wright sees and understands that the guilt rests with some *thing* that is beyond either gender, or race.

All that Wright witnessed and learned changed his thinking about Spain. He writes, "Before going into Spain my ideas about its problems had been mainly political. But my journey and the nature of the reality that I had seen had provoked other and different questions in my mind, questions that went far beyond mere economic and political considerations....Frankly, I had not been prepared for what I had encountered" (191). What Wright encountered was a society so phallocentric in its totalitarianism that it caused him, for the first time, to realize and empathize with women. Wright shared, and realized he shared, a sense of foreignness with these women; he realized that he, like they, could not escape his heritage, a Western heritage that allowed him to condemn the actions of a church and a state. If we look at the corpus of Wright's work, what do we find? I contend that we find this same inability to disregard his heritage—both a sense of *foreignness*, or otherness—as well as an ability to condemn the actions of a church and a state. Where I see a difference between Wright's previous offerings, and those in *Pagan Spain*, is Wright's ability to find some small piece of ground on which to stand in empathy with women; this is a new land for Wright, one he has not visited before, and one that complements his other travels.

Richard Wright was a wanderer; but that desire to wander was rooted in a sense of wonderment. Wright was asked by a young Spanish girl: "You love freedom?" to which he answered, "I do, with all of my heart." She asked, "You will tell the people in America about us?" and he replied, "I'll try; I'll do my best" (170). This is the Richard Wright who told his story to us in everything he wrote; the Richard Wright who believed it was the "sacred duty of creative artists to speak and write ceaselessly about [freedom]" (Kinnamon 226). *Pagan Spain* began as a travelogue, and has managed to transcend this role to become one more piece in the large puzzle that the work of Richard Wright comprises. What is unique about Wright's visit to Spain and the subsequent chronicle of that journey is that it allowed Wright to see that there is more to life than the story of man; there is a story of woman, too, and that story is filled with both suffering and hope. I do not contend that Wright was in any way a feminist, but I do contend that for one brief moment he understood the suffering of women—suffering he had experienced himself—and he empathized and suffered, too. *Pagan Spain* is an integral piece of Wright's puzzlement as a person because it helps us to appreciate Wright as more than the one-dimensional man that he has been made out to be.

Richard Wright with Léopold Senghor

Essay on "French West Africa"
(c. 1959)

"French West Africa"

Behind the Scenes with Richard Wright, the Travel Writer

Virginia Whatley Smith

B y spring of 1959 coinciding with the May 1946 anniversary of his thirteenth year of exile in Paris, France, Richard Wright had made the word "Africa" a familiar term of reference in the majority of his long, nonfictional texts and short essays about his foreign travels during this decade. He especially became interested in the anti-colonial and post-colonial struggles of the continent's various black and brown peoples. Just as he had made the "Negro" in America the major metaphor of his fictions of the 1930s and still gave them central presence in the 1950s, Wright also began to broaden his racial language to include "Negro Africa." By the close of the decade, he started making plans for another travel book on French West Africa to complement *Black Power* (1954), *The Color Curtain* (1956), and *Pagan Spain* (1957). This planned travelogue would lend a fourth, long account of his investigations of the global politics emitting from various African nations during their post-World War II drives for freedom. But despite Wright's attempts in 1959 at garnering financial support to augment the $2,500 advance allocated by his book publisher, according to correspondence dated April 30, 1959 from his American literary agent Paul Reynolds ("Letters"), Wright was forced to abandon plans for his $10,000 project since no additional benefactors had materialized. This was a crisis period for Wright. He was confronting the emerging sixties but away from the impending civil rights turbulences that would grip America and thus validate his life-long crusade of obtaining racial justice and equality for blacks. He was in declining health and in financial distress, and also having trouble getting published and/or locating financial backers for his projects.

Wright died on November 28, 1960, in Paris and his plans for visiting French West Africa never came to fruition beyond the draft stage of his preliminary investigations. Yet, his unpublished manuscript entitled "French West Africa" bears notation as a significant document reflecting certain stages of Wright's typical, behind-the-scenes activities and strategies for producing his narratives of travel. The act of travel is most often initiated owing to the germination of an idea inspiring Wright's need to become mobile. His preliminary activities include conducting research on the prospective site, developing an estimated budget for costs of living during his time in the field (food, hotels, et cetera), and determining modes of transportation to/from the site as well as transportation about the designated area or areas to be covered. Wright next had to consider matters relating to the actual fieldwork experiences such as goals to be accomplished, procedures for gathering data, and contacts to be made. And finally, Wright had to go into the field and then return "home"— that is, to his "fixed abode." At this point, he would begin production of his literary text that already had started with his basic notes on the project and then grown to larger stages of at-home or in-field "first impression" or preliminary draft typescripts. From here followed Wright's writing/typing of the long "travel book"; the growth and/or reduction of the text owing to additional, multiple revisions initiated by the author or suggested by his editors or literary agent; the editing and proofreading of the text by Wright and members of the publishing house inclusive of the galley stage; and finally, the issuance of the hardback or paperback product to Wright's public for assessment. This essay examines the early, behind-the-scenes activities of Wright the travel writer relating to his incomplete project on "French West Africa," for the materials provide insight into Wright's investigatory procedures and reading habits for producing his narratives of travel.

I

To grasp the significance of the global climate of the late 1950s when Wright planned to return to Africa, and to gauge his understanding of and relationship to African and specifically French African culture, it is important to review just how much Wright had become immersed in African cultural politics over a twenty-year period. As far back as 1938, the early stage of Richard Wright's stellar rise to fame after publication of his first short story, "Big Boy Leaves Home," in *Negro Caravan* (1936) that demarcated his shift from a professional poet to a fiction writer, the discourse of "Africa" became a gradual and then standard part of Richard Wright's vocabulary. In a letter of August 13, 1938, Balfour A. Linton, editor of *The African*, a journal published by the Universal Ethiopian Students Association located on West 117th Street in New York, indicates the interest of black Africans in Richard Wright's volatile fictions. Linton specifically speaks about the recent publication of Wright's collection of short stories in 1938, and adds that the organization had been following Wright's career and literary contributions in great earnest, especially his sociological commentary about the black South ("Letter"). The editor expresses interest in forming an alliance with Wright, as would become the standard response of readers to the author's works with release of his novel *Native Son* in 1940 that made Wright the foremost black writer in America. It is not certain if Wright forged a bond with this group, but signs of his interest in continental Africa and black African affairs as an integral force in the shaping of American culture are remarked in Wright's 1941 photographic text, *12 Million Black Voices: A Folk History of the Negro in the United States*. In this picture-word book co-produced with Edwin Rosskam in which Wright bears responsibility for "texts and captions" as well as major control over selection of photographs (4; Smith, "Image" 6), Wright provides a chronological account of the history of slavery in America and starts his analysis on the point of departure and travel away from "home" of the captive Africans, commencing with their sales to Europeans on the shores of Africa. Wright also cites two texts as sources for his information on Africa: *Rum, Romance and Rebellion* by Charles W. Taussig and *History of the American Negro People, 1619–1918* by Elizabeth Lawson (6). However, as far back as 1927–37 during his early years in Chicago while struggling with his apprentice writing, Wright had begun reading the black perspective of history and slavery in forms of slave narratives and historical accounts. Specifically, he read the 1903 edition of W. E. B. Du Bois's masterful work, *The Souls of Black Folk*, which, additionally, is a reference text cited by Lawson (Cayton, "Biography"; Lawson 8). By the time that Wright published *12 Million Black Voices*, he had cultivated a sufficient knowledge of African life and affairs to incorporate references in his writings or to engage in subject-oriented social events.

In the mid-1940s, in fact, Wright's social calendar brought him into further contact with African-related affairs. The publication of his autobiography *Black Boy* in 1945 cast Wright into the swirl of public acclaim and African-related political activities. An invitation for Saturday, January 19, 1946, offers a free lecture on the governmental affairs of Africa by two distinguished speakers, one being W. E. B. Du Bois, noted author and education director of the NAACP, and the other being Mbonu Ojike of Nigeria, West Africa, an author and executive director of the African Academy of Arts and Research. This invitation was sent to Wright's Brooklyn address at 89 Lefferts Place by the sponsoring host, the American Museum of Natural History on Central Park West ("Invitation"). And, by the time that Wright had begun his initial visit to France in 1946 and then physically removed himself from the United States in 1947 to live permanently as an expatriate in Paris, he already had established an alliance with the young South African writer Peter Abrahams. The latter's small packet of letters among Wright's papers in the Yale Collection of American Literature, Beinecke Rare Book and Manuscript Library, indicates a bond forming between them as early as September 28, 1946, when Abrahams wrote from London to Wright at his Paris address of 14 rue Monsieur le Prince to inquire if Wright had read and liked Abrahams's novel *Mine Boy*.

Most important is that Abrahams's letter situates Wright's early connection to the Pan-Africanist movement to which Wright became introduced once he moved to Paris. Abrahams inquires how Wright had enjoyed meeting George Padmore of the West Indies, and also remarks that he understands that Wright would be coming to London. Moreover, in his postscript, Abrahams comments about C. L. R. James and adds that James's friend, a T. R. Makonnen of Manchester, was starting a monthly journal known as *Pan-Africa* and had desires of Wright's becoming a "nominal editor" ("Letters"). Considering the historical significance of the Fifth Pan-African Congress of 1945 held in Manchester, England, a year before Wright's self-removal from America to start a new life in Paris, his arrival on European shores immediately cast him into the milieu of the post-World War II, Pan-Africanist anti-colonialist movement (Azevedo 177).

The Berlin Conference of November 1884–February 1885 met to formalize the partitioning of Africa among fourteen European powers; the Manchester Congress of 1945 met to recover African states from imperialist rulers. The Berlin Conference hosted by Otto von Bismarck, Chancellor of unified Germany, brought together key leaders and delegates from fourteen European nations but excluded representation of Africans in the dismantling of their sovereignties and lands. It was a peaceful coalition in which Mario Azevedo notes: "Interestingly enough, the partition of Africa occurred without causing a single war among the colonial powers— a credit to the Berlin Conference—at least insofar as the strategy of the planners and the participants of the Conference was concerned, namely, a need to divide the continent without resorting to force against one another" (107–9). The British, French, Portuguese, Germans, and the Belgians came away as the leading powers of imperialism although Italy, Portugal, and Spain fared well also. As Basil Davidson notes, "The broad limits of expansion for each of the interested powers... were defined with little trouble at the Berlin colonial conference" (284). Conversely, this Conference inaugurated the master-slave dialectics to follow between intrusive foreigner and oppressed native for the next sixty years. Resistance was always in the mind of native Africans; the ending of World War II unleashed their aggression. As Edward Said notes in his chapter "Themes of Resistance" in *Culture and Imperialism:*

> The slow and often bitterly disputed recovery of geographical territory which is at the heart of decolonization is preceded—as empire had been—by the charting of cultural territory. After the period of "primary resistance," literally fighting against outside intrusion, there comes the period of secondary, that is, ideological resistance, when efforts are made to reconstitute a "shattered community, to save or restore the sense and fact of community against all the pressures of the colonial system," as Basil Davidson puts it. This in turn makes possible the establishment of new and independent stakes [sic]. (209)

The Manchester or Fifth Pan-African Congress of 1945 convened for that purpose, but more so to devise strategies for ideological versus physical resistance to colonialism as noted by Said, although this latter tactic was not ruled out. Says Azevedo:

> Specifically, the Manchester Congress condemned the partition of Africa and the economic exploitation of the continent and the lack of industrial development, advocated a stronger stand against settler colonialism, demanded an end to illiteracy and malnutrition, and supported the independence of Algeria, Tunisia, and Morocco. It further requested the recognition of the rights of syndicates and cooperatives by colonial powers, and approved the demand for independence by West African delegates present at the Congress, and embraced the UN Charter. That many of the participants at this historic Congress made quite notable contributions to the defeat of colonialism proper in Africa a decade or so later only indicates the importance of the Manchester meeting. (177)

The tasks of the conveners were daunting; there was not only the problem of recovery of indigenous customs destroyed or distorted by colonialism, but also the issue of retaining or purging of colonial customs. Says Said of Davidson's observation on the problems confronting leaders of resistance: "Davidson speaks of 'otherworldly' promises made by some in their early phase, for example, rejecting Christianity and the wearing of Western clothes. But all of them respond to the humiliations of colonialism, and lead to 'the principal teaching of nationalism: the need

to find the ideological basis for a wider unity than any known before'" (210). Finding the key to unity was the major issue facing the Manchester attendees, and would
inspire and require their finding of a resolution over the next decade in their struggles to free Africa from European rule. On this point, Said says:

> That is the partial tragedy of resistance, that it must to a certain degree work to recover
> forms already established or at least influenced or infiltrated by the culture of empire. This
> is another instance of what I have called overlapping territories: the struggle over Africa in
> the twentieth century, for example, is over territories designed and redesigned by explorers
> from Europe for generations, a process memorably and painstakingly conveyed in Philip
> Curtin's *The Image of Africa.* Just as the Europeans saw Africa polemically as a blank place
> when they took it, or assumed its supinely yielding availability when they plotted to partition
> it at the 1884–85 Berlin Congress, decolonizing Africans found it necessary to reimagine an
> Africa stripped of its imperial past. (210)

For Wright the new expatriate, circa 1946/1947, these were the anti-colonialist
dynamics undergirding Pan-Africanist intellectual thought following the Manchester Congress of 1945, and influencing the mindsets of the esteemed personages of
George Padmore and C. L. R. James—activist, socialist West Indians from the
Caribbean and longtime, childhood friends now relocated in Britain. Both were
mentioned by Abrahams in his letter to Wright. During the 1930s, James formed
the International African Friends of Abyssinia (IAFA), and Padmore followed later
by founding the International African Service Bureau (IASB), which, according
to Azevedo, was "replaced by the Pan-African Federation in 1944" (176). The "socialist world view and its people" clearly was the predominant ideological
thought unifying the Manchester Congress, and James and Padmore and other
Pan-Africanists "were heavily influenced by the writings of Marx and Lenin" (176).
Such ideological thought was the appeal of these individuals to Wright, a confirmed Marxist although he had fully broken with the Communist Party in 1940
and publicly stated the reasons why in his essay entitled "I Tried to Be a Communist" published by the *Atlantic Monthly* in August 1944 (61). It was this "reimaging
[of] Africa stripped of its imperialist past" as well as forging of its present and
future ideological premises which especially drew Wright into establishing relations
with Abrahams, Padmore, and James during his transition from American citizen
to Parisian refugee. Kwame Nkrumah, who emerged as a "pivotal leader" from the
Manchester Congress in his "wresting [of] political control from the British in
Ghana" (formerly the Gold Coast) from 1947 to its independence in 1957 (Azevedo 177), would become the subject of interest for Wright's first travel narrative
Black Power (1954)—a relationship indirectly spawned from Wright's development

of friendships with Abrahams, Padmore, and James as early as 1946. Abrahams's next letter to Wright dated October 23, 1946, in fact, conveys Padmore's delight at having met Wright ("Letters").

It is not surprising, then, that Richard Wright would eventually go to Africa. His broad-based travels in the 1950s prepare him for future forays that would eventually lead him to dub himself a "Western Man of Color" (*WML* 50). Already his brief, failed marriage to Russian dancer Dhimah Rose Meadman in August 1939 had taken him to Mexico for a honeymoon in 1940. By the end of the decade, Wright was re-married to Ellen Poplar, living as an expatriate in Paris, orchestrating from abroad his writings and publications of his fictions and nonfictions with his American literary agent and publishing house of Harper & Row, and laying plans for the film version of *Native Son* to take place in Argentina. This trip would subsequently expose him from 1949 to 1951 to the Caribbean countries of Trinidad and Haiti; and another South American country, Brazil (Fabre, *UQ* 339; 349–52). Towards the end of his film project, moreover, Wright also began a series of lectures throughout Europe from 1950 to 1956 that would take him to Italy, England, Germany, and Denmark. Ultimately, this lecture series would become *White Man, Listen!* (1957), which includes supplementary remarks about his Afro-Asian travels to Ghana and Indonesia, respectively, from 1953 to 1956. The African experience especially dominates Wright's discourse in this essay collection.

Wright's travel narrative *Black Power* (1954) illustrates Wright's immersion into Pan-Africanist politics as an outsider American, a foreigner residing on European soil, and a Western eyewitness to Kwame Nkrumah's revolutionary Positive Action campaign, later reformulated as the Convention People's Party (CPP) in 1949, to de-colonize Ghana. Even with Wright's blatant criticism of Ghana's primitive customs, absence of modern industry, and handicap of tribal religion, Nkrumah still remained Wright's friend. In many respects, Wright was correct in his advice to Nkrumah that in order for the leader and thus for Ghana to succeed, Nkrumah must link his emerging, post-colonial nation with the industrial world and thus the West. An invitation from the Secretary-General for the All People's Conference to be held December 5–12, 1958 in Accra, Ghana, signifies that Wright still maintained friendly relations with Nkrumah ("APP"). This was the second significant conference held by Nkrumah to promote Pan-Africanism, the first being the Conference of Independent African States in April 1958. The importance of both conferences was that they were held on African soil, another counterresponse to the Berlin Conference of 1884–85 partitioning Africa. Now decisions on the fate of Africa were in the hands of black Africans and being considered on African soil.

George Padmore acted as Nkrumah's African Affairs advisor. It was Nkrumah, however, who made "Ghana the major citadel for the Pan-African movement," and by 1958, influenced demands for independence by African nations under French colonial rule (Azevedo 164; 178).

Wright also received praise for *Black Power* from one of Ghana's leading African scholars. In a letter dated September 28, 1954 from J. B. Danquah at the Department of Public Information, the United Nations, he proceeds to critique Wright's travelogue, but also admits that he had not completely finished the text. Nonetheless, he did desire clarification on some of Wright's remarks which he had observed so far in his reading. On one issue, Danquah observes that "you looked in West Africa for politicians but not for statesmen. I don't blame you for that. A nation's history is longer than the life of a politician, but the statesman builds upon ideals that last, like good poetry" ("Letter"). Danquah confirms the earlier observation noted by Edward Said that "The slow and often bitterly disputed recovery of geographical territory which is at the heart of decolonization is preceded— as empire had been—by the charting of cultural territory" (209). Nkrumah is thus re-charting Ghana's path as a newly reforged cultural territory, and, as Danquah notes, has designed the CPP to define the "political character" of the organization in its representation as "the people's nationalist movement" ("Letter"). Moreover, Danquah remarks upon the "ideals" noted by Said in the latter's statement that "After the period of 'primary resistance,' literally fighting against outside intrusion, there comes the period of secondary, that is, ideological resistance, when efforts are made to reconstitute a 'shattered community'..." (209). Nkrumah's ideal in this circa 1954 time period is to reconstitute a shattered community, that is, Ghana's, as Danquah implies in his correction of Wright's assumptions. Nkrumah, to paraphrase Danquah, is a wise statesman who is building "upon ideals that [will] last, like good poetry." In redefining the geographical territory involved in that ideal, Danquah also tells Wright: "You were immensely impressed or amused to hear an oath taken to Dr. Nkrumah, and you may have noticed that the word 'Ghana' was invoked. Twenty years ago Ghana was not there in Gold Coast politics. I saw we needed such a conception, taking up our glory of the past, and I spent two years in the British Museum Reading Room, searching for Ghana. I found it and made it public property, to break down tribalism for nationalism—the Ghana nation" ("Letter"). This remark illustrates Danquah's own role in the process of nationbuilding through his contributions of intellectual thought and scholarship.

In further critiquing Wright's travel book, Danquah seeks to allay the author's confusion on Ghana's sudden leap to freedom. The politician focuses on Wright's enigma on page 97 when the author states: "After Mr. Baako had gone I marveled how, in one leap, the Gold Coast African had thrown off his chains." Danquah helps Wright to understand how the Ghanaians had accomplished such a magnanimous endeavor. He assures Wright that it was not an overnight "miracle." And since the author had "Padmore's book" in his possession, he could confirm such claims there or seek opinions by some impartial historians such as "Martin Wight's book *The Gold Coast Legislative Council*, or Dr. Bourret's *The Gold Coast*."

Danquah makes a significant observation in his letter to Wright dated September 28, 1954, that brings up the question of Wright's own authority to speak on African affairs besides being a knowledgeable literary critic and writer. His writing of *Black Power* both corroborates and questions that authority. But Dorothy Padmore, wife of George Padmore, vanquishes those doubts. In her letter to Wright dated October 19, 1954, she speaks from the perspective of her own travels throughout Ghana, and positive reaction to Wright's portrayal of the country in *Black Power*. Without knowledge of American reviews, she says that Wright's vivid and "graphic" writing enabled her to see, feel, hear, and smell the forest roads and city streets that he traversed in Accra, Kumasi, and Cape Coast. Moreover, she praises Wright for his deftness at getting "behind the surface of things and [being able] to explain West African man as he is caught today between the forces of his own religion and that foisted upon him by the West" ("Letters").

The books recommended to Wright by Danquah and also the Padmore book which the author had purchased in Ghana speak to the issue of Wright's research techniques and strategies for mastering a subject, this one being Africa. After all, in this climate of the 1950s when Wright was attempting to discern the black African mind, both he and they were considered collectively by skin color as "Negroes" in the eyes of the West. In research performed for his book, *Richard Wright: Books & Writers*, Michel Fabre reconstructs Wright's reading habits from having surveyed Wright's personal library holdings, and identifies, where possible, those documents pertinent to African, and especially, black African writings. After Wright's death, Fabre inspected Wright's personal archives with the aid of Ellen Wright; he also screened some of Wright's manuscripts and catalogued many of the reference texts mentioned by Wright in certain works. As a result, Fabre has compiled a book-length bibliography of the works which Wright had read, had collected on his own, and/or had received from others—which he may or may not have read. Among those cited by Fabre is *Gold Coast: Akan Laws and Customs and the Akim Abuakwa Constitution* (1928), which was written by J. B. Danquah and apparently was purchased by Wright at the University Bookstore, the Gold Coast, sometime in 1953 during

Wright's research activities in Ghana (Fabre 35). Wright also owned three books by George Padmore, one being referred to by Danquah: *Africa: Britain's Third Empire* (1949); *The Gold Coast Revolution: The Struggle of African People from Slavery to Freedom* (1953); and *Pan-Africanism or Communism?: The Coming of Struggle for Africa* (1956), for which Wright later wrote an introduction (123; *UQ* 440). Also Wright owned *The Path of Thunder* (1948) by Peter Abrahams. Wright apparently read the manuscript of Abrahams's book and then recommended that it be published by Harpers according to a letter from Edward Aswell, Wright's publisher at Harper & Row, to Wright dated March 27, 1947 (*B&W* 3). Moreover, Wright owned *The Black Jacobins* (1938) by C. L. R. James, but only purchased and read it in 1951 (79). In addition, he owned *The Dark Child* (1954), an autobiography by Camara Laye (93), and owned and read *The Palm Wine Drunkard* (1952), a work of fiction by Amos Tutuola, which Wright also bought in Accra sometime in 1953 when he purchased Danquah's book (161).

Wright also corresponded frequently with or had personal contact with American blacks who lived abroad, especially those who were permanently living in or temporarily passing through Paris. Relationships with these people kept Wright exposed to African affairs. Such was the case concerning Wright's relationship with St. Clair Drake. Best known for *Black Metropolis* (1945), the famous sociological study that he co-authored with Horace R. Cayton and for which Wright wrote the introduction, Drake became a lifelong friend of Wright's. Drake, too, regarded Wright as a mentor, friend, colleague, and expert on African affairs because of their common ties with Africans and/or French Africans even before Wright went to the Gold Coast in 1953. The trope of "global travel" emerges in Drake's discourse owing to his fieldwork in Kenya while gathering data for his dissertation. And while completing this task, Drake often sent letters to Wright reporting his short residences in London, travels to Argentina, and return to the United States to complete his dissertation on social anthropology at the University of Chicago while teaching at Roosevelt University. For example, in a letter of February 1948 to which is attached a postscript dated 31 March, Drake remarks about Wright's travel to London and their meeting with "George" (Padmore). The sociologist also indicates that he saw Padmore frequently, most recently at a meeting to organize a London protest against atrocities occurring in the Gold Coast during the previous month. He adds that Peter Abrahams and his wife had visited the day before, and they had spent the afternoon discussing this incident and other world events. Drake is part of the Abrahams-Padmore circle and another conduit for linking Wright to the Pan-Africanist movement to decolonize Africa adopted at the Manchester Congress of 1945. Moreover, Drake provides Wright with insight-ful commentary on matters of global politics relating to the Soviet bloc and its emergence as a superpower in the 1950s. In fact, Drake struggles to grasp the build-up himself, and does detect something "ominous" growing in the international theater, especially from the rumblings in Czechoslovakia, Europe, and America. No "liberal" or "fellow traveler," he assures Wright, should be surprised by these events, but Drake himself seems at a loss as to his own "emotional" and "intel-lectual" positions: "I can't see myself supporting a war—even to stop the iron curtain from coming to the channel. And yet I certainly wouldn't like to see com-munism Soviet style sweep over the areas that already have some tradition of civil liberties and the ideals of Western man" ("Letters").

Just as Wright would later express the alarm to African and Asian nations, re-spectively, in his travelogues *Black Power* (1954) and *The Color Curtain* (1956) and then later to the West in *Pagan Spain* (1957) and *White Man, Listen!* (1957) about the growing menaces of Russian imperialism and Spanish Fascism, we hear Drake fore-casting the Russian buildup of power and sensing its threat to the West in this period of the late 1940s. It would be two years later that Wright would begin ac-tively working "in a sort of unofficial protest movement against the cold war" by forming the French-American Fellowship in Paris. Comprised of "black Americans and their white friends of both nationalities," his group met in October 1950 to begin establishing goals, and then swelled to membership of over sixty in the next year inclusive of James Baldwin and other writers, artists, painters, and journalists (Fabre, *UQ* 359–61).

To return to Drake, his file indicates that he was in the process of preparing a draft proposal to develop a documentary film on the Kikuyu tribe of Kenya as well as the Kenya Teacher's College. He sought Wright's opinion on the soundness of the project. Already in this 1948 period, Wright's affiliations with Africans and apparent knowledge of African affairs had drawn people to him for consultation (see also Wright's affiliation with John A. Davis mentioned below). Although gain-ing substantive exposure to global cultures, particularly knowledge of black Africans, Wright was still a misunderstood "Negro" writer to many Americans and still not immune to attacks by the American press. In his letter of August 1, 1949, Drake presents an example of on-going assaults against Wright through the press, remarking to him that he occasionally would see the author's comments in an American communication. However, he was offended by the recent vicious attack on Wright by Sidney Hook in his article for the *Partisan Review*. Drake considers Hook to be both "ignorant" and "unfair," remarking that he "neither understands

you, nor the milieu in which the Parisian intellectual life goes on." Already one
sees a conflict arising from Wright's identity shifts from old to new, narrow to
broad, American to Western intellectual that would culminate in the self-description
he would later append as a "Western Man of Color" in *White Man, Listen!* In another letter, Drake vents his frustrations over America's on-going practices of racial
discrimination towards blacks that had not lessened since Wright had fled abroad.
In his communication of June 10, 1950, Drake tells Wright that he was glad to
leave the turmoil of Argentina, and, upon his return stateside, had "passed" for a
South American in Miami, Florida, in order to get better hotel accommodations.
Even Drake, a renowned sociologist by this time, was subjected to Jim Crow racism
and had to resort to strategies of passing for a non-Negro in order to be treated
with human dignity in America.

In this 1950s tense climate of Russian and American subterfuge as they were
vying for world domination, a time, too, during which Wright, simultaneously,
was adopting a broader, geographic venue for his investigations, it becomes evident
towards the middle and end of the decade that Wright's nonfiction had become his
lucrative form of writing from this exilic threshold. America, in counterresponse
to his criticisms from abroad, became Wright's nemesis. There were unfavorable
American reviews of Wright's existential novel *The Outsider* (1953) and even his two
travel books. He escaped the 1950s McCarthy-era, Communist "witch hunts" conducted by the House on un-American Activities since Wright was abroad, but Ben
Burns of *Ebony* magazine continued his verbal attacks upon Wright and other
blacks in Paris for being expatriots. Despite all this strife, Wright still fared well
economically in Europe. According to Fabre, Wright was "translated, read and
respected throughout Europe. Both books on the Third World came out at this
time [1956] in London, where the British press were particularly true to their principle of 'fair play' concerning *Black Power,* while the German reception of *Schwartze
Macht* and its author had been exceptional. In the Scandanavian countries he had
just visited, as in Paris, Wright was considered an authority on racial problems,
and even *The Color Curtain* was selling better than he had hoped in the United
States. He was also secure financially...." Nonetheless, Fabre also reports the
hidden economic constraints Wright was already facing or about to face. He notes
that "the Harper payments were coming to an end in February [1957], and the
funds that Paul Reynolds had kept in reserve for [Wright] had been almost depleted
by the purchase and repairs of Ailly [Wright's country farm]" (*UQ* 447–8). And
just two, three years later, Wright was torn between which economic path to follow
for his writings. On the one hand, while *White Man, Listen!* (1957) was well-received

by the black press in America, it was ignored or reproached by the white "establishment." In fact, Wright temporarily even felt dissuaded from venturing again into nonfictional/travel writing according to his remarks in a letter to Margrit de Sablonière, his translator, on October 16, 1957. He says to her:

> I suspect that I'll have to stick to fiction for a long time now for, as I told you, my books on world affairs are not really wanted.... My book *White Man, Listen!* has been more or less negatively received in the USA. They hate the book, yet it tells the truth. Then why should I go on writing books that folks will not read? I'm sorry to sound so depressing but one must look facts straight in the face. (qtd in Fabre, *UQ* 456)

On the other hand, he was advised to return to nonfiction/travel writing after the disappointing reception and sales of *The Long Dream* (1958). In a letter to Wright dated December 5, 1958, the same period of his invitation to return to Accra, and from Dr. Hilde Claasen of Claasen Verlag, Wright's German publishers, she explains to the author the reason for his small advancement for *The Long Dream* in comparison to his nonfiction. She reminds him that it is easier to sell large consignments of nonfiction than novels because the trend now is to "move off from pure novels" ("Letter").

With a European publisher presciently gauging the direction of public taste, it now seems logical that Wright would undertake another travel book project toward the close of the decade being that *The Long Dream* had not fared well in reviews or sales. By summer 1959, he would be forced to consider taking on "additional work to meet his expenses" (Fabre, *UQ* 466; 488). Another nonfictional travel account would bode well both professionally and economically for Wright, and he turned his eyes towards French West Africa. Wright already had developed local ties in Paris with French Africans as far back as summer 1946 on his initial move abroad. It was then that he met Léopold Senghor, the Senegalese writer who also introduced him to Aimé Césaire, the West Indian poet. But the activist person among these French-speaking black Africans was Alioune Diop who crystallized bringing together white and black, French, American and African, Africanist scholars inclusive of Wright, André Gide, and Jean-Paul Sartre, to name a few. Diop was the founder of the literary magazine *Présence Africaine* in October 1946, and Wright was one of its charter members who remained affiliated with the organization and magazine as a "frequent contributor and advisor to 1956" (Fabre, *UQ* 316; *B&W* 127). Moreover, by means of an American-based group that linked Présence Africaine, the organization, to the Society of African Culture in America (SACA), a branch of the American Information Committee on Race and Caste (AICRR) later re-named the American Society of Race and Culture (ASRC), Wright established a long-term African/French African/African American triangular relationship with these groups from 1956 to 1959 arising from their intertwined connections that eventually affected Wright's plans for going to French West Africa.

The major vehicle which brought together all of these American-based, black Americans, French Africans, other black Africans in France, England, or continental Africa, and Wright the expatriate Parisian was the First International Conference on Writers and Artists. In a letter dated September 5, 1956, to Wright from John A. Davis of the AICRC, he reminds Wright that a delegation from the United States would be attending the Congress on Writers and Artists to be held in Rome, Italy, September 19–22, 1956, and that "Mme Diop" (wife of Alioune Diop) would be the convener ("Letters" Council; "Letters" Conference). At some point, Davis became alarmed for it appeared that Wright would not be attending the Congress. In an undated letter of 1956 preceding the conference planned for Rome, Italy, Davis expresses his alarm to Wright after having heard from Mercer Cook, the ASAC representative in Paris, that Wright had planned not to participate. Davis reinforces their desire for Wright to participate and lend his knowledge and experience, especially since he is held in such high esteem by the French Africans and knows them better than any other American. Davis ends with a plea to Wright and again reiterates that the conference would not be the same without him ("Letters" Council). Noteworthy in Davis's letter is how Wright is perceived by American blacks as an "expert" on African/French West African affairs, and his presence would be sorely missed should he not attend the conference.

In another letter of November 17, 1956, Davis writes to Wright at 14 rue Monsieur le Prince in response to the past conference, but also to praise Wright for his speech "Tradition and Industrialization: The Tragic Plight of the African Elite" that later was published in *White Man, Listen!* (Fabre, *UQ* 433). Davis commends Wright for "preventing our African friends from returning to the irrationalism and primitivism, and from turning to xenophobia." He encourages Wright to provide the keen insight and guidance that will help them during their "road to national emergence," especially in choosing the things which are the "best and rational in Western culture" ("Letters" Council). The "irrationalism" and "primitivism" that Wright had condemned in his speech obviously were intellectual, political, and religious flaws that others now saw as qualities handicapping the emerging French West African countries as they struggled for independence and modernization. In fact, one of the reasons for the founding of Présence Africaine was to clarify and resolve the conflicted, dual statuses of young African intellectuals too educated to return to the traditionalist practices of their home countries, on the one hand, but not willing to assimilate into European culture, on the other. And in the interstice of this binarism lay the quandry of these African elites of integrating Western technologies into African culture without compromising the purity of customs to neocolonialist inducements. This quandry Alioune Diop pointed out in his editorial, noting particularly that these products of Africa "could and should contribute humanism to the world." Remarks Fabre, "The Africans, Diop stated, considered the spiritual vitality and creative power of the black Americans indispensable to the black world, even if these Blacks had almost totally forgotten their ancestral customs and had not escaped the influence of their confined and dehumanizing social setting" (Fabre, *UQ* 317–18).

One has to recall that towards the conclusion of and after World War II, activists in French-speaking colonies began to clamor for independence, although their end result was much slower than that of the Gold Coast/Ghana. Between 1946 and 1958, a variety of nationalist organizations developed in the French African nations. A labor reform occurred in 1946 abolishing discriminatory labor practices. Under the leadership of Felix Houphouet-Boigny of Côte de Ivoire, the Rassemblement Démocratique Africain (African Democratic Party) that he founded spawned a number of splinter organizations such as the Parti Démocratique de Côte d'Ivoire and Parti Démocratique de la Guinee in 1946 as a result of the group convention in Bamaka (Mali). Reuben Um Nyobe, a trade unionist, formed the Union of the Populations of Cameroon (UPC); Kenneth Kaunda, in 1959, headed the United National Independence Party (UNIP) in Zambia (formerly Northern Rhodesia); and nationalists of Malawi (formerly Nyasaland) founded the Nyasaland National Congress in 1944 that came under leadership of Dr. Hastings Kamuzu Banda in 1958 after his return from England (Azevedo 163–4). All these activities in a swirl of tensions were happening on mainland Africa and at offshoot European organizational groups which drew Wright into their pro-independence drives owing to his many African-related activities, personal and professional relationships, and global travels. From Davis's letter of November 17, 1956 in which he applauds Wright for condemning Africa's return to "irrationalism" and "primitivism," it is evident that Wright is construed as a perceptive intellectual on African affairs to American blacks and to French Africans who all trust his judgment. This portrait of Wright is discernible in Davis's ensuing statement in which he ties Wright's role as a critic and travel writer to that of the ethnographer when Davis remarks to the author that the field had "undoubtedly lost an important social scientist" ("Letters" Council). In the eyes of American blacks, *Black Power* validated Wright's role as a sociological critic, an expert on African affairs, and a voice of authority.

The First International Conference on Writers and Artists actually met at the Sorbonne in Paris, September 19–22, 1956, and out of that meeting was born the Society of African Culture (SAC). Wright was active in drawing up the final resolutions that were born from the ideas of the multinational participants from America, France, England, and both British and French West Africa, to name a few. One concern of conferees was that no delegation was present from South Africa. A particular goal, and only one of many for the members, was for "all Negro intellectuals to unite their efforts in securing effective respect for the rights of Man, whatever his color may be, and for all peoples and nations whatsoever" (Wright "Conference"). Here is the prelude statement inspiring Wright's self-portraiture as a "rootless man," a nationless and universal "Western Man of Color" in *White Man, Listen!* (50). Moreover, after the conference, Davis transmits by a letter dated February 18, 1957 to Alioune Diop, editor of *Présence Africaine*, information pertaining to formation of the Society of African Culture, its Constitution, and list of officials who were appointed at the Paris conference. One thing which Davis stresses to Diop is the importance of having Dr. Horace W. Bond, President of Lincoln University, as a member of the Executive Council because of his affiliations with British West Africa.

As with all organizations, particularly with the geographical dynamics of this one, there came to exist an element of disharmony among members. This is evident in the dispute that ensued and series of telegrams that followed from Davis to Wright. It seems that certain American members felt that they could not participate in SAC America if the organization endorsed the memberships of W. E. B. Du Bois and Paul Robeson. This protest by certain American members leading to group factionalism becomes evident in a telegram that Davis later sends to Wright in 1956 in which Davis flatly states that, despite the endorsement of Présence Africaine, the Americans could not go along with the nominations of Du Bois, Robeson, and another third party. He asks for Wright's intercession. And, in another letter dated February 28, 1957, regarding this same matter, Davis tells Wright that he is transmitting a list of names of the American delegates and the manifesto that they had drafted stating their "fixed positions" to Alioune Diop in order for Wright to have the papers at his disposal when talking to Diop, who would be returning from Dakar in a few days ("Letters" Council). While the members appreciate Du Bois's contributions, especially his premiere, turn-of-the-century ideas of how a "talented tenth" of leaders would bring American blacks out of racial oppression, it seems that Du Bois's political embroilments in Communism and disagreements with the NAACP along with Robeson's pro-Soviet views make some American members feel uncomfortable. One goal of the organization was to establish global connections and these members would be thwarting that effort. Another issue concerned the organization's adopted name of the Society of African Culture and whether the title would be too racially restrictive since the word "African" connotated both color and racial identities. The first line of the proposed constitution deals with questions as to whether the name would hinder the organization's appeal in "non-African" countries such as Cuba, Brazil, the United States, and even Haiti where the origin of black natives is definitely African. Defining "African" was also complicated by the fact that many Africans were actually non-Negro. This is why the prospective title of "Society of Negro and African Culture" would be racially specific ("Letters" Conference).

Amid the flurry of questioning membership, the organization also experienced several name changes in context of its affiliate groups as revealed in conjunction with a loan request by Alioune Diop. In his letter of November 18, 1957, John A. Davis corresponds with Wright about the organization's name change and Diop's request for a $6,000 loan owing to a financial crisis. Davis tells Wright that the Council on Race and Caste in World Affairs, formerly known as the American Information Committee on Race and Caste, was not set up to make loans. There would be the legal issue of losing their tax exempt status. However, Davis points out that it may be possible for the American Society on African Culture, an affiliate of the Council, sometime in the future to set up such business arrangements because of its being a chapter of the Society of African Culture, but only if other chapters would follow in stead. He also advances this idea as a power play, emphasizing to Wright that such a business relationship would only be feasible if "we were a more integral part of the Paris Committee" and the organ, *Présence Africaine.* In fact, Davis suggests that this latter idea would be quite appealing to the American branch and allow for the possibility of their editing one issue of the journal including overseeing the editing of its English version. Most interesting is that Davis, after adamantly rejecting any notion of the organization's loaning of money, recants his statement and indicates to Wright that the organization would attempt to meet Diop's crisis and could raise at least $3,500 of the amount ("Letters").

Davis's letters definitely establish Wright's role as a mediate in the African American/French African/Parisian triadic groups connected to Présence Africaine. Moreover, Davis states in another letter that they, in accordance with an agreement with Diop, hoped to establish a line of communication between the French-speaking and American colleagues. *Présence Africaine* would serve as the international medium, and one or two issues would be published in English. He also asks Wright to submit a 4,000–5,000 word essay on European-educated Africans or the African elite for which the author would receive a $200 payment.

But all was not well with SACA or Présence Africaine. Davis's remarks above suggest an attempt by members to heal internal rifts arising from distrust between the two international groups concerning equalization of power. This latter point is also why Davis, after conferring with Diop, suggests that an American be appointed as a staff member on *Présence Africaine* and asks Wright to suggest a candidate ("Letters" ASAC; "Letters" Council). The Americans apparently sensed this resentment from the French Africans, and in January 1958, felt that the idea was inconceivable. While in some sense filling that mediate position himself, Wright seems to have suggested such a candidate and Mercer Cook eventually fulfilled that function by coming to Paris in August 1958 for advance planning of the Second Conference of Writers and Artists in the Fall. By summer 1958, however, Wright had begun to distance himself from both the Society of African Culture and *Présence Africaine.* He says on his resumé dated October 6, 1956 that he had been one of the "founders of…Présence Africaine, but in 1956 I felt that that organization was secretly coming under the dominance of the French Government and African personalities who were hostile to the concept of African nationalism. I then withdrew my membership." The severance, nonetheless, was not total. Two letters from James T. Harris, assistant executive director of SACA, dated March 21, 1958, and John A. Davis, dated August 1, 1958, indicate their desires for Wright's active participation in the organization. It was their understanding that Wright would be a subgroup delegate of the American Society of African Culture to the Society of African Culture partaking in the Rome Conference, September 19–25, 1958 ("Letters" ASAC). Says Fabre on Wright's distancing of himself from Présence Africaine, "[Wright] felt that the magazine, now dominated by the pro-French, the pro-Catholics, and the antinationalists, was no longer working for its original goal, which should have continued to be the liberation of African culture. In the same way, he considered the American Society of African Culture, which he had helped to found, much too moderate and not sufficiently independent" (*UQ* 489).

Spring 1959 marks the time that Wright would begin initiating efforts to fund his project on French West Africa, but it also indexes the prelude to his experiencing of serious health problems that would become acutely manifested in June. The amoebic dysentery that Wright had unknowingly contracted in 1953 during his trip to Ghana, that silently festered in his body for six long years, began to manifest its symptoms which would rapidly debilitate the author and lead to Wright's death. To understand the gravity of his illness, I turn to St. Clair Drake's letter to Wright dated August 17, 1955 in which Drake describes his own wife's sufferings from amoebic dysentery which she, too, had contracted during their residence in Ghana while Drake was conducting research for his dissertation. Drake remarks upon her health in context of their finally departing Britain and setting sail for America on 11 September. It seems that Elizabeth had endured four weeks of protracted treatment to kill an amoebic infection in her alimentary canal. The Drakes wisely had gone to the Hospital for Tropical Diseases for checkups once they returned to Britain, and her illness was fortunately diagnosed and treatment immediately begun with massive dosages of penicillin that saved her life. Drake indicates their delight at leaving both Africa and Britain, although they would miss Britain's system of socialized medicine ("Letters").

Obviously, Wright did not know about his serious illness; perhaps, he would have had enough of Africa, too. A more important question to ask is, how would Wright have fared if he had gone to French West Africa and experienced his first attack while there? Would he have declined faster? Julia Wright, in her preface to Wright's volume of *Haiku* (1996) edited by Yoshinobu Hakutani, poignantly recalls how Wright physically suffered during the last year of his life, and remarks about how his writing of haiku poetry seemed to function as psychotherapy against the physical pain ravaging Wright's body (vii). This unsuspecting amoebic predator, far more dangerous than the Communist agitators, FBI spies, and collegiate traitors who exacerbated Wright's paranoia during these final twenty-two months of his life, is the culprit, the silent killer, which Wright's readers need to apprehend as far as its siphoning off Wright's strength while he, contradictorily, fought a mighty battle to jumpstart his faltering career.

For example, Wright had a change of attitude towards the Society for African Culture when he began fundraising efforts for his French West Africa project. For this venture, he estimated costs at $10,000 according to an assortment of correspondence related to this project. Africa was again on Wright's mind, and he needed just $7,500 to augment the $2,500 advancement from his publisher of Doubleday. He wrote to John A. Davis of his plans on May 11, 1959. Davis, in his response letter of May 23, 1959, illustrates the self-protective stance of the Society in regards to its "image" being possibly jeopardized because of Wright's customary habit of writing controversial and polemical travel accounts. Besides wanting to cloak the organization's possible funding of Wright's project, despite the author's long-term

affiliation with SACA, Davis assumes the position of a stringent banker protecting his investment, perhaps because of his unclear or lax guidelines for Diop's re-
payment of his previous loan. He responds to Wright's proposition that the book,
morally, would become property of SACA. But he asks Wright to elaborate upon
the technical and legal aspects of such an arrangement since the work could become
a commercial success and earn a substantial amount of money. Should that become the case, says Davis, there should be some arrangement by which SACA
could "recoup" the funds they invested in order to use the money to subsidize
other artists who may be undertaking similar kinds of projects ("Letters" ASAC;
Fabre, *UQ* 490). Between June and August 1959, Wright also solicited funding
support from his British publishers, John Farquharson, Ltd. of London. Several
letters from Innes Rose dated July 3, 1959; July 20, 1959; and August 24, 1959, indicate the interest of The Bodley Head publishers because of negotiations conducted
by Innes Rose through his agency of Farquharson. At first, Bodley Head wants to
know when Wright intends to make the trip, and then his terms. Next, they use a
monetary ploy; in return for providing the remaining advance on *Pagan Spain,* they
request to have "first refusal on [his] African script." Finally in the last letter, The
Bodley Head publishers express excitement to Rose about Wright's trip, and Rose,
in his letter of August 24th, sends the author their first-hand comments. While certain that the book would be extraordinarily interesting, they, like Davis, have their
minds on profit and loss, and the loss seems to loom larger in the area of uncertainty about the work's ultimate success. They, therefore, hedge, noting that Wright's
endeavor depends upon backing from the Ford Foundation. As a consequence,
they take the position of "wait and see," choosing rather to invest later if Ford
backs the author, if he makes the trip, and if he writes the book, at which time
they would be interested in reading it "and should no doubt make an offer for it"
("Letters," Farquharson). Meanwhile, in this summer-time period, news of Wright's
proposed trip reaches South Africa, Abrahams's country. Wright received a letter
dated July 15, 1959 from a Dr. Lothar Lohrisch who belonged to a "Neun Afrika"
cultural group which had heard of Wright's upcoming venture. He proposes to
Wright that the author contribute periodic articles to his newspaper about Wright's
impressions of the French West African countries that he visits. Noticeably,
Lohrisch mentions no monetary compensation to Wright for his work ("Letter").

A number of Wright's other close friends or affiliates also found themselves
devoid of funds to back Wright's project, but made attempts to assist him or
simply ignored the subject. Edmund Wilson the critic had no funds but sought
ways for Wright to raise capital by means of different magazines. In his letter of

July 2, 1959 to Wright, he indicates that he is forwarding Wright's proposal to the *New Yorker*. Wilson also thinks that if the *New Yorker* fails, Wright might find success with *Esquire* or *The Saturday Evening Post* ("Letters"). Another letter from Léopold Senghor dated July 28, 1959, expresses his enthusiasm for Wright's magnificent project and potential plans for visiting Dakar, Senegal. He also indicates that he will inquire if the government of Mali will pay for Wright's stay in "our Federation," and fulfill Wright's request that he be allowed independent meetings with government officials. But Senghor himself now indicates that he may be delayed in New York because of his new appointment as the Minister-Consul of the Communauté in Paris, and, as a result, would be unable to assure Wright's proper greeting in Dakar should Wright depart around 15 October, during the best seasonal climate in Senegal ("Letter"). According to Fabre, Wright met Senghor several times after he became affiliated with Présence Africaine, but there never developed any really strong ties between the two men. There is no indication that Wright read any of Senghor's books, and perhaps only those articles which Senghor contributed to *Présence Africaine* since Wright was never fluent in reading French writings (*B&W* 143). On the other hand, Senghor's letter to Wright does reflect a certain warmth, even affection. Whatever ensued after this correspondence, there is no indication that Wright received subsidies from Senghor or the government of Senegal or Mali. No aid came from social critic Gunnar Myrdal, either, even though he had written the "Foreword" to Wright's second travel book *The Color Curtain* (1956) as indicated by Myrdal's letter of transmittal to Wright dated September 22, 1955. However, Myrdal did not abandon the travel writer; in fact, Myrdal tried to to aid Wright in his endeavors. He actually wrote a private letter to friends on behalf of Wright's cause dated September 17, 1959. In it, Myrdal tells them of Wright's project and his need for $10,000 in financial support. He also expresses sadness when he has to inform Ellen Wright, in a second letter dated October 6, 1959, that his efforts have been to no avail. Myrdal does, on the other hand, offer Wright an alternative. He suggests to Wright an option of the author's coming to India in another letter dated November 2, 1959. In this same letter, he extends his condolences to Wright after hearing about the death of George Padmore who had been a devoted friend of the author ("Letters"). Wright's world at this time period seems to be rife with losses of personal friends, problems of health, and conditions of strained or limited financial aid. Support from foundations is also elusive. Even famed sociologist E. Franklin Frazier whom Wright had known since the 1940s could not intercede successfully enough to garner funds for Wright from the Ford Foundation. Frazier's aide Edward A. Allworth transmits this disappointing missive to Wright dated October 22, 1959 ("Letters"). On his resumé dated October 6, 1959, Wright appends a statement that, as of now, he is a member of "no group or political party." This remark illuminates the void in Wright's professional life at this time, inclusive of severed ties with SACA. By November 1959 marking Padmore's death and Wright's own battles with amoebic dysentery, his plans for "French West Africa" had become a dream of the past.

Arriving back in Paris at 14 rue Monsieur le Prince from Spain, Richard Wright rushed off a letter dated September 29, 1954, to his American literary agent Paul Reynolds. In writing from his "adopted home" address in Paris, France, to his agent in America, and then making the subject of his discussion his recent three-week, research trip "away from home" in Spain, Richard Wright brings up the matter of what constitutes the definition of "home" in travel writing. In *The Politics of Home: Postcolonial Relocations and Twentieth-Century Fiction*, Rosemary Marangoly George defines "home" as "a desire that is fulfilled or denied in varying measure to the subjects (both the fictional characters and reader) constructed in the narrative. As such, 'home' moves along several axes, and yet is usually represented as fixed, rooted, stable—the very antithesis of travel" (12). Her observations are germane to non-fictional works as well. In *White Man, Listen!*, Wright's collection of essays evolving from his travels throughout Europe from 1950 to 1956, and internally remarking upon his travels to Ghana in 1953 and Indonesia in 1955, he portrays himself as both a "homeless" and "nationless" individual. He says in the "Introduction":

> I'm a rootless man, but I'm neither psychologically distraught nor in any wise particularly perturbed because of it. Personally, I do not hanker after, and seem not to need, as many emotional attachments, sustaining roots, or idealistic allegiances as most people. I declare unabashedly that I like and even cherish the state of abandonment, of aloneness; it does not bother me....(xvi–xvii)

Of course, Wright is deliberately self-constructing his public persona of a "Western Man of Color," a global figure and personification unencumbered by nation or country that was born from the ideas and Constitution adopted by the Society of African Culture spawned from the First Congress on Writers and Artists held in Paris, France, September 19–22, 1956. Members adopted an "image" of themselves as "humanists" striving for the "rights of Man, whatever his color may be, and for all peoples and nations whatsoever" (Wright "Conference"; see also remarks in the earlier section of this essay). And Wright was active in drawing up the premises of this seminal manifesto that, not surprisingly, complemented his own philosophies about the "rights of Man," whatever color, as his previous travel narratives *The Color Curtain* involving Afro-Asians and *Pagan Spain* concerning white Spaniards and their oppressed body of non-Catholics—the "white Negroes" dubbed by Wright—attests (*PS* 138–40). Wright the traveler-humanist in this statement from *White Man, Listen!* is also defining "home" as a "psychological," not "physical" space in echo of a trope he had previously devised in his 1941 photographic text *12 Million Black Voices* (30), which, ironically, foreshadows the definition that Rosemary Marangoly George now argues as being a feature of travel writing. She says:

> Today, the primary connotation of "home" is of the "private" space from which the individual travels into the larger arenas of life and to which he or she returns at the end of the day. And yet, also in circulation is the word's wider signification as the larger geographic place where one belongs: country, city, village, community. Home is also the imagined location that can be more readily fixed in a mental landscape than in actual geography. The term "home-country" suggests the particular intersection of private and public and of individual and communal that is manifest in imagining a space as home. Home-country, while widely used in travel documents, personal narratives and fiction, is not quite the object of nationalism as it is usually understood. (11)

One can say all of the above in defining the various nuances and contexts of "home" attendant to Richard Wright's private and public lives. His present, private "fixed" space is his "adopted" home of 14 rue Monsieur le Prince, Paris, France, but his present public, "home-country," on the other hand, is "nowhere" or "anywhere"—an "imagined" or "psychological" space which he occupies in his self-constructed role as a "Western Man of Color." However, all of these permutations of meanings associated with the word "home" also create a chain of differences and/or contradictions, especially in defining "abandoned home"—the United States which he fled in 1946. This "abandoned home/birth place," which would be the meaning affiliated with a passport application in which one declares one's physical place of birth, is made up of the states of Mississippi, Tennessee, Arkansas, Illinois, and New York where Wright was either born or lived temporarily for months or permanently for years as a citizen of America (Wright, "Passport and Visas"). And now as an individual still an American citizen but living in Paris, he not only looks backwards in his fictions to this physical place of "abandoned home/birth place," America, but also looks forward and globally outward towards his re-born "psychological," "home-country"—meaning Paris, Europe, Africa, Asia, Spain, French West Africa, or anywhere his global forays will take him as a traveler-humanist. Another definition of "home" arises in context of Richard Wright's

public/private spaces and those temporary, "away-from-home" residences that he
occupies while in the "field." James Clifford expounds on this very issue in his essay
entitled "Traveling Cultures." Clifford says:

> It may help to view "the field" as both a methodological ideal and a concrete *place* of pro-
> fessional activity. Since the 1920s, a certain kind of research experience, participant obser-
> vation, has been normatively conceived as a sort of mini-immigration. The field is a home
> away from home, a place of dwelling. This dwelling includes work and growth, the devel-
> opment of both personal and "cultural" competence. Ethnographers, typically, are travelers
> who like to stay and dig in (for a time), who like to make a second home/workplace. Unlike
> other travelers who prefer to pass through a series of locations, most anthropologists are
> homebodies abroad. The field as spatial practice is thus a specific style, quality, and dura-
> tion of dwelling. (99)

We have already heard John A. Davis describing Wright as a social scientist
and the loss to the profession because of Wright's chosen role as a writer and literary critic. But he, in great respect, is an ethnographer who goes into the "field"
and collects data. A difference is that Wright defines his "time" at an abode in
the field differently from Clifford's definition which suggests a "fixedness" to the
"home away from home," the in-field "place of dwelling." Wright's letter to Paul
Reynolds dated September 29, 1954 about his exciting, three-week excursion in
the "field"—Spain—pinpoints the author's portrait as that of an ethnographer
but one, contrarily, whose experience has kept him mobile and moving rapidly
from city to city within that "nation" space. The transiency of geographical space
on the Spanish terrain is evident from Wright's remarks to Reynolds in his draft
letter with pencil markings dated September 29, 1954. He provides a catalogue of
the places he had visited—Barcelona, Guadalajara, Madrid, Grenada, Málaga,
Seville, Cordoba, Alaca, et cetera—during 4,000 miles of travel (*UQ* 409–11; "Letters" Reynolds). Moving between and among settings of urban and rural, Wright
declares that this field strategy has enabled him to get a good look at the life of
Spanish people. True, the general country of Wright's temporary "home" has been
"Spain," but the particular features of Spain's disparate regions, cities, and rural
places are incorporated in that broad term for nation and reflect the complexity
of defining "away-from-home" sites. In other field experiences, such as his ten-
week trip to the Gold Coast in 1953, Wright stayed at places longer than three weeks.
He traveled from city to city or village in that experience, too, and was driven
by a chauffeur. Just five months earlier, he had told Reynolds by letter on March
19, 1954: "By going from spot to spot talking to this person and that one, I had to
gather this reality as it seeped into me from the personalities of others. There

might be some merit in that kind of getting and giving a reality, but it might bore the reader. Conrad wrote all of his novels in that roundabout way" (qtd in Fabre, *UQ* 403). By moving from "spot to spot," Wright has found his own research methodology for gathering data. While he may not qualify as Clifford's "fixed" "mini-immigrant" who goes into the field and stays in one place, Wright the transient does turn his "field home" into a workplace wherever he is and for whatever length of time he is at a site.

In other words, Wright is a personification of all of the multiple meanings associated with the genre of travel literature. His preparations for his trip to French West Africa in 1959 evoke all of the connotations associated with the term "home"—at home, fixed home, away from home, field home, home-country, et cetera. It was from his "fixed" home site of 14 rue Monsieur le Prince that Wright commenced making plans; writing letters soliciting entry permits or financial backers; visiting libraries, and reading books about his "away from home" site, its people, and customs; conducting preliminary interviews "at home" before going into the field; and preparing outlines of specific field sites to visit and even a preliminary draft of the "travel book" to come. I. S. MacLaren has remarked upon the various forms of literature that encompass travel writing, and noted that "the decasyllabic couplet, the discontinuous field note, the journal, the diary, the narrative, the report, the letter, the history, the ethnography, the novel, and the combinations of them" all make up its form (qtd in Blunt 20). Most of these kinds of travel literature complement forms of travel writing generated by Wright owing to his somewhat typical Wrightean, pre-publication activities. There are, however, other metanarratives or forms of data which are generated in response to the production of any formalized, genre piece, regardless of the author. These include passports, visas, invitational letters, reference letters, phone logs, automobile contracts, gasoline bills, et cetera. For example, from his experiences in the Gold Coast and again as recently as in Spain, Wright automatically knew that he would need to contract for a chauffeur. He recognizes the difference in the quality and quantity of his data gathering efforts when he is driving himself about versus his being driven about by a chauffeur. Driving is too distracting. Wright tells Reynolds in his letter of September 29, 1954, when projecting his second and third trips to Spain, that he must remain constantly alert to the topography of the foreign terrain—here, Spain's high mountains, steep inclines, narrow roads, and precarious cliffs. He estimates spending $50 per month just for hiring a chauffeur during the three-to-four months that it will take him to cover Spain while learning in-depth about the life and customs of the people ("Letters" Reynolds).

French-speaking Africa was not new in Wright's discourse. He was psychologically and spiritually liberated after his trip to the Gold Coast, and yearned for more adventures. He not only considered the French-speaking countries where he could observe "less advanced technology," but also entertained the idea of traveling to Madagascar, Egypt, and India as options. His method of expression again would be nonfiction, for this genre lent a personal note to his accounts and seemed to appeal broadly to the global audience he sought to reach. Two other French-speaking nations were also being contemplated by Wright, but according to Fabre, "he was afraid that he would have trouble entering the Belgian Congo," on the one hand, and "he wanted to know how *Black Power*" had been received "before setting off for the French-speaking Cameroons," on the other (*UQ* 407–08).

For his trip to French West Africa under production five years later, Wright's preliminary notes indicate that he planned to spend at least four months in the field, and most likely being driven by a chauffeur so that he could devote his full attention to scenes of the countryside, the cityscape, and most importantly, the people and their customs. The geographical locations that he intended to visit are laid out in the outline among Wright's drafts for the project. He anticipated visiting the capital and major cities of West Africa inclusive of Guinea, Dahomey, Benin, Senegal, Mauritania, Mali, Upper Volta, and Niger. In Central Africa, he considered Chad, Central African Republic, Gabon, and the Congo. And one portion of East Africa involved the Sudan (Wright, "Notes—FWA").

An additional sheet in the form of a handwritten telephone log in this same file indicates that Wright began making contacts by phone with his potential sponsors either preceding or following his sending of letters to them. His log consists of eight names with telephone numbers which have lines or check marks by the left side to indicate whether he had made contact. One of the names checked is Gunnar Myrdal's. Other names notated by a horizontal mark include Léopold Senghor and Mike Jesselson. I have indicated in previous remarks that Wright did correspond with Mercer Cook, Gunnar Myrdal, and Léopold Senghor about his project. Timothy Seldes had replaced Edward Aswell at Doubleday, and this was the publishing house partially subsidizing Wright's "French West Africa" endeavor. Around this same period of Wright's attempts at making telephone contacts, he appears to have begun investigating ship passage. At the bottom of this same sheet, he has scrawled "NAB Co, 4PM Thurs; 1 PM Passag[e]." Senghor, it should be recalled, had advised Wright to travel to Africa and specifically to Senegal in October when the climate was better.

Wright's draft letter to Reynolds dated September 29, 1954, when he had just returned from Spain, also forecasts another typical, "at home" activity which Wright would accomplish prior to his going "away from home" into the field. He tells Reynolds in a postscript that he may visit the United Nations in Geneva to acquire information about life in Spain, and then from that point, he would "weave information" from the texts throughout sections of his own book ("Letters" Reynolds). The author's remarks point out two important features of Wright's strategies for writing his narratives of travel. It tells us first that he would go to great lengths in order to obtain preliminary information about his research topic in order to be thoroughly prepared in advance of his actual field experience, even if it entailed his traveling to another country such as Switzerland for information unavailable in Paris. In fact, Wright's habit "at home" was to conduct advanced research by culling information from local sources. In *Richard Wright: Books & Writers,* Fabre provides a list of Wright's favorite bookstores in Paris where the author would go to buy and/or order books once he settled permanently in Paris in 1947. These included: Galagnani on rue Rivoli; Ricour and Chevillet (now closed); the English Bookshop on rue de Seine; Joseph Gilbert in the Latin Quarter; Bretano's on rue de l'Opera; and the old Shakespeare and Company now Mistral Bookstore in the Latin Quarter. On occasions, Wright used the American Library on the Champs-Elysee (x). He also would call on his publishers throughout Europe and even in America to acquire books for him. Presumably, Wright followed these same strategies when compiling his preparatory reading materials for his trip to French West Africa in 1959. Having acquired the appropriate data, Wright would proceed with the second point of extracting/lifting primary passages, scenes, images from the materials and "weaving" them into his work in process (see comments below).

In this same draft letter of September 29, 1954, Wright also expresses two concerns about production of his travel book on Spain: getting permission from the government to conduct research in the indigenous country and then getting a contract from his publisher. He relays to Reynolds that, because of his British and American contacts, he had gotten permission from the government of Spain to conduct research as well as to move about freely. He construes this to mean that he has control over what he thinks and writes ("Letters" Reynolds). This autonomy over his ideas is important to Wright; after all, it was one of the reasons that he broke with the Communist Party in Chicago in 1937. Now, in the later stage of his life, he still demands this uncensored freedom. Senghor's statements to Wright, dated July 15, 1959, suggest that the author already had begun the process of getting internal permissions from government officials in various French West African countries, the Federation of Mali being one. The fact that Wright demanded his right to free expression in speech and writing, however, already had become problematical because of Wright's commentary in both *Black Power* and most recently *Pagan Spain*. This is why Davis, in his letter of May 23, 1959, hedged to commit SACA to Wright's project, stating: "After you have finished the book, it may turn out that we ought not to associate ourselves with it for purely organizational reasons" (qtd in Fabre, *UQ* 490). The prospect of public backlash from Wright's travel book led Davis to design a loophole of distancing the American Society of African Culture from Wright's work and removing the possibility of their being named as sponsors of Wright's production should the final text prove to be too inflammatory and controversial. But Wright could be assertive about principles he wanted enforced or projects he wanted to initiate right away. He says to Reynolds, in this draft letter dated September 29, 1954, that he definitely wanted to hear a response from Harpers within the next ten days so that he would not be held in limbo ("Letters" Reynolds). "At home" in Paris, and for that matter when he was in the field, Wright closely monitored contractual matters concerning the form and content, style, method of payments, advances, and sales of his books. He had a contract from Doubleday and a $2,500 advance for his "French West Africa" project, but that sum was not enough to cover expenses for his ship passage and cost of living four months in the field.

Actually, Wright wrote two versions of this letter to Reynolds regarding his three-week trip to Spain. His first, long polished typescript is dated September 19, 1954. But Wright must have held the letter, marked up the second version dated September 29, 1954 which is shorter, and then perhaps sent version one of September 19th to Reynolds. One paragraph in this September 19th letter is striking, for it illustrates Wright's method of constructing the drafts of his travel accounts that have spawned from his advanced or on-site research and reading. He says to Reynolds that he has written 130 pages of rough notes which he qualifies to mean that they "do not constitute good writing." The author certifies that the contents are unadulterated "raw materials" and that he wrote the draft first hand while in the field. Moreover, should Reynolds desire to show the drafts to Harpers, he has permission to do so. Wright's final remark is that he is enclosing a tentative outline of the proposed book, which may be all that Harpers would desire to see ("Letters" Reynolds).

Maintaining his pattern of text production, Wright also prepared a tentative outline of his book on "French West Africa" that consists of 48 lines of potential topics to be covered. Example headings include: "10. Books/Population"; "15. Rationalism v. Irrationalism in terms of pscyhog or history"; "21. What is the physical ecstacy of the African (see 35)"; "30. Europe in Africa's mind"; "31. Africa in Europe's mind"; "34. 'Call girls' in the Bush"; "43. Attitudes of Africans towards other Africans"; or "44. Attitudes of Africans towards Blacks." This list also includes reminders such as item "46. Ask Dr. Wickert re German contacts" (Wickert is on his phone list); item "47. Ask George [Padmore] re contacts"; and item "48. Ask colonial doctors re circumcision of women in Moslem Africa," et cetera (Wright, "Outline/Prel. Draft—FWA"). These 48 topics are important, for they imply Wright's mode of thinking in this late period of 1959, and suggest the various approaches (psychological, sociological, historical, political, et cetera) from which he would choose to slant his narrative of travel. Africa's problems of rationalism versus irrationalism, the topic he had dissected in *White Man, Listen!*, remains high on the author's list. In terms of the literary approaches which he would use strategically throughout his book on French West Africa, we can gauge by Wright's methodology in his other three travel accounts, and by his remarks in his draft letter to Reynolds on September 29, 1954, regarding his Spanish trip, that Wright's style would be "eclectic." He compares his style to those books on Spain currently being produced, and makes it clear to Reynolds that his focus will be on the psychological and emotional, not political, and with the aim of "dealing with how a nonwestern people who live in Europe work out their life problems, their perspectives" ("Letters" Reynolds).

Wright thus speaks about how the social sciences have infused his creative thinking and benefited his literary career. Just the author's clustering of his 48 exploratory subjects into sectional topics are indices of how his narratives of travel assume some stock patterns of assemblage. *Black Power, The Color Curtain,* and *Pagan Spain* all exemplify Wright's "eclectic style" of synthesizing genres and fields associated disparately with the arts and humanities and with the social and behavioral sciences, and also his standard pattern of dividing his travel texts into sections and then subdividing these sections into parts, chapters, white spaces, or numbered units. Later Wright adds the context information of dedications, epigraphs, preliminary interviews, and background statements.

For "French West Africa," some of these materials exist. Wright's preliminary draft catalogued at the Beinecke consists of 72 numbered, double-spaced typescript pages. The document title "French West Africa" on the first leaf is typed in capital letters and dated May 12, 1959 ("Outline/Prel. Draft—FWA"). The format seems to have evolved from subjects listed in his 48-topic outline. Sections are demarcated by an upside-down triangle of asterisks; overall, Wright has developed six main divisions. For example, Wright opens section 1 (my divisioning for clarity), pages 1–2, "at home" with a statement in the first person that "I began my first, tentative researches into French West Africa while still on French soil." Again, Wright is drawing the reader into his "first impressions" as he had done with *Pagan Spain* and his other travel books. He proceeds to recount his interview with Bud, a French African living in Paris who works as a professional tom-tom player at parties held on the Left Bank by various American and French whites. Wright stages this interview at Tournon Café, 20 rue de Tournon, which is just around the corner from his fourth-floor apartment at 14 rue Monsieur le Prince. This particular café became Wright's favorite place for taking morning coffee and reading the newspaper; he often met friends at this locale for dinner and discussion. Now for "French West Africa," Wright uses the backdrop of his favorite neighborhood haunt to dramatize his interview with Bud around topic "30. Europe in Africa's mind" on his outline. Wright bids Bud to inform him how he and other Africans feel about French colonial rule in Senegal. The directness of the author's query correlates with Wright's plans to make Senegal a central part of his research trip as the correspondence with Senghor confirms. The ensuing conversation between Wright the interrogator and Bud the respondent almost sounds like a dialogue between two black Americans, for Wright portrays Bud as attempting to talk "jive." Although Bud is worldly from having traveled extensively in France, Africa, and England and is seemingly integrated into French culture because of his marriage to a white French woman, he is, nonetheless, living on the brink of poverty. According to Wright's portrait, Bud seems to be representative of the typical, "unlettered African." He subscribes to the Nietzchean "frog" syndrome which Wright describes in *White Man, Listen!* as a state of self-loathing in that an individual sees his mirror reflection as antithetical to Anglo ideals and philosophies of the master group. These self/Other dichotomies are merely linguistic components among a chain of significations relative to definitions associated with psychological dualities of attraction/repulsion and superiority/inferiority stemming from notions of racial power imposed on Africans by colonial rulers. Bud, in this case, fulfills the colonialist's self-perception of white superiority by his believing in cultural signs of his inferiority transmitted by the French whites in power who rule above him in all aspects of society. Wright again uses the device of a dramatic scene found in his other travel accounts to illuminate his reactions to the interview subject. Here through Bud he demonstrates the dialectical tensions still undergirding race relations between the white colonial imperialists and their oppressed native subjects dating back to the Berlin Conference of 1884–85. Although Bud sounds extremely dense, he articulates the native's indomitable will to resist subjugation as mentioned earlier by Edward Said in this essay. To demonstrate, Wright sees Bud as a representation of Africa's dispute with Europe and the dangerous element who eventually will rise up in resistance to the white adversary.

In section 2, now separated by triple asterisks as a division and consisting of pages 3–12, Wright begins his weaving process common to the production of his travel accounts by integrating external texts with his field data and personal responses. For example, he shifts his attention to exploring item "31. Africa in Europe's mind" and items "18–20. Relations between White & Native" ("Outline/Prel. Draft—FWA"). He begins his account by integrating comments from books by European authors that he has located, including the places and dates of publication of the work. Some books which he intended to purchase or borrow from a library are noted on paper in the same files where he lists the countries that he wished to visit. He notes three books: *French West Africa* by Virginia Thompson and Richard Adloff; *Islam in West Africa* by John Spencer Trimingham; and *Freedom and Authority in French West Africa* by Robert Delavignette ("Notes—FWA"). All provide Eurocentric views of Africa, and the one on *Islam in West Africa* leads into Wright's reminder to himself to inquire about item 48 concerning gathering evidence from doctors about practices of female circumcision in Moslem countries of black Africa. Consistent with the style of his other travel narratives, Wright takes his reader along with him on his readings and musings as he had done with the Falange Española or political book of etiquette for Spanish girls and women in *Pagan Spain* (36). With "French West Africa," he directs his first, in-depth reading to the *Africa Emergent* by W. M. MacMillan and deliberately includes citation information for footnoting purposes (Pelican Books, 1949). And, by extracting quotations and citing page numbers, Wright thus adopts a "call-response" technique in which he provides the reader with MacMillan's verbatim statements and thereafter gives his alter ego's "reactions" to those remarks. For example, he leads off with a simple statement such as "Macmillan gives his summary of why Africa is such a problem to the Europeans who try to reform it" (3–4). He then extracts a 120–150 word passage and embeds it into his text. Here is the sample statement he excises from page 20 of MacMillan's work:

> In all their history Africans have been caught in a vicious circle which defeats and discourages the best administration. Poor and ill-equipped because they are backward, they remain backward because they are too poor to better their equipment. The only civilization worth boasting of is the fruit of many peoples' experience pooled by the travel and intercourse

from which the Negroes as a whole were cut off—far more completely than the peoples of the most secluded corners of Europe. Almost destitute of world knowledge, Africans could afford neither medical help nor mechanical equipment, nor the schooling that would enable them to use these. Their poverty—first fully revealed by Livingstone—is still neither their fault nor an imposed misfortune; it is a fact of geography and economics.

As Wright proceeds to explore the topics on his list by number and subject, his voice becomes more and more pronounced, and his qualifying statements become longer and longer.

In section 3, pages 12–18, Wright turns to the artistic aspect of African culture which he ties in with reformed sexual practices in Africa. He looks at Geoffrey Gorer's book on *African Drums* which Wright identifies as being published by Penguin Books, 1935. The author links his items 35 and 21 to Gorer's remarks on the sexual habits of Africans that contrast to practices of homosexuality and lesbianism in European culture. Like his fictions and travel accounts of *Black Power* and *Pagan Spain*, a culture's sexual practices are important to Wright, the prudish researcher. But he does something insightful by demonstrating that definitions of sex and sexuality are inherently related to power and that the source of this power resides within religion and its institutions. Certainly this is a pre-Foucaultian assumption since Wright is temporally assessing prevailing theories of the 1940s/50s in context of their applications to African culture, and is excavating, weighing, and assessing hierarchies of power which he links to religion. This is why Wright is attracted to Gorer's placing of blame for racial discrimination and deviant codings imposed on Africans in the hands of missionaries and, at the highest level, the Catholic Church. The author surmises that present-day charges of aberrant sexual practices in African culture stem from biased Westerners and specifically English, American, and Australian missionaries who made Negro Africans believe that their indigenous natural sexual practices were sinful (Wright's page 16).

Section 4, pages 18–45, is a long analysis. Wright here decides to use two texts by Laurent Van der Post entitled *Venture into the Interior* and *The Dark Eyes of Africa* which he appraises as quite illuminating in many ways. An example is this line which he takes from *Venture* when Van der Post says, "It may be that the Europeans of Kenya are trying to live a fantasy. Perhaps they pursue, in the un-English setting of Africa, a dream of English country life which has long ceased to exist even in Britain." This passage relates to distance perceptions in that many poor Europeans who have gone to the colonies have ended up living better than at home. And, from their adopted home, they, in turn, have proceeded to measure their lives in context of values from the distant home country which now has assumed

fantastical proportions, but in reality, is really nonexistent. Colonialists, Wright
is showing, suffer intraracially with their own kind of Nietzchean frog perspectives. This selected passage is why Wright proceeds next to examine the moral
tensions between Africans and Europeans, for it is the European's tendency away
from home to blame his unrealities on the African, so Van der Post says again,
and therefore "to shoulder him with our fears and our sin, to call it a black, a native,
an African problem" (20; Wright's pages 18–21). In his extensive response statement,
Wright actually affirms a familiar premise which Van der Post has now inferred,
and which is that the white race will never heal until it has embraced its own
black brothers.

Several things now occur in Wright's interpretative processes: he starts to integrate psychological theory, and also to insert his "existentialist ego" into the text.
In other words, like his other travel books, particularly that of *White Man, Listen!*,
Wright's selfhood, his ego, is becoming the focus of this fourth travel account.
There is a contrapuntal foregrounding of his "reactions," and backgrounding of
the secondary author's statement or incident. For example, he turns to the ideas
of Ladislas Segy and his text entitled *African Sculpture Speaks* published by Lawrence
Hill & Company, New York, 1955. Wright begins to examine practices of magic
and the roles of masks and sculptures in this process which incorporates disparate
themes of secret societies, death, and rituals.

Another book which Wright incorporates into this section is Diedrich Westermann's *The African Today and Tomorrow* published by International African Insti-
tute, Oxford University Press, 1949. Wright focuses on Westermann's analysis of
economics, the value of land, and the seizure of land from the natives by whites.
Wright sees that Westermann has shown that the white man has deliberately mis-
lead the natives in order to steal their lands. They are inundated with propaganda
about their lower class statuses as laborers, and how they should expect low wages
as farm laborers and have no assumptions about owning their land or their homes
(35; Wright's page 33). In this section, Wright also begins to examine Moslem religion, and repeats his interrogations of human sexuality and even beastiality according to Westermann's point of view (Wright's page 39).

Section 5, consisting of pages 45–57, brings in contemporary world issues of
the 1950s concerning the cold war conflicts between the superpowers of Russia
and America over Africa. While quarreling over the natives, neither group envisions
Africans as autonomous people who may someday rise up in mass and take the
center stage of modern history (Wright's page 45). Not only does Wright's language resound of Marxist dialectics, but his ideas are contemporaneous with

Wright's earlier alarm to the East about the "snakelike coil" of Western tyranny in *White Man, Listen!* But the West, according to Wright, is underestimating the post-World War II reactionary mindset of Africans. This involves, according to Said, first physiological, and then ideological resistances of native Africans to European colonization. Here especially, Wright's "ego" once again subsumes the problem in order to foreground his "reactions." His response compares to a similar justification that he provides in the opening pages of *The Color Curtain* when he supplies seven reasons to his spouse as to why he should attend the Bandung Conference in Indonesia. Now magnifying his personal "I-ego" as the foreground subject in "French West Africa" (Erickson 25; Bugental 30), he cites reasons of his own level of tolerance, his being an American Negro, his emerging from the lowest economic class in American society, his being largely self-taught, and his having experienced firsthand the precepts of American democracy and Russian Communism as justifications for his self-appointment as the spokesperson for those "who live beyond the moral pale of both America and Russia" (Wright's page 46). Westermann, in essence, has become a minuscule figure in comparison to Wright's enlarged ego as the self-appointed "Twentieth Century Western Man of Color" policing the West. And he points to reactionary movements against the West now taking place inside Ghana, citing the stridency of Ghana's secret circle as one such group (Wright's page 53).

In the last part, section 6, pages 57–72, Wright shifts from his evaluation of the social sciences and turns his attention to the humanities. He provides a critical analysis of the African novel entitled *The Palm Wine Drinkard* by Amos Tutuola and published by Faber and Faber, London, 1953. Most interesting is Wright's opening "reaction" to this African work, for he finds himself estranged to the form, structure, and thematic elements of the novel. In fact, it is in the guise of the outsider or foreigner, a role which he had assumed in his other major travel accounts, that he approaches Tutuola's novel. Thus, in situating dualities of self/Other; foreigner/native; outsider/insider, et cetera, Wright falls into the familiar persona of his narratives of travel. For example, he cannot understand how African novelists develop character portraits devoid of a central personality in the story (Wright's page 58). Based upon literary techniques and subject matter in this novel by an African writer, and the work's being contrary to the familiar forms which he has been trained to recognize in Western culture, Wright sets up binary oppositions of strange versus familiar with his opening comment. Through his alternating use of reveal/conceal codes in which a word is stated or antithetically implied by indirection, he thereby is complicating the character portrait of his persona, the everchanging, contradictory tourist, investigator, researcher, and/or outsider. One finds such rhetorical devices in his photographic text *12 Million Black Voices* in which Wright deconstructs the "strange" and "familiar" meanings of the word "Negro" from the perspective of blacks in counterresponse to notions of whites (30). His linguistic performance in "French West Africa" as the mystified "stranger" is evident when Wright remarks that after having read the first 63 pages of Tutuola's novel, he still has not fathomed an inner spirit motivating the addicted hero beyond hunger, thirst or sex, or some magical creatures. Having already condemned the handicap of tribal religion in the platforms of African nations striving for independence, Wright here inserts that aspect of "irrationalism versus rationalism" that the modern African must fight. A source of frustration for the author is that the African hero is no Bigger Thomas self-empowered to move things on his own volition, but a character who must use one agent to move another object or else take flight (Wright's page 58). This African hero has no existentialist will. And, to illustrate something comprehensible and logical to him, Wright inserts two lines from Blake's poem "Tiger, Tiger Burning Bright" as an example of a familiar narrative and action. Just as he, an atheist, had preferred hearing Paul Laurence Dunbar's song "When Malindy Sings" to the Gold Coast's Christian hymn in *Black Power* (134), he again assumes the role of the naive Westerner and outsider and turns to a Western narrative to counteract the nonsensical, strange beings and magical spirits elusive to him in Tutuola's text.

Tutuola's novel serves as a catalyst that provides Wright with an excuse to return to more rational material in which he can apply some of his knowledge from the social sciences. He decides now to focus on two items pertaining to Moslem religious practices and specifically the habits of black Moslems in Algeria and North Africa. He returns to his readings of Westermann's text where the latter provides a long section on Moslem religion, Arab invasions in North Africa, Islamic practices in Fulani, Hausa, and Somali cultures, and the roles which women occupy in these societies. This is also the section where Wright posts a reminder to himself to examine practices of female circumcision, although it is not developed here in this preliminary draft. What he proceeds to do, however, is to incorporate two other authors in this section who, too, examine African religious customs. One text by Saloman Reinach called *Orpheus* piques Wright's interest once again about magical practices and animal worship from prehistoric times to the Middle Ages. The second book by L. S. B. Leakey entitled *Mau Mau and the Kikuyu* and published by Metheun and Company, 1952, suggests the influence of St. Clair Drake on Wright's thinking because of Drake's field experiences in Kenya. Another text examined by Wright is Wulf Sack's *Black Hamlet* published by Little, Brown and Company, Boston, 1947, which pertains to tribal thinking and explores African beliefs and spiritual powers. Lastly, Wright takes note of a book by H. G. Woodley entitled *Certified—An Autobiographical Study* published by Victor Gollancz, London, 1947, that also provides information about the tribal mentality of Kenyan Africans.

Overall, Wright's "French West Africa" project would have added a powerful dimension to his already complete trilogy of travel books. His plans indicate that the French African colonies in their transitions from colonial subjugation to post-colonial independence were his central focus with Senegal being his starting point. From that geographic position, Wright appears to have thoughts of traveling to Central and Northern Africa according to his notes, outline, and preliminary draft. Not only do these project materials reflect the depth and breadth of Wright's knowledge of French African affairs, but his "Introduction" to the French edition of *White Man, Listen!*, which he wrote in February 1959 as he envisioned his fourth travel book project, reflects the prescience of his mind. He notes that Guinea, Ghana, Liberia, Sudan, and Ethiopia are free countries and that Togo, Nigeria, Somalia, French Cameroon, and the Rhodesian Federation will soon be liberated states, too. He predicts that when emotions subside after these nations have achieved their full independencies, there will have to be compromises made by both Africans and Europeans. Most of all, there ultimately will have to be a change in attitudes on both sides as, to use a term of Edward Said, these "shattered communities" stand on their own principles and on their own recovered lands as freed people on the brink of modern history ("To French Readers").

The word "Africa," a term familiar in Wright's discourse as far back as 1938, now serves as a marker signifying the growth of the author's mind from the narrow space of his American birth to his universal place as a self-appointed Pan-Africanist and, more importantly, a "Western Man of Color" and global humanist. His project files, although incomplete, are significant in that the small assemblage of papers continues to illuminate Wright's style of producing his narratives of travel in the 1950s. They, in essence, validate his development of a particular, Wrightean form of travel writing. He again indicates how frames of language achieve new meanings in time and space, and by contextuality of race, class, and gender owing to its utterance at that particular moment and specific locale. More-over, his behind-the-scenes activities relating to all his narratives of travel including Wright's "French West Africa" project illuminate why terms of "home," "fixed home," "adopted home," "home-country," "psychological home," and "field home" may bear semantics intrinsic to Anglo travel literature, but acquire new meanings in the discourse of Richard Wright the travel writer of the 1950s.

Notes

S. Shankar, "Richard Wright's *Black Power*"

1. This essay has benefited from the careful attention of a number of readers. Barbara Harlow, Helena Woodard, Anannya Bhattacharjee, Luc Fanou, Hosam Aboul-Ena, Louis Mendoza, Purnima Bose, Rachel Jennings, Ann Cvetkovich, Barbara Foley, and Luis Marentes especially looked at earlier drafts of this essay and made numerous helpful comments and bibliographic suggestions.

2. In *"Black Power* Revisited: In Search of Richard Wright," Jack B. Moore presents his discoveries from his journey to Ghana some years after Wright. Moore went to Ghana to meet some of the people who appear in *Black Power*. He interviewed James Moxon, Hannah Kudjoe, and Kofi Baako. All three challenge some of what Wright says in *Black Power* about various incidents that took place on his visit. Moore's conclusion based on this (a conclusion he also suggests in "The Art of *Black Power*") is that *Black Power* "is sometimes profitably read as a novel" (185). Moore seems to be working with a certain conventional understanding of fiction and nonfiction in making these comments.

3. "What Is Africa to Me?" was one of the earlier suggested titles for *Black Power*. See Michel Fabre's *The Unfinished Quest of Richard Wright* (401). The Countee Cullen poem from which this title is taken continues to appear as an epigraph to the book.

4. The detailed discussion of "economy" as applicable to texts forms a part of my book entitled *Textual Traffic: Colonialism, Modernity and the Economy of the Text* (NY: SUNY P).

5. Wright's faith in the "Westernized elite" of the "Third World" is in stark contrast to the innumerable African writers (such as Chinua Achebe, Ayi Kwei Armah, Wole Soyinka, Ngugi wa Thiong'o and Chinweizu, to name only a few) who have, on the contrary, expressed deep disillusionment in such an elite. However, it is also true that the careers of most of these writers are later than that of Wright.

6. In this matter of names ("Gold Coast" and "Ghana"), we can find conveniently summarized the relationships between colonialism and nationalism respectively, on the one hand, and

the territory, geographical and otherwise, that they contest, on the other. Colonialism identifies the land by the commodity it produces; nationalism, casting its glance backwards, reclaims a history by reappropriating the name of an ancient kingdom.

7. In this context, see also Wright's story "Man, God Ain't Like That...." In this story, Babu, a superstitious African, takes his white employer John to be God. The story is a critical examination of both European racism and African superstition. Unfortunately, Wright also reproduces some of the Africanist stereotypes regarding Africa in his story.

8. More about this word "pathetic" below.

9. This is not to say that Christianity goes uncriticized in *Black Power*. Wright, in fact, finds the Christianity of the Gold Coast to be anemic when compared to the pagan religion and the instrument of colonialism (132–35).

Jack B. Moore, "No Street Numbers in Accra"

1. Once again, I am pleased to thank the American Philosophic Society for enabling me to retrace Wright's steps in Ghana. All ellipses mine.

2. I am indebted to Casey Blanton for discussing with me travel literature and Bakhtin's theories relating to the genre.

John Lowe, "Richard Wright as Traveler/Ethnographer"

1. Since then, several anthropologists have copiously documented the highly sexual nature of rituals and popular folkculture in Spain, especially Stanley Brandes (1980). I am indebted to Michel Fabre for his careful reading of this essay and for his usual, generous suggestions.

2. Wright typed "protest"—was this a Freudian slip? Did he actually mean "protect"?

3. As James L. Peacock tells us, the lore of social science teems with this syndrome, probably because our ordinary lives are so fragmented; the requirement that one focus intently on a group through participation in it can often be exhilarating; yet, as Peacock remarks, "the job of the anthropologist is, finally, not merely to experience or even join the group, but to analyze and understand it. To achieve that end, the participant must remain observer" (58).

4. For an analysis of Wright's employment of burning and lynching scenes and metaphors in his fiction, see Trudier Harris's gripping study entitled *Exorcising Blackness*.

5. An example of how emotion can be rendered precisely through pictures may be found in one of Wright's pictures; he crops the figure presented (a hooded figure) to focus on the bare feet under a white robe, positioned on the rough pavement. The attachment note reads, "many marched barefooted to make themselves suffer as they felt that their God had suffered." I should mention, too, that not all of the photos that summon up emotion appear intended for "expose" functions; a lovely one of a handsome priest in white, accompanied by two older men with their hands clasped behind them, bears the lyrical notation, "Incense bearers swung with slow rhythms their vessels of silver, veiling the air."

6. Wright was always aware of the uses of nudity in mythic presentations; a typed note on flypaper is in one of the folders at the Beinecke Library, Yale, stating "Some of the statues of

Las Fallas in Valencia in 1955. Nudity ranked high on the elaborately done and artistically wrought monuments (4 photos)."

7. As such, however, it situates Wright quite differently from many ethnographers, who all too often, Malinowski once said, are dealing with vanishing societies. "Ethnology is in the sadly ludicrous, not to say tragic position, that at the very moment when it begins to put its workshop in order, to forge its proper tools, to start ready for work on its appointed task, the material of its study melts away with hopeless rapidity" (Malinowski xv).

Dennis F. Evans, "The Good Women, Bad Women, Prostitutes and Slaves of *Pagan Spain*"

1. The only other instance in which Wright consciously portrays one of his anti-heroes as a white character is in *Savage Holiday*. Margaret Walker, in her critical biography, *Richard Wright: Daemonic Genius*, considers Wright's portrayal of Erskine Fowler to be Wright's own autobiographical desire to be white (245).

2. See for instance, Maria K. Mootry's essay, "Bitches, Whores, and Women Haters: Archetypes and Topologies in the Art of Richard Wright," in Richard Macksey and Frank E. Moorer, eds., *Richard Wright: A Collection of Critical Essays*. Englewood Cliffs, NJ: Prentice-Hall, 1984, 117–27; Nagueyalti Warren's essay, "Black Girls and Native Sons: Female Images in Selected Works by Richard Wright," in C. James Trotman, ed., *Richard Wright: Myths and Realities*. New York: Garland, 1988, 59–77; or Margaret Walker's critical biography, *Richard Wright: Daemonic Genius*. New York: Warner, 1988, 117–18, 184–85, and 246–48.

3. Kristeva creates a dense multilayered metaphor focusing on the role of the foreigner in life and in literature. Her most basic point is that we are all, at one time, exposed to the hatred and objectification that is often aimed at foreigners:

> Foreigner: a choked up rage deep down in my throat, a black angel clouding transparency, opaque, unfathomable spur. The image of hatred and of the other, a foreigner is neither the romantic victim of our clannish indolence nor the intruder responsible for all the ills of the polis.... Strangely, the foreigner lies within us: he is the hidden face of our identity, the space that wrecks our abode, the time in which understanding and affinity founder. By recognizing him within ourselves, we are spared in detesting him in himself. A symptom that precisely turns "we" into a problem, perhaps makes it impossible, the foreigner comes in when the consciousness of my difference disappears, unamenable to bonds and communities (1).

Wright can appreciate the hatred aimed at women in Spain because he, like they, knows what it feels like to be "the image of hatred and of the other." The irony lies in Wright's experiencing less overt hatred when he is away from his native land; he and the women of Spain both experience more oppression as foreigners at home than they do abroad. Yet, both Wright and the women he empathizes with can never escape this burden of being the foreigner.

4. In fact, many critics, including Wright's own agent Paul Reynolds, assert that it is Wright's fiction, and more specifically, his American fiction that is most creative. Michel Fabre in *The Unfinished Quest of Richard Wright* quotes from a letter Reynolds sent to Wright in January, 1956:

Why was that the most creative period in your life up till now, and why, since then, have the sources of your creativeness seemed to dwindle? It seems to me—and of course I am only guessing now—that as you have found greater peace as a human being, living in France, and not been made incessantly aware that the pigmentation of your skin sets you apart from other men, you have at the same time lost something as a writer. To put it another way, the human gain has been offset by a creative loss (432).

Reynolds's claim is that "Wright at Home" is a more forceful, politically motivated, creative artist than is "Wright as foreigner," and that his creativity and forcefulness are directly related to Wright's having been oppressed by his own native society. In other words, Wright is made *foreigner* in his own country, and this gives him the creative incentive necessary to create the forceful sociopolitical fiction that he produced. Yet, there is a price to be paid for this literary forcefulness, and that price includes the subordination and subjugation of women.

Works Cited

Abrahams, Peter. "The Blacks." *Black African Voices.* Ed. James E. Miller, et al. Glenview, IL: Scott, Foresman and Company, 1970. 20–35.

———. "Letters." JWJ MSS 3, Box 93, File 1161. Yale Collection of American Literature. Beinecke Rare Book and Manuscript Library. New Haven, CT.

Adams, Percy G. *Travel Literature and the Evolution of the Novel.* Lexington, Kentucky: UP of Kentucky, 1983.

All People's Conference. "Invitation." December 5–12, 1958. JWJ MSS 3, Box 93, File 1157. Yale Collection of American Literature. Beinecke Rare Book and Manuscript Library. New Haven, CT.

Allworth, Edward A. "Letter." October 22, 1959. JWJ MSS 3, Box 97, File 1340. Yale Collection of American Literature. Beinecke Rare Book and Manuscript Library. New Haven, CT.

American Museum of Natural History. "Invitation." January 19, 1946. JWJ MSS 3, Box 93, File 1157. Yale Collection of American Literature. Beinecke Rare Book and Manuscript Library. New Haven, CT.

Angelou, Maya. *All God's Children Need Traveling Shoes.* New York: Random-Vintage, 1987.

Appiah, Kwame Anthony. "A Long Way from Home: Wright in the Gold Coast." *Richard Wright.* Ed. Harold Bloom. NY: Chelsea House, 1987. 173–90.

Armah, Ayi Kwei. *The Beautyful Ones are Not Yet Born.* NY: Collier, 1990.

Ashcroft, Bill, et al. "Introduction." *The Empire Writes Back: Theory and Practice in Post-Colonial Literatures.* NY: Routledge, 1989. 1–13.

Azevedo, Mario. *Africana Studies: A Survey of Africa and the African Diaspora.* Durham, NC: Carolina Academic P, 1993.

Baker, Carlos. Ed. *Ernest Hemingway, Selected Letters, 1917–1961.* NY: Scribner's, 1981.

Bahktin, Mikhail. *The Dialogic Imagination.* Austin: U of Texas P, 1981.

Baldwin, James. *Nobody Knows My Name.* NY: Dell, 1963.

"Bishop Prevented from Going to Lambeth." *Christian Century.* 6 August 1958. n.p.

Blunt, Alison. *Travel, Gender, and Imperialism: Mary Kingsley and West Africa.* NY: Guilford, 1994.

Blyth, R. H. *Haiku.* 4 Vols. Tokyo: Hokuseido, 1949.

———. *A History of Haiku.* 2 Vols. 1963. Tokyo: Hokuseido, 1964.

Boas, Franz. "Race Problems in America." *The Shaping of American Anthropology, 1883–1991. A Franz Boas Reader.* Ed. George W. Stocking, Jr. NY: Basic Books, 1974. 318–30.

Boyi-Mudimbe, Elizabeth. "Travel Representation and Difference, or How Can One Be a Parisian?" *Research in African Literature.* 23.3 (1992): 25–37.

Brignano, Russell C. *Richard Wright: An Introduction to the Man and His Works.* Pittsburgh: U of Pittsburgh P, 1970.

Bugental, James F. T. *The Search for Existential Identity.* San Francisco: Jossey-Bass, 1976.

Burgum, Edwin Berry. "The Art of Richard Wright's Short Stories." *Quarterly Review of Literature* 1 (Spring 1994): 198–211.

Butor, Michel. "Travel and Writing." *Mosaic* (1974): 1–16.

Butterfield, Stephen. *Black Autobiography in America.* Amherst, MA: U of Massachusetts P, 1974.

Campbell, James. *Exiled in Paris.* NY: Scribner's, 1995.

Camus, Albert. *The Stranger.* Trans. Stuart Gilbert. NY: Vintage-Random, 1954.

Cappetti, Carla. *Writing Chicago: Modernism, Ethnography, and the Novel.* NY: Columbia UP, 1993.

Carpenter, Frederic Ives. *Emerson and Asia.* Cambridge: Harvard UP, 1930.

Carr, Raymond. "See Those Bullfights." Review of *Pagan Spain. The London Observer.* 20 March 1960. 20.

Cayton, Horace. "Discrimination—America: Frightened Children of Frightened Parents." *Twice-A-Year* 12–13 (1945): 262–69.

———. "Richard Wright Biography." The Vivian Harsh Collection. Woodson Public Library. Chicago, IL.

Charbonnier, Georges. "Richard Wright, for Whom Do You Write?" *Conversations with Richard Wright.* Eds. Keneth Kinnamon and Michel Fabre. Jackson: UP of Mississippi, 1993. 224–29.

Claasen, Hilde. "Letter." December 5, 1958. JWJ MSS 3, Box 93, File 1261. Yale Collection of American Literature. Beinecke Rare Book and Manuscript Library. New Haven, CT.

Clifford, James. *The Predicament of Culture: Twentieth-Century Ethnography, Literature, and Art.* Cambridge: Harvard UP, 1988.

———. "Traveling Cultures." *Cultural Studies.* Eds. Lawrence Grossberg, et al. NY: Routledge, 1992. 96–116.

———. and George R. Marcus. Eds. *Writing Culture: The Poetics and Politics of Ethnography.* Berkeley: U of California P, 1986.

Cobb, Nina K. "Richard Wright and the Third World." *Critical Essays on Richard Wright.* Ed. Yoshinobu Hakutani. Boston, MA: G. K. Hall, 1982. 228–39.

Collier, John, Jr. "Photography in Anthropology: A Report on Two Experiments." *American Anthropology.* 59 (1957): 843–59.

Collins, Patricia Hill. *Black Feminist Thought: Knowledge, Consciousness, and the Politics of Empowerment.* NY: Routledge, 1991.

———. "Learning from the Outsider Within: The Sociological Significance of Black Feminist Thought." *Taking Sides: Clashing Views on Controversial Issues in Race and Ethnicity.* Ed. Richard C. Monk. Guilford, CT: Dushkin, 1994. 15–23.

Conrad, Joseph. *Heart of Darkness.* 3rd Ed. NY: W. W. Norton, 1988.

Crapanzano, Vincent. "Hermes' Dilemma: The Masking of Subversion in Ethnographic Description." *Writing Culture: The Poetics and Politics of Ethnography.* Eds. James Clifford and George E. Marcus. Berkeley: U of California P, 1986. 51–76.

Dadié, Bernard Binlin. *An African in Paris.* Urbana: U of Illinois P, 1994.

Daniel, E. Valentine and Jeffrey M. Peck. Eds. "Culture/Contexture: An Introduction." Berkeley: U of California P, 1996. 1–33.

Danquah, J. B. "Letter." September 28, 1954. JWJ MSS 3, Box 96, File 1288. Yale Collection of American Literature. Beinecke Rare Book and Manuscript Library. New Haven, CT.

Davidson, Basil. *Africa in History.* 1966. New York: Collier/MacMillan, 1991.

Davis, Charles T. and Michel Fabre. *Richard Wright: A Primary Bibliography.* Boston: G. K. Hall, 1982.

Davis, John A. "Letters." American Society of African Culture. JWJ MSS 3, Box 93, File 1173. Yale Collection of American Literature. Beinecke Rare Book and Manuscript Library. New Haven, CT.

———. "Letters." Conference on Negro Writers and Artists. September 19–22, 1956. JWJ MSS 3, Box 104, File 1557. Yale Collection of American Literature. Beinecke Rare Book and Manuscript Library. New Haven, CT.

———. "Letters." Council on Race and Caste. JWJ MSS 3, Box 96, File 1276. Yale Collection of American Literature. Beinecke Rare Book and Manuscript Library. New Haven, CT.

De Certeau, Michel. *The Writing of History.* NY: Columbia UP, 1988.

De Vera, Cuevas. "Letter." n. d. JWJ MSS 3, Box 53, File 651. Yale Collection of American Literature. Beinecke Rare Book and Manuscript Library. New Haven, CT.

Dorst, John. "Rereading *Mules and Men:* Toward the Death of the Ethnographer." *Cultural Anthropology.* 2, 3 (1987): 305–18.

Douglass, Frederick. *Narrative of the Life of Frederick Douglass, An American Slave, Written By Himself.* Eds. William L. Andrews and William S. McNeely. 1845. NY: W. W. Norton, 1997. 12–80.

Drake, St. Clair. "Letters." JWJ MSS 3, Box 96, File 1302. Yale Collection of American Literature. Beinecke Rare Book and Manuscript Library. New Haven, CT.

Du Bois, W. E. B. *The Souls of Black Folk.* 1903. NY: Penguin, 1989.

Durdin, Tillman. "Review of *The Color Curtain.*" *New York Times Book Review.* 26 September 1954.

Elkins, Stanley M. *Slavery: A Problem in American Institutional and Intellectual Life.* 1959. Chicago: University of Chicago P, 1976.

Emerson, Ralph Waldo. *Journals of Ralph Waldo Emerson, 1821–1871.* Ed. E. W. Emerson and W. E. Forbes. Boston: Houghton Mifflin, 1911.

Erickson, Erik H. *Identity and the Life Cycle.* 1959. NY: W. W. Norton, 1980.

Fabre, Michel. *From Harlem to Paris: Black American Writers in France, 1840–1980.* Urbana: U of Illinois P, 1991.

———. *Richard Wright: Books & Writers.* Jackson: UP of Mississippi, 1990.

———. *The Unfinished Quest of Richard Wright.* Trans. Isabel Barzun. NY: William Morrow, 1973.

———. *The World of Richard Wright.* Jackson: UP of Mississippi, 1985.

Fanon, Frantz. *Black Skin, White Masks.* NY: Grove Weidenfeld, 1967.

Farquharson, John, Ltd. "Letters." JWJ MSS 3, Box 99, File 1407. Yale Collection of American Literature. Beinecke Rare Book and Manuscript Library. New Haven, CT.

Feshbach, Seymour and Bernard Weiner. *Personality.* 2nd ed. 1982. Lexington, MA: D. C. Heath, 1986.

Foucault, Michel. *The Archaeology of Knowledge and the Discourse of Language.* NY: Pantheon, 1972.

———. *Discipline and Punish.* 1977. NY: Vintage, 1979.

———. *The Uses of Pleasure: Volume 2 of the History of Sexuality.* Trans. Robert Hurley. NY: Pantheon, 1985.

Friede, Donald. "Letters." JWJ MSS 3, Box 108, File 1697. Yale Collection of American Literature. Beinecke Rare Book and Manuscript Library. New Haven, CT.

Frieden, Ken. *Freud's Dreams of Interpretation.* Albany, NY: SUNY P, 1990.

Frus, Phyllis. *The Politics and Poetics of Journalistic Narrative: The Timely and the Timeless.* Cambridge: Cambridge UP, 1994.

Fussell, Paul. *The Norton Book of Travel.* NY: W. W. Norton, 1987.

Gates, Henry Louis, Jr. "Binary Oppositions in Chapter One of *Narrative of the Life of Frederick Douglass, An American Slave, Written By Himself.*" *Afro-American Literature.* Ed. Dexter Fisher and Robert B. Stepto. NY: MLA, 1979. 212–32.

Gayle, Addison. *Richard Wright: Ordeal of a Native Son.* Garden City, NY: Anchor, 1980.

Geertz, Clifford. *The Interpretation of Cultures.* NY: Basic Books, 1973.

George, Rosemary Marangoly. *The Politics of Home: Postcolonial Relocations and Twentieth-Century Fiction.* Cambridge: Cambridge UP, 1996.

Gikandi, Simon. *Maps of Englishness: Writing Identity in the Culture of Colonialism.* NY: Columbia UP, 1996.

Gilroy, Paul. *The Black Atlantic: Modernity and the Double Consciousness.* Cambridge: Harvard UP, 1993.

Greenfield, George. "Letters." JWJ MSS 3, Box 99, File 1407. Yale Collection of American Literature. Beinecke Rare Book and Manuscript Collection. New Haven, CT.

Gruesser, John C. "Afro-American Travel Literature and African Discourse." *BLAF* 24 (Spring 1990): 5–20.

Hakutani, Yoshinobu. *Richard Wright and Racial Discourse.* Columbia: U of Missouri P, 1996.

Harris, Trudier. *Exorcising Blackness: Historical and Literary Lynching and Burning Rituals.* Bloomington: Indiana UP, 1984.

Hemingway, Ernest. *The Dangerous Summer.* NY: Scribner's, 1985.

———. *Death in the Afternoon.* NY: Scribner's, 1932.

Howe, Irving. *A World More Attractive.* NY: Horizon, 1963.

Hughes, Langston. *The Big Sea.* 1940. NY: Hill and Wang, 1963.

Ivy, James W. "Spanish Journey." "Review of *Pagan Spain.*" *Crisis* (May 1957): 314–15.

Jahn, Jahnheinz. *A History of Neo-African Literature: Writing in Two Continents.* NY: Grove, 1968.

James, C. L. R. "Black Power." *The C. L. R. James Reader.* Ed. Anna Grimshaw. Oxford, UK: Blackwell, 1992. 362–74.

Jefferson, Thomas. *Notes on the State of Virginia.* Boston: Lily and Wait, 1832.

Keene, Donald. *World Within Walls: Japanese Literature of the Pre-Modern Era, 1600–1868.* NY: Grove P, 1976.

Kerstiens, Thomas. *The New Elite in Asia and Africa: A Comparative Study of Indonesia and Ghana.* NY: Frederick A. Praeger, 1966.

Kinnamon, Keneth and Michel Fabre. *Conversations with Richard Wright.* Jackson: UP of Mississippi, 1993.

Kristeva, Julia. *Strangers to Ourselves.* Trans. Leon S. Roudiez. NY: Columbia UP, 1991.

Kurebayashi, Kodo. *Introduction to Dogen Zen.* Tokyo: Taiho Rinkaku, 1984.

Lawson, Elizabeth. *History of the American Negro People, 1619–1918.* NY: Works Book Shop, 1939.

Legvold, Robert. *Soviet Policy in West Africa.* Cambridge: Harvard UP, 1970.

Linton, Balfour. "Letter." August 13, 1938. JWJ MSS 3, Box 93, File 1157. Yale Collection of American Literature. Beinecke Rare Book and Manuscript Library. New Haven, CT.

Logue, Ellen. "Review of *The Color Curtain.*" *Books on Trial.* 14 (1956): 351.

Lohrisch, Lothar. "Letter." July 15, 1959. JWJ MSS 3, Box 93, File 1163. Yale Collection of American Literature. Beinecke Rare Book and Manuscript Library. New Haven, CT.

MacMillan, W. M. *Africa Emergent.* London: Faber and Faber, 1938.

Marcus, George. "The Finding and Fashioning of Cultural Criticism in Ethnographic Research." *Dialectical Anthropology: Essays in Honor of Stanley Diamond.* Ed. Christine Ward Gailey. Gainesville: UP of Florida, 1992. 2 vols. *The Politics of Culture and Creativity.* 77–101.

Margolies, Edward. *The Art of Richard Wright.* Carbondale: Southern Illinois UP, 1969.

Mbiti, John. *African Religions and Philosophy.* Garden City, NY: Doubleday, 1970.

Mead, Margaret. *Anthropology, a Human Science: Selected Papers, 1939–1960.* Princeton: Van Nostrand, 1964.

Melville, Herman. *Typee.* NY: Viking, 1981.

Merton, Robert K. "Insiders and Outsiders: A Chapter in the Sociology of Knowledge." *Taking Sides: Clashing Views on Controversial Issues in Race and Ethnicity.* Ed. Robert C. Monk. Guilford, CT: Dushkin, 1994. 4–14.

Mitchell, W. J. T. "Space, Ideology, and Literary Representation." *Poetics Today* 10 (Spring 1989): 91–102.

Moore, Jack B. "The Art of *Black Power:* Novelistic or Documentary." *Revue Francaise d' Etudes Americaines* 31 (Feb. 1987): 79–91.

———. "*Black Power* Revisited: In Search of Richard Wright." *Mississippi Quarterly* 41 (Spring 1988): 161–86.

Murphy, Carl. "Letter." January 30, 1941. JWJ MSS 3, Box 93, File 1164. Yale Collection of American Literature. Beinecke Rare Book and Manuscript Library. New Haven, CT.

Myrdal, Gunnar. *1944. An American Dilemma.* NY: McGraw-Hill, 1964.

———. "Letters." JWJ MSS 3, Box 101, File 1481. Yale Collection of American Literature. Beinecke Rare Book and Manuscript Library. New Haven, CT.

Padmore, Dorothy. "Letters." JWJ MSS 3, Box 103, File 1521. Yale Collection of American Literature. Beinecke Rare Book and Manuscript Library. New Haven, CT.

———. "Letter." March 13, 1963. *The World of Richard Wright.* Ed. Michel Fabre. Jackson: U of Mississippi P, 1985. 256–61.

Peacock, James L. *The Anthropological Lens: Harsh Light, Soft Focus.* NY: Cambridge UP, 1986.

Pile, Steve and Nigel Thrift. *Mapping the Subject.* NY: Routledge, 1995.

Pratt, Mary Louise. "Fieldwork in Common Places." *Writing Culture: The Poetics and Politics of Ethnography.* Eds. James Clifford and George Marcus. Los Angeles: U of California P, 1986. 27–50.

———. *Imperial Eyes: Travel Writing and Transculturation.* NY: Routledge, 1992.

———. "Scratches on the Face of the Country; or, What Mr. Barrow Saw in the Land of the Bushmen." *"Race," Writing and Difference.* Ed. Henry Louis Gates, Jr. 1985. Chicago: U of Chicago P, 1986. 138–62.

"Red Rag to Spain." "Review of *Pagan Spain.*" *Literary Supplement. The London Times.* n.p., n.d. JWJ MSS 3, Box 59, File 689. Yale Collection of American Literature. Beinecke Rare Book and Manuscript Library. New Haven, CT.

Reilly, John M. "Richard Wright and the Art of Non-Fiction: Stepping Out on the State of the World." *Callaloo* 9.3 (Summer 1986): 507–20.

———. "Richard Wright's Discovery of the Third World." *Minority Voices* 2 (1978): 47–53.

Reynolds, Paul R. "Letters." JWJ MSS 3, Box 104, File 1539. Yale Collection of American Literature. Beinecke Rare Book and Manuscript Library. New Haven, CT.

Rosaldo, Renato. "From the Door of His Tent: The Fieldworker and the Inquisitor." *Writing Culture: The Poetics of Ethnography.* Eds. James Clifford and George E. Marcus. Berkeley: U of California P, 1986. 77–97.

Rose, Innes. "Letters." JWJ MSS 3, Box 99, File 1407. Yale Collection of American Literature. Beinecke Rare Book and Manuscript Library. New Haven, CT.

Said, Edward. *Culture and Imperialism.* NY: Alfred Knopf, 1993.

Sartre, John Paul. *Black Orpheus.* Trans. S. W. Allen. Paris: Présence Africaine, 1976.

Senghor, Léopold. "Letter." July 28, 1959. JWJ MSS 3, Box 106, File 1606. Yale Collection of American Literature. Beinecke Rare Book and Manuscript Library. New Haven, CT.

Smith, John. *The Generall Historie of Virginia. The Norton Anthology of American Literature.* Ed. Paul Lauter, et al. Vol. I. Lexington, MA: D. C. Heath, 1990. 186–94.

Smith, Virginia Whatley. "Image, Text, and Voice: Opposition of Meanings in the Wright-Rosskam Photographic Text." *OBSIDIAN II* (Fall/Winter 1996): 1–27.

———. "Interviews with Charles E. Wright." August 16–19, 1999. Natchez, MS.

———. "Interviews with Ellen Wright." January 1988 and February 1992. Paris, France.

Snelling, Paula. "Import of Bandung." *Progressive* 19 (June 1956): 39–50.

Stein, Gertrude. *Four Saints in Three Acts.* NY: Random House, 1934.

———. *Tender Buttons.* NY: Claire Marie, 1914.

Stepto, Robert B. *From Behind the Veil.* Urbana: U of Illinois P, 1991.

Stott, William. *Documentary Expression and Thirties America.* NY: Oxford UP, 1973.

Strout, Richard. "Richard Wright's Spanish Excursion." "Review of *Pagan Spain.*" *The New York Republic.* 18 February 1957. 136.

Swan, Oliver G. "Letters." JWJ MSS 3, Box 104, File 1539. Yale Collection of American Literature. Beinecke Rare Book and Manuscript Library. New Haven, CT.

Targ, William. "Letters." JWJ MSS 3, Box 108, File 1697. Yale Collection of American Literature. Beinecke Rare Book and Manuscript Library. New Haven, CT.

Taussig, Charles W. and Philip Kappel. *Rum, Romance and Rebellion.* London: Jarolds, 1928.

Twain, Mark. *Adventures of Huckleberry Finn.* 1884. Boston: Houghton Mifflin, 1962.

Van den Abbeele, Georges. *Travel as Metaphor: From Montaigne to Rousseau.* Minneapolis: U of Minnesota P, 1992.

Vladisav, Jan. "Exile, Responsibillity, Destiny." *Literature in Exile.* Ed. John Glad. Durham: Duke UP, 1990.

Walker, Margaret. *Richard Wright: Daemonic Genius.* NY: Warner, 1988.

Webb, Constance. *Richard Wright: A Biography.* NY: G. P. Putnam's Sons, 1968.

Weiss, M. Lynn. "*Para Usted:* Richard Wright's *Pagan Spain.*" *The Black Columbiad: Defining Moments in African American Literature and Culture.* Ed. Werner Sollars and Maria Diedrich. Cambridge: Harvard UP, 1995. 212–225.

Williams, Eric. *Capitalism and Slavery.* Chapel Hill: U of North Carolina, 1944.

Williams, Stanley. *The Spanish Background of American Literature.* 1955. NY: Archon, 1968.

Wilson, Edmund. "Letters." JWJ MSS 3, Box 108, File 1687. Yale Collection of American Literature. Beinecke Rare Book and Manuscript Library. New Haven, CT.

Wright, Julia. "Introduction." *Haiku: This Other World.* Ed. Yoshinobu Hakutani and Robert Tener. NY: Arcade, 1998.

Wright, Richard. "Adventure and Love in Loyalist Spain." "Review of *The Wall of Men*" by William Rollins, Jr. *New Masses* (8 March 1938): 25–26.

———. "Almos' A Man." *Harper's Bazaar* (Jan. 1940): 401.

———. *American Hunger.* NY: Harper & Row, 1983.

———. "Between the World and Me." *The Poetry of the Negro: 1746–1949.* Eds. Langston Hughes and Arna Bontemps. Garden City, NY: Doubleday, 1949. 156–58.

———. "Big Boy Leaves Home." *Uncle Tom's Children.* 1936. NY: Harper & Row, 1965. 17–53.

———. *Black Boy: A Record of Childhood and Youth.* 1945. NY: Harper/Perennial, 1993.

———. *Black Power.* 1954. London: Dennis Dobson, 1956.

———. "Blueprint for Negro Writing." *Richard Wright Reader.* Eds. Ellen Wright and Michel Fabre. 1937. NY: Harper & Row, 1978. 36–49.

———. *The Color Curtain: A Report on the Bandung Conference.* London: Dennis Dobson, 1956.

———. "Conference on Negro Writers and Artists, September 19–22, 1956." JWJ MSS 3, Box 104, File 1557. Yale Collection of American Literature. Beinecke Rare Book and Manuscript Library. New Haven, CT.

———. "Contact Sheets/Photos—*Black Power.*" JWJ MSS 3, Box 22, File 340–47. Yale Collection of American Literature. Beinecke Rare Book and Manuscript Library. New Haven, CT.

———. *Conversations with Richard Wright.* Ed. Keneth Kinnamon and Michel Fabre. Jackson: UP of Mississippi, 1993.

———. *Eight Men.* 1961. NY: Thunder's Mouth P, 1987.

———. "Film Negatives—*The Color Curtain.*" JWJ MSS 3, Box 29, File 419. Yale Collection of American Literature. Beinecke Rare Book and Manuscript Library. New Haven, CT.

———. "Fire and Cloud." *Uncle Tom's Children.* NY: Harper & Row, 1938. 221–317.

———. "French West Africa." JWJ MSS 3, Box 5, File 86. Yale Collection of American Literature. Beinecke Rare Book and Manuscript Library. New Haven, CT.

———. "Guggenheim Application." JWJ MSS 3, Box 99, File 1408. Yale Collection of American Literature. Beinecke Rare Book and Manuscript Library. New Haven, CT.

―――. "How *Uncle Tom's Children* Grew." *Columbia U Writer's Bulletin* 2 (May 1938): 15–17.

―――. "I Choose Exile." JWJ MSS 3, Box 29, File 419. Yale Collection of American Literature. Beinecke Rare Book and Manuscript Library. New Haven, CT.

―――. "Inaugural Invitation, Bandung Conference." JWJ MSS 3, Box 113, File 1813. Yale Collection of American Literature. Beinecke Rare Book and Manuscript Library. New Haven, CT.

―――. "I Tried to be a Communist." *Atlantic Monthly* (August 1944): 71–70; (September 1944): 48–56.

―――. "Letter to Mr. Cole, Editor." *The Daily Echo.* June 24, 1954. JWJ MSS 3, Box 22, File 341. Yale Collection of American Literature. Beinecke Rare Book and Manuscript Library. New Haven, CT.

―――. *The Long Dream.* NY: Doubleday, 1958.

―――. "Man, God Ain't Like That." *Eight Men.* Cleveland: World, 1961. 163–92.

―――. *The Man Who Lived Underground.* 1944. Cleveland: World, 1961. 27–92.

―――. *Native Son.* 1940. NY: Perennial/Harper, 1966.

―――. "Notes—French West Africa." JWJ MSS 3, Box 111, File 1749. Yale Collection of American Literature. Beinecke Rare Book and Manuscript Library. New Haven, CT.

―――. "Outline—*Pagan Spain.*" JWJ MSS 3, Box 53, File 652. Yale Collection of American Literature. Beinecke Rare Book and Manuscript Library. New Haven, CT.

―――. "Outline/Preliminary Draft—French West Africa." JWJ MSS 3, Box 53, File 786. Yale Collection of American Literature. Beinecke Rare Book and Manuscript Library. New Haven, CT.

―――. *The Outsider.* 1953. NY: Perennial/Harper & Row, 1965.

―――. *Pagan Spain.* NY: Harper & Row, 1957.

―――. "Passport and Visas." JWJ MSS 3, Box 117, File 1881. Yale Collection of American Literature. Beinecke Rare Book and Manuscript Library. New Haven, CT.

―――. "Photographs—*Pagan Spain.*" JWJ MSS 3, Box 54, File 655–57. Yale Collection of American Literature. Beinecke Rare Book and Manuscript Library. New Haven, CT.

―――. "Questionnaire—*The Color Curtain.*" JWJ MSS 3, Box 31, File 434. Yale Collection of American Literature. Beinecke Rare Book and Manuscript Library. New Haven, CT.

―――. Resumé. JWJ MSS 3, Box 8, File 164. Yale Collection of American Literature. Beinecke Rare Book and Manuscript Library. New Haven, CT.

―――. "Return to Paradise—Notes." JWJ MSS 3, Box 30, File 433. Yale Collection of American Literature. Beinecke Rare Book and Manuscript Collection. New Haven, CT.

―――. *Savage Holiday.* 1954. NY: UP of Mississippi, 1994.

―――. "Semana Santa." *Pagan Spain.* JWJ MSS 3, Box 29, File 421. Yale Collection of American Literature. Beinecke Rare Book and Manuscript Library. New Haven, CT.

―――. "Superstition." *The World of Richard Wright.* 1931. Jackson: UP of Mississippi, 1985. 217–28.

―――. "Tarbaby's Dawn." JWJ MSS 3, Box 6, File 150. Yale Collection of American Literature. Beinecke Rare Book and Manuscript Library. New Haven, CT.

―――. "To French Readers." JWJ MSS 3, Box 661, File 784. Yale Collection of American Literature. Beinecke Rare Book and Manuscript Library. New Haven, CT.

———. "Travel Diary—*Pagan Spain.*" JWJ MSS 3, Box 55, File 658–661. Yale Collection of American Literature. Beinecke Rare Book and Manuscript Library. New Haven, CT.

———. "Typescripts—*Pagan Spain.*" JWJ MSS 3, Box 54, File 652–685. Yale Collection of American Literature. Beinecke Rare Book and Manuscript Library. New Haven, CT.

———. *12 Million Black Voices: A Folk History of the Negro in the United States.* NY: Viking, 1941.

———. *Uncle Tom's Children.* 1940. Harper & Row, 1965.

———. *White Man, Listen!* 1957. NY: Anchor/Doubleday, 1964.

Young, Timothy. "Richard Wright Papers." April 1994. Yale Collection of American Literature. Beinecke Rare Book and Manuscript Library. New Haven, CT.

Contributors

Ngwarsungu Chiwengo is associate professor of English and director of the World Literature Program at Creighton University. She has published articles on both African and African American literature and several book reviews. Currently, she is working on a book about the South African writer Peter Abrahams.

Dennis F. Evans just completed a Ph.D. in eighteenth-century British literature at the University of North Texas. He is currently working on his first book: "The Afro-British Slave Narratives: The Rhetoric of Freedom in the Kairos of Abolition," examining the British abolition in the context of Christian and secular rhetorical models of kairos.

Yoshinobu Hakutani is professor of English at Kent State University. He is the author or editor of many books on Richard Wright, Theodore Dreiser, and cross-culturalism. His books include *Critical Essays on Richard Wright*; *The City in African-American Literature* co-edited with Robert Butler; *Richard Wright and Racial Discourse*; and Richard Wright's *Haiku: This Other World*, co-edited with Robert Tener.

Keneth Kinnamon is the Ethel Pumphrey Stephens Professor of English at the University of Arkansas. He is a distinguished Wright scholar and known for his publication of *A Richard Wright Bibliography: Fifty Years of Criticism and Commentary, 1933–1982*. His most recent work is *Conversations with Richard Wright* which he co-edited with Michel Fabre. He is currently working on a book to be titled "Hemingway and Politics."

John Lowe, professor of English at Louisiana State University, is author of *Jump at the Sun: Zora Neale Hurston's Cosmic Comedy*, editor of *Conversations with Ernest Gaines* and *Redefining Southern Culture*, and co-editor of *The Future of Southern Letters*. He is currently completing *The Americanization of Ethnic Humor*, a cross-cultural, multidisciplinary examination of changing patterns in American comic literature.

Jack B. Moore currently is graduate director in the Department of English, the University of South Florida, where he has also held a long-time appointment in the Department of American Studies. He has published books and critical essays on W. E. B. Du Bois, Joe DiMaggio, John Updike, and Chester Himes, and several on Richard Wright. His opinion pieces on race, sports, and the American scene are regularly distributed by the *Newsday–Los Angeles Times* syndicate.

S. Shankar teaches in the Department of English, Rutgers University (Newark). He is the author of a novel, *A Map of Where I Live*, a work of cultural criticism entitled *Textual Traffic: Colonialism, Modernity and the Economy of the Text*, and articles which have appeared in a variety of journals.

Virginia Whatley Smith is an associate professor of English at the University of Alabama at Birmingham. She has published essays in *African American Review*, *OBSIDIAN*, and *Mississippi Quarterly* as well as the MLA *Approaches to Teaching Wright's* Native Son. She currently is working on a second book entitled "Richard Wright's Re/Construction of Blackness: An Intellectual Biography of His Life Through His Writings."

Index